Windows Phone 7 Silverlight Cookbook

All the recipes you need to start creating apps and making money

Jonathan Marbutt

Robb Schiefer Jr.

BIRMINGHAM - MUMBAI

Windows Phone 7 Silverlight Cookbook

First published: August 2011

Production Reference: 1180811

Published by Packt Publishing Ltd.
Livery Place
35 Livery Street
Birmingham B3 2PB, UK

ISBN 978-1-849691-16-1

www.packtpub.com

Cover Image by Asher Wishkerman (wishkerman@hotmail.com)

Credits

Authors

Jonathan Marbutt

Robb Schiefer Jr.

Reviewers

Cory Smith

Kelum Peiris

Tom McLeod

Acquisition Editors

David Barnes

Steven Wilding

Development Editor

Hithesh Uchil

Technical Editor

Pallavi Kachare

Copy Editor

Leonard D'Silva

Project Coordinator

Zainab Bagasrawala

Proofreader

Aaron Nash

Indexer

Monica Ajmera

Graphics

Geetanjali Sawant

Production Coordinator

Alwin Roy

Cover Work

Alwin Roy

Foreword

I am delighted that Jonathan and Robb undertook the task of writing this book. Both Jonathan and Robb have been involved in the .NET community for a number of years and developed a passion for the Windows Phone. With this book, they have decided to share their knowledge and experience with their readers to help developers dive into doing more with Windows Phone.

When we began rebuilding the Phone, the goal was to do this over multiple releases and keep iterating on feedback rapidly to take the platform forward. In doing so, the platform evolved with the developers consuming it and aligned to their needs. The premise of using platforms like Silverlight and XNA as the basis was founded by the need to make it simple and familiar, and also enable rapid development of a large volume of high quality applications. We also attempted to stitch together the end-to-end story Microsoft had to offer between the tools, the platforms, the phone operating system, and the various services in the company.

When I was approached to write this foreword by Scott Guthrie and Jonathan, I was personally skeptical given the risk of capturing so much in so little. By reading the book, I have personally had a refresher of the various constructs we have enabled over the year and feel that the authors have done a good job telling the end-to-end story.

The book embodies the basic construct of Windows Phone development, namely, to simplify and enable. Jonathan and Robb have taken the essence of what is required to get started and develop applications rapidly which is a key to mobile development. The market continues to evolve rapidly and hence the need for efficient development strategies including quick learning.

I hope the readers of this book learn and are able to develop high quality and attractive applications to help differentiate themselves in the highly competitive market.

Akhil Kaza
Development Manager Silverlight for Windows Phone

About the Authors

Jonathan Marbutt at the early age of ten, began to learn building simple games to amuse his friends and family. Twenty years later, he still has the passion for technology and development. Jonathan loves to share his passion with other developers by writing for his blog and various books as well as speaking at many user groups and technology conferences. Throughout the past three years, Jonathan's focus has primarily been on working with Silverlight and its most recent version for Windows Phone 7. Through this newest version for Windows Phone 7, Jonathan has been able to work on many high profile applications that are rated as some of the most downloaded applications.

Jonathan is also currently the Vice President and Co-founder of WayCool Software, Inc. based in Birmingham, AL which provides solutions for non-profit organizations. Jonathan has also been providing consulting services through his latest venture JM TechWare, Inc. where he helps provide both User Experience and architectural guidance on Silverlight, Windows Phone 7, and WPF applications. In addition to development, Jonathan has co-authored *Visual Basic 2010 and .Net 4,* published by Wrox Press.

Thank you to my beautiful wife Jennifer for being by my side while writing this book and putting up with the late nights that I worked to get it done. Thank you for supporting me and always being there for me. You are truly the love of my life.

Thank you to my precious little girl, Kathryn, for always brightening my day and making me enjoy the little things in life. Thank you for always making me laugh and always having a smile no matter what is going on. I love you so much and and love getting to be there to watch you grow up.

Thank you to my parents for encouraging me at an early age to pursue my passion and providing me the means to do so. I wouldn't be the person I am today without your help.

Robb Schiefer Jr. is a follower of Christ, husband to the perfect wife, and father of two beautiful girls. Coincidentally, he is also a successful .NET software developer which is a better qualification for writing a programming book.

His development career started while working part-time during college where he learned graphic design basics and built simple data-driven PHP websites. After college, he worked for a small startup on a VB6 application for educators and learned .NET by jumping head first into building a complimentary ASP.NET site. Since then, he has worked as a .NET developer for a market leading, privately held corporation with a global presence. This enterprise environment has provided many unique challenges and learning opportunities. He currently leads a development team in the company's latest development efforts, mentors many developers, and plays a leading role in planning the company's .NET architecture.

Prior to the announcement of Windows Phone 7, he had little experience with Silverlight, but always wanted to learn it. WP7 provided the perfect opportunity to learn Silverlight in a defined space and on a smaller scale. He currently has several apps in the marketplace and has plans for many more (if he ever gets this book done).

I would first like to thank my wonderful wife for her continual support and love (especially while writing the book). Also for her work at home with our two precious girls and in the future, number three. And four? I couldn't ask for a better wife, thank you and I love you. Second I would like to thank Jonathan for his friendship and for asking me to write the book with him. Lastly, thanks to the .NET/Silverlight/Windows Phone development community, Microsoft for finally having a decent smartphone OS which is a joy to work with and the followers of my blog.

About the Reviewers

Tom McLeod started writing software for fun 16 years ago and has been enjoying it ever since. He has written software for HP48 series calculators and a rainbow of UNIX flavors. Since earning a degree in trombone performance, he has worked on a variety of .NET projects. When he's not developing software, he enjoys producing episodes of The Deucecast podcast and being a father and photographer to his two young daughters. He can be contacted through leftylabs.com.

Kelum Peiris is a Mobile Software Developer with Polar Mobile, a company that provides an industry-leading platform to enable top-tier media publishers to easily and quickly launch mobile apps for every major Smartphone. At Polar Mobile, Kelum is primarily involved in developing the Windows Phone platform which will be used to deploy more than 500 apps in year 2011. He is a recent graduate from the University of Waterloo, Ontario, Canada where he specialized in Mobile Development and Real-Time Operating Systems. Kelum has a keen interest in advance concepts in Object Oriented Programming and Design Patterns and he is a clean code addict.

Colin Smith is an experienced mobile developer, musician, and startup guy currently working with a wide range of technologies. He is a co-founder and Mobile Lead of Cardinal, a startup focused on social music sharing, discovery, and analytics. He is currently the Technical Lead / Lead Developer of iOS applications at Shaw Communications as well. You may know him as Smixx, creator of the Developers rap song.

I'd like to thank my lovely wife Chelsea for putting up with the long hours and sleepless nights that went into reviewing this book while getting a startup off the ground and holding down a fulltime job as well, couldn't have done it without you!

www.PacktPub.com

Support files, eBooks, discount offers and more

You might want to visit www.PacktPub.com for support files and downloads related to your book.

Did you know that Packt offers eBook versions of every book published, with PDF and ePub files available? You can upgrade to the eBook version at www.PacktPub.com and as a print book customer, you are entitled to a discount on the eBook copy. Get in touch with us at service@packtpub.com for more details.

At www.PacktPub.com, you can also read a collection of free technical articles, sign up for a range of free newsletters and receive exclusive discounts and offers on Packt books and eBooks.

http://PacktLib.PacktPub.com

Do you need instant solutions to your IT questions? PacktLib is Packt's online digital book library. Here, you can access, read and search across Packt's entire library of books.

Why Subscribe?

- ▶ Fully searchable across every book published by Packt
- ▶ Copy and paste, print and bookmark content
- ▶ On demand and accessible via web browser

Free Access for Packt account holders

If you have an account with Packt at www.PacktPub.com, you can use this to access PacktLib today and view nine entirely free books. Simply use your login credentials for immediate access.

Instant Updates on New Packt Books

Get notified! Find out when new books are published by following @PacktEnterprise on Twitter, or the *Packt Enterprise* Facebook page.

I would like to dedicate this book to someone who didn't know anything about software development and often called me a nerd. For 23 years she lived life to the fullest and laughed louder than anyone in the world. To my sister Bebe, who went to be with the Lord. I love you.

Robb Schiefer Jr.

Table of Contents

Preface

In this book, you will discover the latest development technology from Microsoft for the Windows Phone 7. We will cover all that you need to get a variety of applications developed. Throughout this book you will find many simple examples that stand by themselves to help provide quick reference to many of the common needs for a Windows Phone developer.

What this book covers

Chapter 1, Layout and Design, covers the most common ways to lay out your Windows Phone application that will provide you with the basics for designing applications. We will cover the basics of Expression Blend and its important role in Windows Phone Application development.

Chapter 2, Creating Animation, explains that understanding the basics of animations is no longer a tool just for designers, but it can play an important role in your application to give it the polish to make your application stand out from the crowd. Through this chapter, we will cover the basics of creating simple animations with both Storyboards and Visual State Manager.

Chapter 3, Behaviors and Events, explains now that you have the design aspects down for your application, it is time to give the user a way to interact with the application. In Windows Phone development, much of the initial interaction can be fired by both behaviors and events. We will show you some built in behaviors as well as developing custom behaviors.

Chapter 4, DataBinding 101/MVVM, covers the basic understandings of databinding in Silverlight as well as the MVVM design pattern as most apps have some data to populate and display. With MVVM, you can architect your application for much easier maintenance as well as easier testing and design time support for data.

Chapter 5, Services, Data, and RSS, explains that once you have a great understanding of how to structure an application to show data as well as the basics of databinding, it is now time to dig into pulling data from services. In this chapter, we will cover the basics of using WCF services as well as building a simple RSS reader.

Chapter 6, Location Services: Are you lost? Start using GPS coordinates and other location information from the phone in your apps with this chapter. We cover how to efficiently use location services, utilize the emulator for debugging your app, and using the built-in mapping control.

Chapter 7, Push Notifications to the Phone, shows how poling for data every 10 minutes is so 1995. This chapter covers setting up push notifications to the phone. Learn how the Microsoft Push Notification Services work and how you can leverage them to make your app the coolest on the block. Topics include start tile notifications, toast notification, and even a helper class to get you going faster.

Chapter 8, Launchers and Choosers, launches your app into Windows Phone 7 with tight integration through Launchers and Choosers. Start using the phone's core features like sending e-mails, starting up the web browser, and working with the camera or stored photos in this chapter. Learn how these APIs can be utilized with ease to make your app shine.

Chapter 9, Sensing with Sensors, covers the various sensor APIs to find what makes smartphones smart. Learn how to use the accelerometer, microphone, and touchscreen in your apps for a truly engaging end-user experience.

Chapter 10, Preparing Apps for the Marketplace: It's time to get rich and famous. It's time to share your app with the world in the Windows Phone Marketplace. Learn all the ins and outs of submitting an app to the marketplace and benefit from our experience. Topics include avoiding failed verifications, adding trial support, creating icons, and a step-by-step walkthrough of app submission.

What you need for this book

For this book, you will need the following:

- ► Visual Studio Express for Windows Phone
- ► Expression Blend for Windows Phone
- ► Windows Phone SDK

The tools can be downloaded for free at `http://developer.windowsphone.com`.

Who this book is for

This book is for both the hobbyist and professional developer wanting to begin development for Windows Phone development. Throughout the book we tried to take the most simplistic approach for complex problems to provide you with the quickest reference to many common scenarios.

Conventions

In this book, you will find a number of styles of text that distinguish between different kinds of information. Here are some examples of these styles, and an explanation of their meaning.

Code words in text are shown as follows: "After finding the control in the assets window, drag-and-drop them onto your `control.Blend`."

A block of code is set as follows:

```
<VisualTransition GeneratedDuration="0:0:1">
  <VisualTransition.GeneratedEasingFunction>
    <ExponentialEase EasingMode="EaseInOut"/>
  </VisualTransition.GeneratedEasingFunction>
</VisualTransition>
```

When we wish to draw your attention to a particular part of a code block, the relevant lines or items are set in bold:

```
<Storyboard>
      <DoubleAnimation Duration="0" To="26"
      Storyboard.TargetProperty="(FrameworkElement.Height)"
      Storyboard.TargetName="textBlock" d:IsOptimized="True"/>
</Storyboard>
```

New terms and **important words** are shown in bold. Words that you see on the screen, in menus or dialog boxes for example, appear in the text like this: "We need to create a new Windows Phone Application after clicking **New Project** in Visual Studio".

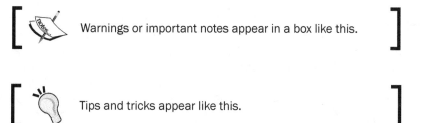

Warnings or important notes appear in a box like this.

Tips and tricks appear like this.

Reader feedback

Feedback from our readers is always welcome. Let us know what you think about this book—what you liked or may have disliked. Reader feedback is important for us to develop titles that you really get the most out of.

To send us general feedback, simply send an e-mail to `feedback@packtpub.com`, and mention the book title via the subject of your message.

If there is a book that you need and would like to see us publish, please send us a note in the **SUGGEST A TITLE** form on `www.packtpub.com` or e-mail `suggest@packtpub.com`.

If there is a topic that you have expertise in and you are interested in either writing or contributing to a book, see our author guide on `www.packtpub.com/authors`.

Customer support

Now that you are the proud owner of a Packt book, we have a number of things to help you to get the most from your purchase.

Downloading the example code

You can download the example code files for all Packt books you have purchased from your account at `http://www.PacktPub.com`. If you purchased this book elsewhere, you can visit `http://www.PacktPub.com/support` and register to have the files e-mailed directly to you.

Errata

Although we have taken every care to ensure the accuracy of our content, mistakes do happen. If you find a mistake in one of our books—maybe a mistake in the text or the code—we would be grateful if you would report this to us. By doing so, you can save other readers from frustration and help us improve subsequent versions of this book. If you find any errata, please report them by visiting `http://www.packtpub.com/support`, selecting your book, clicking on the **errata submission form** link, and entering the details of your errata. Once your errata are verified, your submission will be accepted and the errata will be uploaded on our website, or added to any list of existing errata, under the Errata section of that title. Any existing errata can be viewed by selecting your title from `http://www.packtpub.com/support`.

Piracy

Piracy of copyright material on the Internet is an ongoing problem across all media. At Packt, we take the protection of our copyright and licenses very seriously. If you come across any illegal copies of our works, in any form, on the Internet, please provide us with the location address or website name immediately so that we can pursue a remedy.

Please contact us at `copyright@packtpub.com` with a link to the suspected pirated material.

We appreciate your help in protecting our authors, and our ability to bring you valuable content.

Questions

You can contact us at `questions@packtpub.com` if you are having a problem with any aspect of the book, and we will do our best to address it.

1
Layout and Design

In this chapter, we will cover:

- ▶ Creating simple navigation
- ▶ Using Positioning controls
- ▶ Discovering the various input controls
- ▶ Introduction to ViewStateManager
- ▶ Customizing ViewState of standard buttons
- ▶ Understanding the panorama control
- ▶ Using the pivot control

Introduction

When Microsoft announced the Windows Phone 7, they made a bold move to drop the legacy of Windows CE. By doing this, they decided to leverage Silverlight as the foundation of their mobile user interface. Many people relate Silverlight with applications that have been used for events such as the Olympics to deliver high definition videos. What most people don't realize is that the real power of Silverlight is to develop rich applications that go beyond the traditional Windows Forms type development. With Silverlight, they have built-in rich support for both designers and developers to build applications together in environments that they are both familiar with.

Microsoft also took another bold move in the tooling by providing both Expression Blend 4 and Visual Studio 2010 for Windows Phone for free. This choice was to give developers and designers the easiest way to begin developing for Windows Phone 7. Both of these tools provide a rich atmosphere to spark creativity among designers while giving developers the tools to get the job done.

In this chapter, we will familiarize ourselves with the basic tools of developing a Windows Phone 7 Silverlight Application. These skills will help you throughout the rest of the book by giving you the fundamentals for building any Silverlight Application on Windows Phone 7.

Downloading the tools

Before you begin to write your first line of code or design your first user interface for Windows Phone 7, you will need to download and install the Visual Studio and Expression Blend. These tools are offered completely free by Microsoft and can be downloaded at `http://developer.windowsphone.com`. You will also need the latest version of the Zune software if you will test your application on a physical device. The Zune software can be downloaded from `http://www.zune.net/en-us/products/software/download/`.

Understanding the tools

There are several pieces to the tools that you will download, and each serve their own role.

Visual Studio 2010 Express

Visual Studio 2010 Express provides an environment that is especially designed for the programming side of an application. This doesn't mean that if you are a designer you shouldn't use Visual Studio, but use it to supplement your skills with Blend. There are many areas that Visual Studio offers that Blend does not offer, including:

- **InteliSense**: If you have ever used Visual Studio, then you will be familiar with this feature. This provides you with very rich auto complete features when you are typing in the code behind files.

- **Debugging**: Visual Studio provides many advance debugging features that aren't offered in Blend. This includes the ability to set break points to step through your code while it is running. Visual Studio also provides the ability to debug your application on the phone versus the emulator whereas Blend does not allow breakpoint support for debugging.

Expression Blend for Windows Phone

Microsoft Expression Blend for Windows Phone offers a tool that is more intended for the designing of user interfaces. While Visual Studio does provide drag-and-drop type design for user interfaces, there are many areas that Visual Studio is not well suited for, including:

- **Animation**: Expression Blend provides a variety of ways to create simple and complex animations. Or if you have been using Adobe Flash or other animation tools, this will be very familiar to you as Blend uses Timeline-based animations as well as other transition types.

- ▶ **Vector-graphics support**: Expression Blend also provides a vector-graphics support for creating your UI. Microsoft has also included support for importing existing assets from Adobe Illustrator and Photoshop.

- ▶ **Visual state editing**: Blend provides a simple interface for setting visual states on controls that Visual Studio does not.

- ▶ **Template editing**: Blend also offers a rich interface for editing templates and creating templates without having to know how to do it in the code.

- ▶ **Sample data**: The sample data features of Blend allow you to quickly mock up user interfaces that might be attached to a database and see how the controls look without having the actual database connection in place.

The many features of Expression Blend create an environment for developing rich user experiences on Windows Phone. It is an essential tool for both the developers and designers and comfortable for them to use too.

Windows Phone Emulator

The Windows Phone Emulator provides you with a virtual machine that emulates the Windows Phone operating system. This is used to provide a test environment that is almost identical to the runtime of the phone devices.

Also included in the download

There are several other items included in the download that enable you to run the items above to develop Windows Phone applications; these include:

- ▶ Silverlight 4 SDK
- ▶ .NET Framework 4
- ▶ XNA Game Studio 4.0

The XNA Game Studio is an extensive technology that is created for developing more complex games and will not be covered in this book. The XNA framework is an alternative library for building Windows Phone 7 applications. It doesn't support the layout controls and event-driven input suitable for line-of-business applications, but uses input and graphics methods useful for more complex games. Because of the extent of the XNA framework, it will not be covered in this book but see `http://msdn.microsoft.com/en-us/wp7trainingcourse_wp7xna_unit.aspx` for some great example on getting started with XNA.

Creating simple navigation

If you are developing a Windows Phone application, the odds are you will have more than one page which you want to show to the user. Luckily for us, Microsoft has provided a basic navigation framework for navigating from one screen to another. This type of navigation is very similar to how you would navigate from one web page to another. It supports query strings similar to websites. This simple navigation example will be used throughout the book as a starting point for many other examples. This is a popular way to build applications that a user can easily navigate.

We will create a business information application that simply displays information about a fictional company called ACME and allows you to navigate from one screen to another easily. We will include the following pages:

- Home
- About ACME
- Contact ACME
- Locations
    - Corporate Office
    - Satellite Office

Although this application is very simple, it is designed to give you the fundamental building blocks for creating a complex Windows Phone application.

Getting ready

Before we begin, we need to create a new Windows Phone Application after clicking **New Project** in Visual Studio:

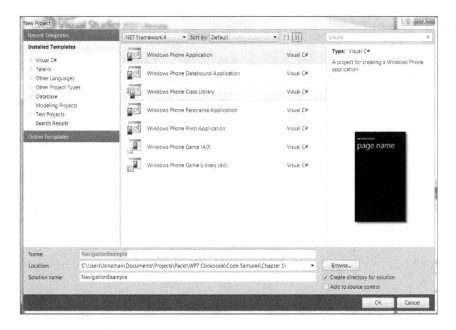

How to do it...

Now that you have created the Navigation Project, in the following example, you will see the basic structure of the application on the right-hand side of Visual Studio:

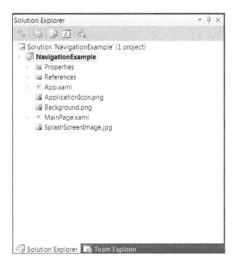

Add some folders to the structure of the application by right-clicking on the **NavigationExample** project in the **Solution Explorer**, selecting **Add | New Folder,** and then renaming the folder as **Views.**

1. Now, to add the first pages to the application, right-click on the new **Views** folder, select **Add | New Item**, then select the Windows Phone Portrait page, enter `About.xaml` as the name, and click **OK**.

2. Repeat this step for the **Contact** page, naming it as `Contact.xaml`:

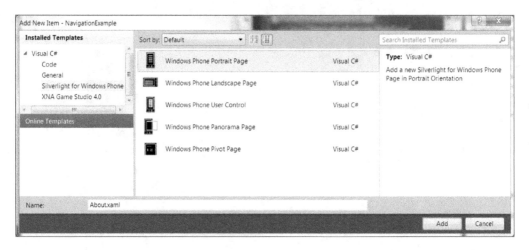

3. We will then repeat steps 1 and 2 for creating a sub folder named **Locations** under the **Views** folder and adding two more Windows Phone Portrait pages named `CorporateOffice.xaml` and `SatelliteOffice.xaml`. This will create a project that should look like this:

In the previous steps, we had only spent time in Visual Studio. Now it is time to swap over to Expression Blend. OK, so you may be asking yourself, "Can't I just stay in Visual Studio?". The answer is yes you can, but you will find it much easier to do many of the design-related items like adding controls and setting properties of controls in Blend. The good news is that Blend and Visual Studio both use the same project files, so you can leave both Visual Studio and Blend open with the same project and they will update each other when you save the files:

1. To open this project in Blend, right-click on the `MainPage.xaml` and select **Open in Expression Blend...**.

2. The first things you will want to change are the two TextBlocks at the top of the page. To do this, simply double-click on the text to begin editing the text on the top-most label and enter the text **ACME Co.**. Then double-click the larger TextBlock and type **Home**.

3. Now that we have the home page labels renamed, let's do the same thing for the sub pages by double-clicking on them in the solution explorer, double-clicking the TextBlocks, and entering appropriate titles. For the **Corporate Office** page, enter **ACME Co.** as the upper title and **Corporate Office** in the larger TextBlock. Also do this for the Satellite Office page.

4. What we want to do now is provide a basic navigation of the `MainPage.xaml` to the About, Contact, and Location Pages by using the `HyperlinkButton` control. We do this by clicking the **assets** button at the bottom of the tool box on the left-hand side of Blend. This will expand and give you a search box where you can search for `HyperLinkButton`:

After finding the control in the assets window, drag-and-drop them onto your `control.Blend`.

5. Once you have the hyperlinks on your design surface, double-click on them to edit the text of the first one as **About**, the second as **Contact**, and the last one as **Locations**. This should create a screen that looks like the following:

6. Enable each of these links to navigate to the corresponding pages when a user touches the link on the phone. This is easily done by selecting the hyperlink button, and then on the properties window setting the `NavigationUri` property to the corresponding `page`, as seen in the following screenshot:

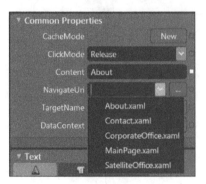

7. In this example, we are selecting the `NavigationUri` for the **About** button. Simply select the `About.xaml`. Repeat this step for the **Contact** and **Locations** links.

8. Now run the application by hitting *F5*. You can now see that clicking on the items in the emulator navigates to the corresponding pages in your application. This includes using the back button that is located on the phone.

How it works...

This simple form of navigation works by utilizing the underlying navigation framework built into the application. In Silverlight, pages are defined in the `System.Windows.Controls.Page` class. The Windows Phone Portrait Page items you added to the solution are instances of a subclass of the type, `Microsoft.Phone.Controls.PhoneApplicationPage`. It defines phone-platform-specific events and properties including the BackKeyPress event, which is raised when the phone's hardware back button is pressed.

When you set the `NavigationUri` property of each link, what is actually happening is that it is setting this property in the XAML, as you can see in the following code:

```
<Grid x:Name="ContentPanel" Grid.Row="1" Margin="12,0,12,0">
        <HyperlinkButton Content="About" Grid.Row="1" NavigateUri="/
NavigationExample;component/Views/About.xaml"/>
        <HyperlinkButton Content="Contact" Grid.Row="2"
NavigateUri="/NavigationExample;component/Views/Contact.xaml"/>
        <HyperlinkButton Content="Locations" Grid.Row="3"
NavigateUri="/NavigationExample;component/Views/CompanyLocations.
        xaml"/>
</Grid>
```

Downloading the example code

You can download the example code files for all Packt books you have purchased from your account at `http://www.PacktPub.com`. If you purchased this book elsewhere, you can visit `http://www.PacktPub.com/support` and register to have the files e-mailed directly to you.

As you can see, it doesn't just set the `NavigationUri` to a simple file path like you might expect if you have done web development before. Instead it is setting it to a path that includes the namespace of the project. In this case, the namespace is *NavigationExample*. This allows you, in more complex examples, to navigate to controls that are merely referenced in other assemblies.

There's more...

While this navigation is simple, you usually want to pass some information from one control to another. You can do this with a query string much like you would do in a traditional web application. For example, your `NavigateUri` may look something more like this:

```
"/NavigationExample;component/Views/DetailsPage.xaml?selectedItem=2"
```

Then on your details page, you would need to retrieve the value by handling the query string in the navigation load of your `DetailsPage.xaml`, as seen in the following code:

```
protected override void OnNavigatedTo(NavigationEventArgs e)
    {
        string selectedIndex = "";
        if (NavigationContext.QueryString.
        TryGetValue("selectedItem", out selectedIndex))
        {
            int index = int.Parse(selectedIndex);
            DataContext = App.ViewModel.Items[index];
        }
    }
```

This provides you with the basic functionality for passing values from one page to another.

Using Positioning controls

Once you begin developing Windows Phone 7 applications, you will need to be aware of the various basic layout controls. Each of these controls provides different ways to present your data. These controls include the following:

  ▶ **Grid**: The Grid control provides a layout system that can use rows and columns as well as margins to place a control. Grids are the most flexible of the layout controls.

  ▶ **Canvas**: The canvas control provides a simple coordinate based layout method for child controls.

  ▶ **Stack Panel**: The StackPanel control provides a simple horizontal or vertical "stacking" layout. This stacking method will place child controls in order of their declaration in the XAML.

There are also two other layout controls that supplement the three primary controls. These controls differ a little more because they only allow one child control compared to the Grid, Canvas, and Stack Panel that allow unlimited number of child controls. These two controls are as follows:

  ▶ **ScrollViewer**: This control is primarily used to add horizontal and vertical scroll bars to a control that is larger than the area provided to present its child control.

  ▶ **Border**: This control provides a simple border to a control. While this control is one of the most basic, it does give you the ability to create nice rounded borders for controls that may not have that option.

Now that you have read about the basic options for laying out controls, let's look into how to use them to modify our existing navigation application to add more content.

Getting ready

This example will carry forward some of the key concepts from the Navigation application to provide an improved UI.

How to do it...

Let's start with the home page to give it a more finished look. You should have something that looks similar to the following screenshot:

As you can see, it isn't very exciting, but will give you a few foundation steps that are sometimes assumed that you understand. Hopefully, this will get you familiar with the tool in a new way if you are an experienced developer but if you are new to development, it will help you ease into it.

1. Select the border control from the toolbox on the far-left side. Click and hold the current container control (fourth button from the bottom),which will then pop up the selection of other container controls, as shown below:

2. Now that you have selected the **Border** control, draw it to fill most of your control. From the property window, select **Brushes** and set the **BorderBrush** color to white by clicking on the top-left side of the color picker gradient in the Editor and the **Background** to blue. Now the border is covering the existing buttons. We need to place the hyperlink controls into the border control, but if you remember, the border control and scrollviewer controls can have only one child.

    With that, let's actually add a stack panel inside the **Border.** This time you will want to add it a little differently than we had added other controls. I want to show you that there is another way to add controls, especially when you want to add controls as a child of another control.

3. Add a stack panel to the border by simply selecting the border on your design surface. Now select the stackpanel control on the toolbox so that it is the default container control and then double-click on it. This will add the stackpanel as the child control of the border.

    Now that we have seen how to add a new control as a child of an existing control, let's move the hyperlink buttons as children of the stack panel.

4. To do this, we are actually going to use the **Objects and Timelines** window. This window gives you a representation of what is going on with the layering and grouping of your control. Currently, this window should look similar to the following screenshot:

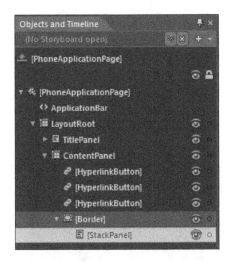

5. To move the three HyperlinkButtons, click the top one in the **Objects and Timeline** window, then press *Shift*, and select the last one. Now you can move all three **HyperlinkButtons** at once instead of moving them individually. In this window, drag the buttons to the stack panel. This will change your document outline to look similar to the following screenshot:

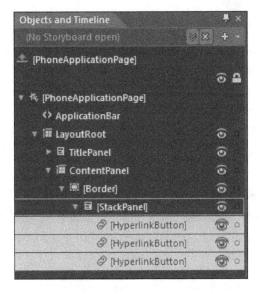

6. While we have these three controls selected, lets set their margins. One thing that is nice in both Blend and Visual Studio is that you can set properties of multiple selected controls at the same time. So while you have these properties selected, go to the **margins** section in the **Layout** section list and set the margins to look like the following:

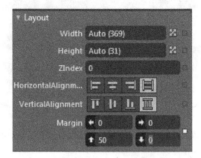

As you can see, this gives you a nice evenly spaced menu by using the StackPanel control. This combination of layout controls gives you the flexibility to design almost any UI that you would need.

How it works

Through the various layout controls you can see that they each offer their own unique features to layout your controls as needed. You can use various combinations of all of these to create any layout you could possibly dream of.

As you have seen in this recipe, the primary layout controls offer a variety of simple layouts by using things such as Grids, Canvas, and the StackPanel. The Grid offers both relational positioning from margins or offering column and row based layouts. The canvas offers a more exact layout that is not adjusted by the container it is in and finally the StackPanel offers a simple stack of child elements.

Discovering the various input controls

As with any application there is usually the need to capture some type of user input. This may be in the form of gathering data like a user name or password or even just capturing a website address. If you have ever done windows application development, these types of items can be captured through two very popular controls, namely, the Textbox and the PasswordBox. While both of these still exists in Windows Phone 7, the Textbox control has a few tricks up its sleeves. One of the biggest tricks is the ability to optimize input on the screen for various types of user input set by input type. In this example, we will take a contact form to take traditional contact information from a user but optimize the keyboard for various inputs like phone, address, e-mail, and a few others.

Getting ready

To get ready for this part of the project, we will be editing the `Contact.xaml` in our example for this chapter to take some basic contact information for a customer. To begin, let's open the `Contact.xaml` in Expression Blend.

How to do it...

For the most part, we have the `Contact.xaml` open in Expression Blend. We will want to begin to layout our control to take the following information:

- First Name and Last Name
- Phone Number
- E-mail Address
- Website Address
- Address Information (Address, City, State, Zip)
- Comments

For the most part, this doesn't seem like anything out of the ordinary for building a form. We will leverage some of the techniques we learned for laying out controls in the layout example to build a very consistent UI:

1. Start by setting the Scrollbars to be Auto on the ContentPanel. This will automatically show the scrollbars once our form has grown past the possible viewable area on the screen, which can be found by expanding the Layout section and setting the `VerticalScrollBarVisible` in the properties window.

2. Now let's select the **ContentPanel** in our `Contact.xaml` file's design surface. Then double-click the Grid control from the toolbox. As you can see, it creates a Grid control that is placed inside the **ContentPanel**, but one little problem—it doesn't actually fill the **ContentPanel.** By default, Blend creates a Grid with a few standard settings already set like height, width, and alignment. For our purposes, we actually want to reset those by right-clicking the Grid that you just created and clicking **Auto Size | Fill**. This will remove the default height, width, and alignment settings, which will cause the new Grid to fill its parent container.

3. Now we will need to build our layout for controls. Since this is a very simple control, we will just place the controls on the screen. We will want to place both **Textboxes** and **Textblock** controls to identify which inputs are for each textbox. Drag the controls on the screen to look like this:

How it works

In this recipe, we discovered many of the basic input controls. These controls use simple input and place them in properties, which you can access from your code behind. This provides the easiest way of getting data input from your users.

Now that you have created your first form for data input, I am sure you can see the simplicity of creating forms. There's more to creating Windows Phone 7 applications than just adding textboxes on a form. We will use this form later for actually sending feedback. So go ahead, run the application, and navigate to the **Contact** page to find that you can add data using the controls.

There's more...

As users get savvier with their mobile devices, they also have higher expectations for the application to know more about what they are doing. For example, in the form we just created, users will need to have data input that is more catered to the actual data they are inputting. By this I mean, if you are asking a user to input a phone number, don't show them a keyboard with the alphabet on it so they have to switch to the number and symbol keyboard. Wouldn't it make sense to simply show a numeric input?

So how do you customize these inputs? It is actually very simple. In Blend, select the phone number text box you created before. In the properties window, there is a property called `InputScope`; change this to `TelephoneNumber`. Now run the application and navigate to the contact page and try entering a phone number. Notice that instead of the standard keyboard, you get the number pad. This is a simple way to ease user input in your application with no code.

Now let's set a few others to be more optimized for that type of input:

- **First Name textbox**: Set `InputScope` to `PersonalGivenName`
- **Last Name textbox**: Set `InputScope` to `PersonalSurName`
- **Email textbox**: Set `InputScope` to `EmailUserName`
- **Web Site textbox**: Set `inputScope` to `Uri`
- **Address textbox**: Set `InputScope` to `AddressStreet`
- **City textbox**: Set `InputScope` to `AddressCity`
- **State textbox**: Set `InputScope` to `AddressStateOrProvince`

So you may ask yourself, do I have to do this for every textbox? And the answer is no. But the question is should you do this, and the answer is yes. While this little tweaking doesn't seem to make a huge difference on some input, it is actually highly optimized to give the user the best keyboard for that input, even when it comes to other cultures and languages.

Also, while setting `InputScope` in Blend gives you a drop-down of a good number of input scopes, there are actually many that aren't displayed that are even more specialized. Here is the list of `InputScope` instances:

AddressCity	Address CountryName	AddressCountry ShortName	AddressState OrProvince
AddressStreet	Alphanumeric FullWidth	Alphanumeric HalfWidth	ApplicationEnd
Bopomofo	Chat	CurrencyAmount	CurrencyAmount AndSymbol
Currency Chinese	Date	DateDay	DateDayName
DateMonth	DateMonthName	DateYear	Default
Digits	EmailNameOr Address	EmailSmtpAddress	EmailUserName
EnumString	FileName	FullFilePath	Hanja
Hiragana	Katakana FullWidth	Katakana HalfWidth	LogOnName
Maps	NameOr PhoneNumber	Number	NumberFullWidth
OneChar	Password	PersonalFullName	PersonalGivenName
Personal MiddleName	Personal NamePrefix	Personal NameSuffix	PersonalSurname
PhraseList	PostalAddress	PostalCode	Private
Regular Expression	Search	Srgs	TelephoneAreaCode
Telephone CountryCode	Telephone LocalNumber	TelephoneNumber	Text
Time	TimeHour	TimeMinorSec	Url
Xml	Yomi		

ViewStateManager introduction

Many of the concepts set in this chapter will help provide you with a foundation to build highly customized controls that are sharp and provide various user feedback. We are all aware of how buttons react when you mouse over them in a standard windows application; most of the time they change color or highlight. This change of state is similar to using the ViewStateManger in a Windows Phone application.

The various controls that are included with Silverlight for Windows Phone have visual states associated with them. These states can be customized easily through the templates, but what if you want to create different states for your custom control? We do this with the Visual State Manager. For our first example, we will customize our current navigation example to build different states when selecting a location on the location screen. This is a way to add visual differences without creating another control for the different content.

Getting ready

We are going to carry our navigation example through to this example. We will be taking the `Location.xaml` and adding a few custom states to it. We will also introduce the concept of behaviors in this recipe so that we can switch between our custom visual states.

How to do it...

Let's start by opening the `CompanyLocations.xaml` in Expression Blend. We want to create a simple way to hide and show the location details once they are clicked. Traditionally in other types of development, you might do this by creating code that manually changes the visibility properties of the details and moves the other pieces out of the way. But instead we are going to actually use unique view states for this:

1. Now that we have the `CompanyLocations.xaml` open, let's drag four text block controls onto the design surface, two for the headers and two for the details. Let's lay it out to look something like the following screenshot:

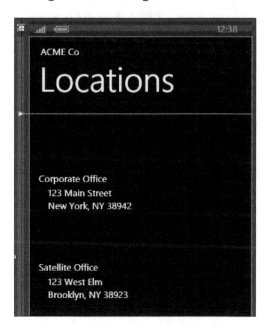

2. As you can see, this isn't very exciting. So let's do a little more to it by adding two more text blocks that are rotated 90 degrees that also say the location name. As well as that, let's move the address information off screen and make the text larger for the headers so it looks more like this:

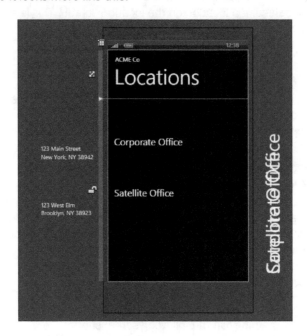

Now what we want to do is make it so that when you touch the **Corporate Office** text, the appropriate information displays the corporate office information. Then when you click on the **Satellite Office**, the information for it displays the satellite office information. And on top of that we are going to pretty much do this with zero code (actually, there is code in the XAML but we will show you that afterwards).

3. To create the states, we have to go to the **States** window in the top left of Blend to create a new state group. Click on the **Add state group** button in the top-right side of that window and name the state group as **LocationStates**. Then add two states, namely, **CorporateState** and **SatelliteState.** This will cause your state group to look something like the next screenshot:

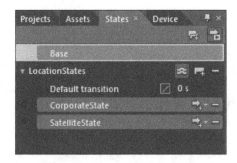

4. To make the states, select the **CorporateState,** which will put this into a recording mode for the state, as seen by the red dot in the top right of the design surface. This does not mean it is recording your every move, but does mean it is recording any changes to the selected state compared to the base state. So let's lay out both the CorporateState and SatelliteState. You can lay them out as shown in the following screenshot:

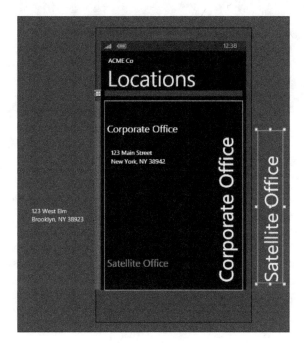

And the Satellite Office view is shown in the following screenshot:

5. Now that we have the individual states, we need to make it to where you actually touch the text that it switches. First let's switch back to the base state so that any changes we make effect all states.

6. Now let's begin to create the way we want it to change once clicked. To do this, we are going to use a behavior that is included with Blend. So from your assets window, search for *GotoStateAction* and drag that to both the **Corporate Office** and **Satellite Office** text. Now let's set the options for this. As you can see in your objects and timeline window, it adds the child elements to the text. You can select these objects and set the `StateName` property to the appropriate state for the text.

7. At this time, let's run the application. From what you can see now when you click the individual text on the location, it will swap to the appropriate state.

How it works...

The concept of visual state manager is actually quite simple and very flexible. The XAML markup it creates is actually very simple, as we can see below:

```
<VisualStateManager.VisualStateGroups>
        <VisualStateGroup x:Name="LocationStates">
```

```xml
            <VisualState x:Name="CorporateState">
              <Storyboard>
                <DoubleAnimation Duration="0" To="-54" Storyboard.
TargetProperty="(UIElement.RenderTransform).(CompositeTransform.
TranslateY)" Storyboard.TargetName="textBlock" d:IsOptimized="True"/>
                <DoubleAnimation Duration="0" To="208" Storyboard.
TargetProperty="(UIElement.RenderTransform).(CompositeTransform.
TranslateY)" Storyboard.TargetName="textBlock1" d:IsOptimized="True"/>
                <DoubleAnimation Duration="0" To="264" Storyboard.
TargetProperty="(UIElement.RenderTransform).(CompositeTransform.
TranslateX)" Storyboard.TargetName="textBlock2" d:IsOptimized="True"/>
                <DoubleAnimation Duration="0" To="-50.219" Storyboard.
TargetProperty="(UIElement.RenderTransform).(CompositeTransform.
TranslateX)" Storyboard.TargetName="textBlock3" d:IsOptimized="True"/>
                <DoubleAnimation Duration="0" To="-69.781" Storyboard.
TargetProperty="(UIElement.RenderTransform).(CompositeTransform.
TranslateY)" Storyboard.TargetName="textBlock3" d:IsOptimized="True"/>
                <DoubleAnimation Duration="0" To="0.4"
Storyboard.TargetProperty="(UIElement.Opacity)" Storyboard.
TargetName="textBlock1" d:IsOptimized="True"/>
              </Storyboard>
            </VisualState>
            <VisualState x:Name="SatelliteState">
              <Storyboard>
                <DoubleAnimation Duration="0" To="0.4" Storyboard.
TargetProperty="(UIElement.Opacity)" Storyboard.TargetName="textBlock"
d:IsOptimized="True"/>
                <DoubleAnimation Duration="0" To="-84" Storyboard.
TargetProperty="(UIElement.RenderTransform).(CompositeTransform.
TranslateY)" Storyboard.TargetName="textBlock" d:IsOptimized="True"/>
                <DoubleAnimation Duration="0" To="-28" Storyboard.
TargetProperty="(UIElement.RenderTransform).(CompositeTransform.
TranslateY)" Storyboard.TargetName="textBlock1" d:IsOptimized="True"/>
                <DoubleAnimation Duration="0" To="282" Storyboard.
TargetProperty="(UIElement.RenderTransform).(CompositeTransform.
TranslateX)" Storyboard.TargetName="textBlock4" d:IsOptimized="True"/>
                <DoubleAnimation Duration="0" To="-46.219" Storyboard.
TargetProperty="(UIElement.RenderTransform).(CompositeTransform.
TranslateX)" Storyboard.TargetName="textBlock5" d:IsOptimized="True"/>
                <DoubleAnimation Duration="0" To="-69.781" Storyboard.
TargetProperty="(UIElement.RenderTransform).(CompositeTransform.
TranslateY)" Storyboard.TargetName="textBlock5" d:IsOptimized="True"/>
              </Storyboard>
            </VisualState>
          </VisualStateGroup>
        </VisualStateManager.VisualStateGroups>
```

What you will notice is that for every element we moved in a state, it is actually creating `DoubleAnimation` for the movement with the new value in the **To** property. So, let's take one animation and break it down:

```
<DoubleAnimation Duration="0" To="-54" Storyboard.
TargetProperty="(UIElement.RenderTransform).(CompositeTransform.
TranslateY)" Storyboard.TargetName="textBlock" d:IsOptimized="True"/>
```

It is broken down to these items:

- ▶ **Duration**: Currently set to 0, this is the time period that this animation should play for.
- ▶ **To**: This is the new value of the property being set in the animation. In this case, we are changing the TranslateY property.
- ▶ **Storyboard.TargetProperty**: This gives the dependency property reference that needs to be set.
- ▶ **Storyboard.TargetName**: The name of the element being animated.

There's more...

ViewStateManager is probably one of my favorite things to use in Blend, mostly because it has a nice feature to create simple animations without really having to know how to animate. To do this, you need to do two things, change the EasingFunction on the state group and the duration. We will change the duration to one second and to an exponential easing function, as you can see below:

As with any change in Blend, this also adds the following to your XAML:

```
<VisualStateGroup.Transitions>
        <VisualTransition GeneratedDuration="0:0:1">
          <VisualTransition.GeneratedEasingFunction>
            <ExponentialEase EasingMode="EaseInOut"/>
          </VisualTransition.GeneratedEasingFunction>
        </VisualTransition>
      </VisualStateGroup.Transitions>
```

Now when you run your application, you will get a simple animation that adds a nice finishing touch to your locations screen. The two best things to do are play with the timings and change the easing functions. Each easing function will give you a pretty different animation that can be tweaked for your specific desired outcome.

Understanding the panorama control

Up to this point, almost everything we have talked about gives you a basic understanding of developing user interfaces in Silverlight regardless of whether it is intended for the phone or for the web. With the introduction of Windows Phone 7, Microsoft introduced two new controls, namely, the panorama and pivot controls. These two controls provide the rich sliding motion that is very common in many of the Windows Phone 7 interfaces.

The panorama control allows you to create content beyond the extent of the physical device.

Getting ready

To get started with the panorama control in Visual Studio, create a new project and select the **Windows Phone Panorama Application**:

This will create a new project which is already setup and ready to go for using the panorama control. You do not have to use this project template to use this control. It is just a good starting point if this is the desired design of your application.

How to do it...

Now let's do a little customization to the current application to give you a feel of how the control works. As you can see when running the application, as you drag the interface to the left or right side the content, header, and background, all move independently as to give it a much more fluid look and feel.

Let's do some simple customization to this project. Let's first change the text that says *My application* to say *ACME Company*:

1. To do this, select the panorama control in the design surface in Visual Studio and then set the property of the title to *ACME Company* in the property window, which is found by right-clicking the panorama control and clicking **Properties** as follows:

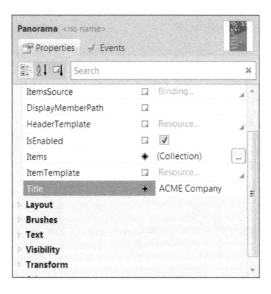

Now let's make the data in the two panes a little more interesting. For the first one, let's mimic what we have done in earlier recipes and give the locations of ACME Company.

2. To do this, navigate to the `SampleData/MainViewModelSampleData.xaml` and double-click on it. Let's change the data to look more like this:

```
<local:MainViewModel
    xmlns="http://schemas.microsoft.com/winfx/2006/xaml/
    presentation"
    xmlns:x="http://schemas.microsoft.com/winfx/2006/xaml"
    xmlns:local="clr-namespace:PanoramaExample"
    SampleProperty="Sample Text Property Value">
```

```
<local:MainViewModel.Items>
    <local:ItemViewModel LineOne="Main Office" LineTwo="123
    Main St. New York, NY" LineThree="(123) 123-1234"/>
    <local:ItemViewModel LineOne="satellite  Office"
    LineTwo="123 Elm St. Bronx, NY" LineThree="(123)
    321-1234"/>
</local:MainViewModel.Items>

</local:MainViewModel>
```

3. Rebuild the application by right-clicking the project and selecting the rebuild option. You will see that this updates the design surface. Now let's run the application and see how this looks in the emulator. The first thing you will notice is that the emulator and the design time don't match! Don't worry, this was expected.

4. To change the actual runtime data, let's open up the **ViewModels | MainViewModel. cs**. Let's delete the lines from the section under the comment about inserting sample data and let's insert it with real sample data. Let's consolidate it to just two lines that look like this:

```
this.Items.Add(new ItemViewModel() { LineOne = "Main Office",
    LineTwo = "123 Main St. New York, NY", LineThree = "(123)
    123-1234" });
this.Items.Add(new ItemViewModel() { LineOne = "Satallite Office",
    LineTwo = "123 Elm St. Bronx, NY", LineThree = "(123)
    321-1234" });
```

Now when you run it, the data is correct.

How it works...

Now this has also been an extremely simple overview of not only the Panorama control but also some basic data binding techniques and architecture that is called **MVVM** (**Model-View-View Model**), which we will cover in much greater depth in a later chapter.

As far as the actual `Panorama control`, it is actually very simple. The panorama control is made up of the control that can only contain Panorama Item controls, those which can hold other controls. This is very similar to how the other controls we have used in the chapter work, except it renders differently and offers a more specialized interface.

You can see the extent of the XAML here:

```
<!--Panorama control-->
    <controls:Panorama Title="ACME Company">
        <controls:Panorama.Background>
            <ImageBrush ImageSource="PanoramaBackground.png"/>
        </controls:Panorama.Background>
        <!--Panorama item one-->
```

```
<controls:PanoramaItem Header="first item">
    <!--Double line list with text wrapping-->
    <ListBox Margin="0,0,-12,0" ItemsSource="
      {Binding Items}">
        <ListBox.ItemTemplate>
            <DataTemplate>
                <StackPanel Margin="0,0,0,17" Width="432">
                    <TextBlock Text="{Binding
                        LineOne}" TextWrapping="Wrap"
                        Style="{StaticResource
                        PhoneTextExtraLargeStyle}"/>
                    <TextBlock Text="{Binding LineTwo}"
                        TextWrapping="Wrap"
                        Margin="12,-6,12,0"
                        Style="{StaticResource
                        PhoneTextSubtleStyle}"/>
                </StackPanel>
            </DataTemplate>
        </ListBox.ItemTemplate>
    </ListBox>
</controls:PanoramaItem>

<!--Panorama item two-->
<!--Use 'Orientation="Horizontal"' to enable a panel that
    lays out horizontally-->
<controls:PanoramaItem Header="second item">
    <!--Double line list with image placeholder and text
        wrapping-->
    <ListBox Margin="0,0,-12,0" ItemsSource="
        {Binding Items}">
        <ListBox.ItemTemplate>
            <DataTemplate>
                <StackPanel Orientation="Horizontal"
                    Margin="0,0,0,17">
                    <!--Replace rectangle with image-->
                    <Rectangle Height="100" Width="100"
                      Fill="#FFE5001b" Margin="12,0,9,0"/>
                    <StackPanel Width="311">
                        <TextBlock Text="{Binding
                           LineOne}" TextWrapping="Wrap"
                           Style="{StaticResource
                           PhoneTextExtraLargeStyle}"/>
                        <TextBlock Text="{Binding
                           LineTwo}" TextWrapping="Wrap"
                           Margin="12,-6,12,0"
                           Style="{StaticResource
                           PhoneTextSubtleStyle}"/>
                    </StackPanel>
                </StackPanel>
            </DataTemplate>
```

```
        </ListBox.ItemTemplate>
      </ListBox>
    </controls:PanoramaItem>
  </controls:Panorama>
```

Using the pivot control

Now that you have used the panorama control, you will find the pivot control almost identical in usage. Where the panorama control acts almost as one unified control, the pivot control acts almost like a traditional tab control that you would see in any other application.

Getting ready

Similar to the panorama control, there is a project template for creating a pivot control application. Let's start by creating a Pivot Control Application in Visual Studio. Also, because these items are so similar, let's actually repeat the steps of changing the sample data and the view model runtime data in the project that you did in the previous example.

How to do it...

Now that you have updated the application to almost mimic the panorama control, let's actually run it. You should get something that looks like the following screenshot:

Now when you click on the word **second**, it jumps to the second content and the tab for the first moves to left and off the screen after the second tab. Unlike the pivot control that acts as a tab control, the panorama acts as a single sliding image. The pivot control also does not have the option for the background that moves independently from the content.

How it works...

If you begin to look at the XAML, you will notice that it is almost identical to the panorama control, as you can see below:

```
<phone:PhoneApplicationPage
    x:Class="PivotExample.MainPage"
    xmlns="http://schemas.microsoft.com/winfx/2006/xaml/presentation"
    xmlns:x="http://schemas.microsoft.com/winfx/2006/xaml"
    xmlns:phone="clr-namespace:Microsoft.Phone.
        Controls;assembly=Microsoft.Phone"
    xmlns:shell="clr-namespace:Microsoft.Phone.
        Shell;assembly=Microsoft.Phone"
    xmlns:controls="clr-namespace:Microsoft.Phone.
        Controls;assembly=Microsoft.Phone.Controls"
    xmlns:d="http://schemas.microsoft.com/expression/blend/2008"
    xmlns:mc="http://schemas.openxmlformats.org/
        markup-compatibility/2006"
    mc:Ignorable="d" d:DesignWidth="480" d:DesignHeight="768"
    d:DataContext="{d:DesignData SampleData/MainViewModelSampleData.
        xaml}"
    FontFamily="{StaticResource PhoneFontFamilyNormal}"
    FontSize="{StaticResource PhoneFontSizeNormal}"
    Foreground="{StaticResource PhoneForegroundBrush}"
    SupportedOrientations="Portrait"  Orientation="Portrait"
    shell:SystemTray.IsVisible="True">

    <!--LayoutRoot is the root grid where all page content is
        placed-->
    <Grid x:Name="LayoutRoot" Background="Transparent">
        <!--Pivot Control-->
        <controls:Pivot Title="MY APPLICATION">
            <!--Pivot item one-->
            <controls:PivotItem Header="first">
                <!--Double line list with text wrapping-->
                <ListBox x:Name="FirstListBox" Margin="0,0,-12,0"
                    ItemsSource="{Binding Items}">
                    <ListBox.ItemTemplate>
                        <DataTemplate>
                            <StackPanel Margin="0,0,0,17" Width="432">
```

```
                            <TextBlock Text="{Binding
                              LineOne}" TextWrapping="Wrap"
                              Style="{StaticResource
                              PhoneTextExtraLargeStyle}"/>
                            <TextBlock Text="{Binding LineTwo}"
                              TextWrapping="Wrap"
                              Margin="12,-6,12,0"
                              Style="{StaticResource
                              PhoneTextSubtleStyle}"/>
                        </StackPanel>
                    </DataTemplate>
                </ListBox.ItemTemplate>
            </ListBox>
        </controls:PivotItem>

        <!--Pivot item two-->
        <controls:PivotItem Header="second">
            <!--Triple line list no text wrapping-->
                <ListBox x:Name="SecondListBox" Margin="0,0,-12,0"
                  ItemsSource="{Binding Items}">
                    <ListBox.ItemTemplate>
                        <DataTemplate>
                            <StackPanel Margin="0,0,0,17">
                                <TextBlock Text="{Binding
                                  LineOne}" TextWrapping="NoWrap"
                                  Margin="12,0,0,0"
                                  Style="{StaticResource
                                  PhoneTextExtraLargeStyle}"/>
                                <TextBlock Text="{Binding
                                  LineThree}" TextWrapping="NoWrap"
                                  Margin="12,-6,0,0"
                                  Style="{StaticResource
                                  PhoneTextSubtleStyle}"/>
                            </StackPanel>
                        </DataTemplate>
                    </ListBox.ItemTemplate>
                </ListBox>
        </controls:PivotItem>
    </controls:Pivot>
</Grid>

<!--Sample code showing usage of ApplicationBar-->
<!--<phone:PhoneApplicationPage.ApplicationBar>
    <shell:ApplicationBar IsVisible="True" IsMenuEnabled="True">
        <shell:ApplicationBarIconButton IconUri="/Images/
        appbar_button1.png" Text="Button 1"/>
        <shell:ApplicationBarIconButton IconUri="/Images/
        appbar_button2.png" Text="Button 2"/>
        <shell:ApplicationBar.MenuItems>
            <shell:ApplicationBarMenuItem Text="MenuItem 1"/>
```

```
            <shell:ApplicationBarMenuItem Text="MenuItem 2"/>
        </shell:ApplicationBar.MenuItems>
    </shell:ApplicationBar>
</phone:PhoneApplicationPage.ApplicationBar>-->

</phone:PhoneApplicationPage>
```

The main thing to note is where it declares the pivot control. It essentially is declared as `controls:Pivot` instead of `controls:Panorama`. So now you are probably asking yourself "When should I use which one?". There are a couple of rules to consider:

Use the panorama control:

 ▶ When you want to use a sliding background image

 ▶ When you want to have all the child controls to be almost dragable to where you can peek at them from another control

Use the pivot control:

 ▶ When you need to have the application bar (panorama control cannot have an application bar on the same screen)

 ▶ You want to create the illusion of a tab control

Other things to keep in mind:

 ▶ The panorama control can be much more memory intensive to use, especially depending on the number of panorama items and the background used

 ▶ The pivot control is much more memory optimized for when you want a great number of child pivot items

2
Creating Animation

In this chapter, we will cover:

- ▶ Using ViewStateManager to create simple animations
- ▶ The basics of timelines
- ▶ Using timelines that change based on user interaction

Introduction

As we have seen in *Chapter 1*, Microsoft has provided a rich set of tools for creating Windows Phone applications and this chapter will take us beyond simply laying out controls by adding animation. For many developers, animation is an afterthought, but it can be an important part of any application, especially a Windows Phone 7 application by conveying the status of the application and things like loading, waiting, and connection status. Because of the disconnected nature of a Windows Phone 7 application when building applications that connect to services on the Internet, these connections may be slower than usual where the user is located.

Also, as animations become a more important part of our applications, it is a necessity for both developers and designers to have an understanding of how animations work, specifically on the windows phone. In this chapter, we will work entirely in Expression Blend to create our animations. This is due to the fact that Visual Studio does not offer any animation tools other than writing it from scratch in your XAML.

We will expand on some of the basic examples of animations from *Chapter 1* to bring more dynamic animations but also provide some practicality to the animations.

Using ViewStateManager to create simple animations

As we have seen in the previous chapter, ViewStateManager allows us to create some simple animations. Now we want to take things a lot further by adding various animations to one control. We will be adding some simple animations to a list box to provide a much customized look and feel.

We will also begin to customize various levels of templates on a few controls to create something that doesn't even look remotely like the standard control.

Getting ready

Let's start by opening Expression Blend and creating a new Windows Phone Application. The other thing we want to go ahead and do is create some sample data for the project to simulate this application actually having some real world data in it. You can do this by navigating to the **Data** tab, clicking the first button with the plus sign, and then selecting **New Sample Data**. When it prompts you for the **Data Source Name**, simply set it to **MySampleData**:

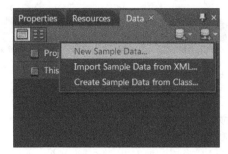

Once you have created your sample data source, we can add additional information to it via the **Data** tab and modify it to be something a little more useful. For this example, we will be modifying the sample data that might be found in a store locator. For this we will need to delete the two properties that are currently in the sample data and add a few of our own. We will be adding the following:

- Store Name
- Store Address
- Store Phone Number
- Manager Name

To do this, simply right-click on the **Property1** and click on **Remove Property**, then do the same for **Property2**. Now click the plus button on the collection row to add four new properties. You can then name the properties to correspond with what we need to keep track of, namely, ManagerName, StoreAddress, StoreName, and StorePhoneNumber.

The next step is to make this sample data seem a little more real; next to the ManagerName property, click the icon that has ABC on it. Then from the format, select **Name**. This will populate the sample data with fake names in the **ManagerName** field. Let's now do the same with the other fields; set them to the following:

- Store Name: Company Name
- Store Address: Address
- Store Phone Number: PhoneNumber

Now you have created your first sample dataset. This is an extremely powerful tool for prototyping applications before you have a database associated with it.

How to do it...

While you now have some data, we need to actually make it do something that will let you animate it. So to start with, we are going to create a listbox on the main control with the data:

1. To do this, drag the **Collection** property in the data window to the main part of your screen, as shown in the following screenshot:

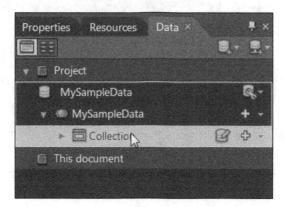

Now that you have a really simple UI, our goal with this UI is to simply show the store name when viewing the entire list, and if you select a single item, then display the details on the store. We want to animate from the non-selected to the selected version of the selected item.

2. If you have created any other forms of Windows development in .NET, you may have some misconceptions of how you might accomplish this in the world of Silverlight and Windows Phone 7. To accomplish this, we will need to edit the item template for the listbox that we just created. Editing the template is fairly simple but it is not very easy to find your first time, so to find where to edit it, we need to right-click on the listbox and navigate to **Edit Additional Templates | Edit Generated Items | Edit Current**:

 Performing this step will take you to the template editing mode, this is probably one of the most important skills you can learn when creating a Silverlight application. This is because many controls are highly customizable but only through templates. Template editing is one thing that you can only do in Blend with design assistance. While you can edit the raw XAML in Visual Studio, the design experience is much richer in Expression Blend.

3. Back to the task at hand to customize the selected state and the base state; what you will quickly find is that the ItemTemplate doesn't actually contain the states. The states are actually contained in the ContainerTemplate. So the only reason I had to open the generated item template is to cut the content to paste it into the ContainerTemplate. So let's select all the textblocks defined in the ItemTemplate and press *Ctrl + X*.

4. To jump back to editing the main control so we can edit the ContainerTemplate, click on the listbox text in the top-left of the design surface as follows:

This will take you back to editing the root control.

5. To move the controls we just selected from the ItemTemplate, we must right click on the listbox then **Edit Additional Templates | Edit Generated Item Container (ItemContainerStyle) | Create Empty**. As you have probably guessed, this will create an empty template for the ItemContainerStyle, which will provide us with the necessary states to get the result we were looking for.

6. But before we can start editing the states, we must change the LayoutRoot to a listbox. There is a very easy way to do this—simply right-click the grid in the **Objects and Timeline** window and **Change Layout Type | Stackpanel**. Now paste the controls into the stackpanel so that we can begin setting the animation for the selected item.

   If you select the **States** window, you will see the entire list of possible states for the ItemContainerStyle. See the following screenshot:

In this exercise, we are only concerned with editing the base state and the **Selected** state. So let's begin with the base state which actually isn't a state at all but the default setting for all states.

7. In our base state, we only want to show the store name, so we will select all the TextBlocks except the TextBlock bound to the store name. To hide these controls, we could set the visibility to **collapsed**, but this would not work to achieve the animation of expanding the details.

8. In a standard Silverlight application, you can set the visibility to collapsed and use fluid layout to help with the animation, but unfortunately you don't have fluid layout in WP7 Silverlight applications.

   Since we can't use the visibility, set the height of the textblocks to 0 by selecting all but the **StoreNameTextBlock** at the same time and in the property window set the height to 0.

9. The next step is to set the selected state by clicking on the Selectedstate in the States window. This will set the design surface into recording mode for the current state. We can now select the TextBlocks in the objects and timeline window and set the height to 26.

10. To see the effect this has on the application, let's run it by pressing *F5*. Once the application launches, try selecting one of the individual companies. As you can see, it will expand as you probably expected but it isn't all that exciting. Now we will want to add some animation to this selection process.

11. Let's go back to Expression Blend to add simple animation to the expanding process. We will want to go back into the editing of the ItemContainer template. Go to the SelectionStatesviewstate group and set the time to 1 second and select any of the easing functions, as shown below:

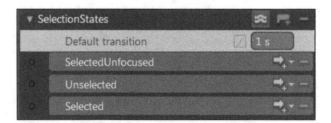

12. To see how this affected our application, let's run it by hitting *F5*. Now when you select the item, you will see it animate. This is the simplest form of animation that you can do in Windows Phone applications.

How it works...

Although this is a very simple form of animation, there are some fundamentals that you might want to consider when creating `ViewStateManager` animations. The animation is actually based on the differences between the base state and the state you are animating to. For this example, we are actually only setting a few properties that are different, in this case, height of the individual textboxes.

There are a couple of ways to actually see where this gets set; one is a nice little visual in Expression Blend and the other is knowing where to find it in the XAML. So to see the place where it gets set in the individual state changes, let's revisit editing the selected state. Now let's examine the objects and timeline window:

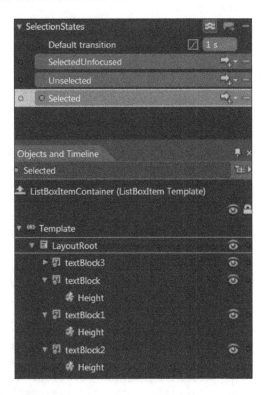

You will see that there are red dots over every textblock that is different from the base state. If you expand those individual textblocks, you can see that you are setting the height. This is very useful when you start making more complex animations with the `ViewStateManager`.

You can also examine this in the XAML that follows:

```
<phone:PhoneApplicationPage.Resources>
    <DataTemplate x:Key="ItemTemplate">
        <StackPanel/>
```

```
          </DataTemplate>
          <Style x:Key="ListBoxItemContainer" TargetType="ListBoxItem">
            <Setter Property="Background" Value="Transparent"/>
            <Setter Property="BorderThickness" Value="0"/>
            <Setter Property="BorderBrush" Value="Transparent"/>
            <Setter Property="Padding" Value="0"/>
            <Setter Property="HorizontalContentAlignment" Value="Left"/>
            <Setter Property="VerticalContentAlignment" Value="Top"/>
            <Setter Property="Template">
              <Setter.Value>
                <ControlTemplateTargetType="ListBoxItem">
                  <StackPanel x:Name="LayoutRoot"
                      Background="{TemplateBinding Background}"
                  HorizontalAlignment="{TemplateBindingHorizontalAlignment}"
                  VerticalAlignment="{TemplateBindingVerticalAlignment}">
                    <VisualStateManager.VisualStateGroups>
                      <VisualStateGroup x:Name="CommonStates">
                        <VisualState x:Name="Normal"/>
                        <VisualState x:Name="MouseOver"/>
                        <VisualState x:Name="Disabled"/>
                      </VisualStateGroup>
                      <VisualStateGroup x:Name="SelectionStates">
                        <VisualStateGroup.Transitions>
                          <VisualTransitionGeneratedDuration="0:0:1">
                            <VisualTransition.GeneratedEasingFunction>
                              <ExponentialEaseEasingMode="EaseInOut"/>
                            </VisualTransition.GeneratedEasingFunction>
                          </VisualTransition>
                        </VisualStateGroup.Transitions>
                        <VisualState x:Name="Unselected"/>
                        <VisualState x:Name="Selected">
                          <Storyboard>
                            <DoubleAnimation Duration="0" To="26"
                      Storyboard.TargetProperty="(FrameworkElement.Height)"
                      Storyboard.TargetName="textBlock" d:IsOptimized="True"/>
                            <DoubleAnimation Duration="0" To="26"
                      Storyboard.TargetProperty="(FrameworkElement.Height)"
                      Storyboard.TargetName="textBlock1" d:IsOptimized="True"/>
                            <DoubleAnimation Duration="0" To="26"
                      Storyboard.TargetProperty="(FrameworkElement.Height)"
                      Storyboard.TargetName="textBlock2" d:IsOptimized="True"/>

                          </Storyboard>
                        </VisualState>
                      </VisualStateGroup>
```

```
        </VisualStateManager.VisualStateGroups>
        <TextBlock Text="{Binding StoreName}"
          Margin="0,10,0,0"/>
        <TextBlock x:Name="textBlock" Text="{Binding
          ManagerName}" Height="0"/>
        <TextBlock x:Name="textBlock1" Text="{Binding
          StoreAddress}" Height="0"/>
        <TextBlock x:Name="textBlock2" Text="{Binding
          StorePhoneNumber}" Margin="0,0,0,10" Height="0"/>
      </StackPanel>
    </ControlTemplate>
  </Setter.Value>
  </Setter>
  </Style>
</phone:PhoneApplicationPage.Resources>
```

The key concept to notice is the `DoubleAnimation` tag under the `VisualState` tag. This tag is just the code that explains which state to set and what properties you are changing.

The basics of timelines

While `ViewStateManager` is an outstanding way to create simple transitions for controls based on the current state of the control, sometimes you actually need more traditional animation techniques. If you have ever created a Flash application, then this will be very similar to what you are used to.

In this example, we will create a simple animation that will demonstrate animating various properties including position and brush settings. We will just be creating a simple one that could represent a loading animation.

Getting ready

To get started we simply need to open Expression Blend and start a new Windows Phone application. This will be our foundation for animation.

How to do it...

Create a circle in each corner of the screen as follows:

We are now going to animate each circle to move from one corner to the other.

1. To begin, let's create a blank storyboard by clicking on the plus sign in the Objects and Timeline window. As you will notice, this layout isn't ideal for creating animations because you can't see the entire timeline. To switch to the animation layout view, press *F6*; this will toggle between Animation and Design views.

2. Before we begin animating, we need to set the first keyframe so all controls start at their current point. We do this by clicking on the insert **keyframe** button on the timeline window. As you will notice, it will only set the keyframe for the selected object you are working with. Do this for each circle.

3. Examine the storyboard that was just created and decide how long you want to make our animation. For this example, we will be going to use the 3- second mark by clicking on 3 seconds on the timeline. This will move the yellow mark to this point. Now if you modify anything on the design surface, it will create a keyframe at this point.

4. Drag the top-left circle over the bottom-left circle; and then the bottom-left to the bottom-right; the bottom-right to the top-right, and finally the top-right to the top-left.

5. Hit the play button on the timeline view to preview the storyboard animation. What you will see is each circle animating from one corner to the next. Now we need to actually make this animate when the application starts. We will want to exit the recording mode by hitting the red circle next to Recording on the design surface.

6. Place a basic behavior by dragging-and-dropping the `ControlStoryBoardAction` onto the design surface. Start it on load by setting the property EventName to loaded.

Now when you run your application, the animation should play.

How it works...

The XAML is actually defining `DoubleAnimations` similar to the XAML that was developed for the state changes. You can see the code below:

```
<Storyboard x:Name="Storyboard1">
        <DoubleAnimationUsingKeyFrames Storyboard.
TargetProperty="(UIElement.RenderTransform).(CompositeTransform.
TranslateX)" Storyboard.TargetName="ellipse">
            <EasingDoubleKeyFrameKeyTime="0" Value="0"/>
            <EasingDoubleKeyFrameKeyTime="0:0:3" Value="-7.5"/>
        </DoubleAnimationUsingKeyFrames>
        <DoubleAnimationUsingKeyFrames Storyboard.
TargetProperty="(UIElement.RenderTransform).(CompositeTransform.
TranslateY)" Storyboard.TargetName="ellipse">
            <EasingDoubleKeyFrameKeyTime="0" Value="0"/>
            <EasingDoubleKeyFrameKeyTime="0:0:3" Value="544.5"/>
        </DoubleAnimationUsingKeyFrames>
        <DoubleAnimationUsingKeyFrames Storyboard.
TargetProperty="(UIElement.RenderTransform).(CompositeTransform.
TranslateX)" Storyboard.TargetName="ellipse3">
            <EasingDoubleKeyFrameKeyTime="0" Value="0"/>
            <EasingDoubleKeyFrameKeyTime="0:0:3" Value="402"/>
        </DoubleAnimationUsingKeyFrames>
        <DoubleAnimationUsingKeyFrames Storyboard.
TargetProperty="(UIElement.RenderTransform).(CompositeTransform.
TranslateY)" Storyboard.TargetName="ellipse3">
            <EasingDoubleKeyFrameKeyTime="0" Value="0"/>
            <EasingDoubleKeyFrameKeyTime="0:0:3" Value="-1.5"/>
        </DoubleAnimationUsingKeyFrames>
        <DoubleAnimationUsingKeyFrames Storyboard.
TargetProperty="(UIElement.RenderTransform).(CompositeTransform.
TranslateY)" Storyboard.TargetName="ellipse2">
            <EasingDoubleKeyFrameKeyTime="0" Value="0"/>
            <EasingDoubleKeyFrameKeyTime="0:0:3" Value="-544.5"/>
```

```
        </DoubleAnimationUsingKeyFrames>
        <DoubleAnimationUsingKeyFrames Storyboard.
TargetProperty="(UIElement.RenderTransform).(CompositeTransform.
TranslateX)" Storyboard.TargetName="ellipse2">
            <EasingDoubleKeyFrameKeyTime="0" Value="0"/>
            <EasingDoubleKeyFrameKeyTime="0:0:3" Value="1.5"/>
        </DoubleAnimationUsingKeyFrames>
        <DoubleAnimationUsingKeyFrames Storyboard.
TargetProperty="(UIElement.RenderTransform).(CompositeTransform.
TranslateX)" Storyboard.TargetName="ellipse1">
            <EasingDoubleKeyFrameKeyTime="0" Value="0"/>
            <EasingDoubleKeyFrameKeyTime="0:0:3" Value="-391.5"/>
        </DoubleAnimationUsingKeyFrames>
        <DoubleAnimationUsingKeyFrames Storyboard.
TargetProperty="(UIElement.RenderTransform).(CompositeTransform.
TranslateY)" Storyboard.TargetName="ellipse1">
            <EasingDoubleKeyFrameKeyTime="0" Value="0"/>
            <EasingDoubleKeyFrameKeyTime="0:0:3" Value="-4.5"/>
        </DoubleAnimationUsingKeyFrames>
    </Storyboard>
```

This animation defines what object is moving and the amount of time taken to start and stop each animation. For example, if you take the following code that is used in the above example:

```
<DoubleAnimationUsingKeyFrames Storyboard.TargetProperty="(UIElement.
RenderTransform).(CompositeTransform.TranslateX)" Storyboard.
TargetName="ellipse">
        <EasingDoubleKeyFrameKeyTime="0" Value="0"/>
        <EasingDoubleKeyFrameKeyTime="0:0:3" Value="-7.5"/>
    </DoubleAnimationUsingKeyFrames>
```

You can see that we are defining an animation that uses keyframes called a `DoubleAnimationUsingKeyFrames`. This type of animation requires a `Storyboard. TargetProperty`, which is used to set the beginning and ending values for the defined property, in this case, the TranslateX property. As a child element of the `DoubleAnimationUsingKeyFrames`, you must define the keyframes for the animation which tells us to set the Target Property at a specific time in the animation. In this case, we want to Translate X to 0 at the beginning of the timeline and -7.5 at the end of the timeline which is at three seconds.

There's more...

While this animation is fairly straightforward, you may have the need to make the transition a little more interesting than just moving the items to their desired spot in a set amount of time. So we can actually adjust the easing function the way we set it in the `ViewStateManager` example but apply it to each item's transition.

To do this, open your storyboard in the Object and Timeline window and click on the individual keyframes at the end of the timeline. You can now select an easing function that you would like to use in this animation. For each of these keyframes, set the easing function to BackInOut. Now run the application.

Using timelines for feedback to users

As we have seen so far, animations are a simple way of adding some visual interest to your application. But we have only seen so far the ability to add animations in a non-user driven animation. With any application, most animations are going to be user driven or respond to users.

In this example, we will take our previous example on a timeline and another sample timeline and place buttons to react to each button.

Getting ready

Since we are using the existing timeline example, we are going to simply expand it by adding an additional storyboard that we can swap between. Open the existing application and go to your objects and timeline window. Click the plus button to add an additional storyboard.

This additional storyboard will be used to flip the individual circles using projection. Select all four circles and insert a keyframe at the zero timeframe and another keyframe at two second timeframe. While on the two second time slot, set the Projection settings of all four circles to X=180 and Z=180. You can play the animation from the timeline and see that the circles rotate on the X and Z axes.

How to do it...

Drag-and-drop two buttons onto the screen as follows:

Now drag-and-drop the same `ControlStoryBoardAction` behavior we used to have the animation start when the application was loaded but to both the buttons. On the commands, set the Storyboard to Control for button one to Storyboard 1 and button two to Storyboard 2.

When you run the application, you can see that it will run the animation when you click on the buttons. Also, you will notice that each storyboard is independent of the other so you can actually run both storyboards at the same time. This is only possible when both storyboards aren't setting the same properties. If you do have two storyboards that edit the same properties, then the storyboard that was started last will set the property last.

How it works...

The animation as in the previous examples is being set within the XAML which is often more than you would ever write yourself. It is good to have a basic understanding of how animations work as we covered in the previous recipe. When editing timelines, it will add and adjust animations like the following code:

```
<DoubleAnimationUsingKeyFrames
 Storyboard.TargetProperty="(UIElement.RenderTransform)
.(CompositeTransform.TranslateX)"
Storyboard.TargetName="ellipse">
  <EasingDoubleKeyFrameKeyTime="0" Value="0">
    <EasingDoubleKeyFrame.EasingFunction>
      <BackEaseEasingMode="EaseOut"/>
    </EasingDoubleKeyFrame.EasingFunction>
  </EasingDoubleKeyFrame>
  <EasingDoubleKeyFrameKeyTime="0:0:3" Value="-7.5">
    <EasingDoubleKeyFrame.EasingFunction>
      <BackEaseEasingMode="EaseInOut"/>
    </EasingDoubleKeyFrame.EasingFunction>
  </EasingDoubleKeyFrame>
</DoubleAnimationUsingKeyFrames>
```

If you examine your XAML from this example, you will see that it has added a large amount of code to create this animation. It is good to examine how it uses this to build the various animations.

3
Behaviors and Events

In this chapter, we will cover:

- ▸ Understanding events
- ▸ Understanding basic behaviors
- ▸ Custom behavior
- ▸ Physics engine behavior

Introduction

Throughout the two previous chapters, we learned how to lay out our applications and add some simple animations to them. We have added some simple interactivity using both events and behaviors. Events are a classic way of adding interactivity, and if you have any background in WinForms development, then you will be used to this type of development. But with Silverlight, you will find that behaviors tend to lend themselves to an easier way of doing things by allowing you to define a majority of things directly in the XAML.

Essentially, behaviors are a way to attach an action to an event of a control without having to write code in your code behind. This is great for assigning events like `NavigateToPage` or `PlaySound`, which can be a few lines of code in your code behind, when you can just drag-and-drop the behavior onto the design surface and have a much richer editing experience.

Understanding events

If you have done some programming in the past, you should find yourself very comfortable using an event. Events are a simple way of saying "something happened" against which you can write the code to handle it. A very classic type of event is handling an OnClick event where a user clicks a button or in the case of Windows Phone, a user touches a button. In our first example, we will carry out a very basic handling of this event type.

Getting ready

To get started with this example, create a very basic windows phone application in Visual Studio like we have in the previous chapters. This will just be the standard windows phone application type, as shown in the following screenshot:

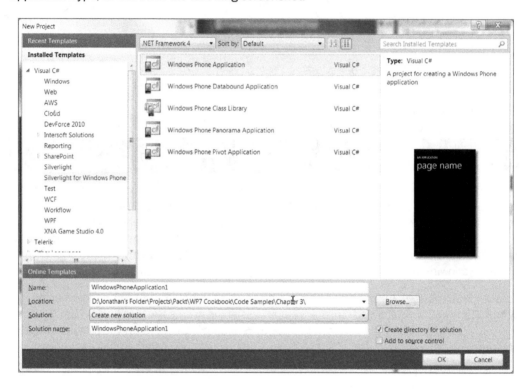

How to do it...

Now that we have a simple starting point we can begin to implement behaviors.

1. Let's change the XAML for the content panel to the following:

```
<!--ContentPanel - place additional content here-->
  <StackPanel x:Name="ContentPanel" Grid.Row="1"

   Margin="12,0,12,0">
      <Button Height="100" Content="Say Hello"/>
      <TextBlock x:Name="txtBlock" Height="200"/>
  </StackPanel>
```

   This will give us a stack panel with both a button and a textblock. We need to create the classic Hello World example to show how to add interactivity to the button. We will do this by adding a Click event.

2. Start typing the word "Click" after the property for content. Intelisense will prompt you to create an event handler, and you can do that by pressing the *Enter* key, so the final result will look like this:

```
<Button Height="100" Content="Say Hello" Click="Button_Click"/>
```

   What also happened when you let it create the event handle for you, is that it created a method in the `MainPage.xaml.cs` that looks like this:

```
private void Button_Click(object sender, RoutedEventArgs e)
{
}
```

 This has given you the foundation for handling the event. If you are an experienced developer, this will seem very basic to you, but it is a good reminder of how to wire up events in XAML. Unlike win forms and other similar technologies, you have to explicitly assign the handler in the XAML.

3. Now that we have some code, let's make it do something. This will be easy to do by editing the method that was created for you and setting the property for the textblock's content. We will do this by changing the method call as follows:

```
private void Button_Click(object sender, RoutedEventArgs e)
{
    txtBlock.Text = "Hello From My Event Handler";
}
```

4. Now when we run the app and click on the button, we should get the following:

How it works...

This is the most basic form of interaction but handles the foundation of many key concepts in C# and Windows Phone development. If this is your first time developing applications, you can see the simplicity of the event-driven model. With every control, there is a set of events and properties. To discover some of the events for a control, simply select it on the design surface and look at the events window in Visual Studio or Blend. As you can see in the following screenshot, the button is selected to show you the various events possible on a textbox:

With every control there are many common events like GotFocus, Loaded, MouseEnter, MouseLeave, and several others. But every control has specific events associated with it, like the TextChanged event on the textbox which fires anytime the text is changed. By using these events, you can do much more to increase your interactivity, whether that is validating a password's security level when a user is typing, or knowing when a user simply clicks on a control.

In an event, you can do very complex scenarios that aren't necessarily a fit for a behavior that we will cover in the next example.

There's more...

There will be times when you need to assign events to objects and controls in your code behind and not your XAML. To do this, you can do some simple code like the following to assign the event handler in code:

```
btn.Click += Button_Click;
```

And to remove the event handler, you can simply change the += to -=, like the following:

```
btn.Click -= Button_Click;
```

When assigning an event handler, type the event name and += and then press the *Tab* key twice. This will automatically create the event handler with the correct arguments for you.

Understanding basic behaviors

As we have seen with the events handler example, you can assign event handling logic through XAML to associate the event handler as well as the ability to do it in your code behind. In this example, we will cover a very similar type of thing but with only XAML and in Blend. We will repeat the exact same example but with behaviors.

Getting ready

We will need to create a Windows Phone application, but this time in Expression Blend for easier drag-and-drop capabilities. So let's create the project in Blend using the following screenshot as a reference:

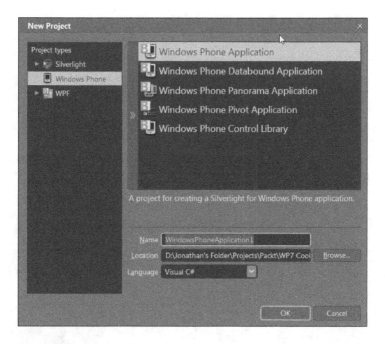

How to do it...

Now that we have our basic application that we can use for a test bed to use some built in behaviors by using tools built into Blend.

1. Let's drag-and-drop both a button and a textblock onto the design surface. We will have something that looks like this:

2. Instead of adding an event handler to change the text block, we are going to use a simple behavior that is called `ChangePropertyAction`, and you can drag this onto your button:

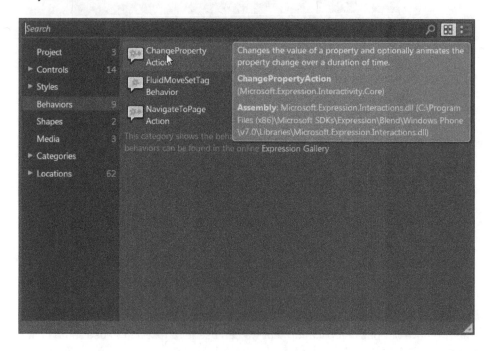

From here, you will see the properties of the action in your properties window. It has a few things to note—a set of properties for Trigger, Common Properties that define the target, and some Animation Properties.

3. Click the **Target** icon:

4. And then simply click the textblock on the design surface. It is almost like you are aiming the textblock. Now let's set the property by hitting the drop-down next to **PropertyName** and selecting **Text**. Once we have the property name selected, we can enter a value. Let's enter **Hello from behavior**.

5. When you run the application, you can see that this works exactly as expected. When you click on the button, it will change the text of the textblock. We did this all without writing any background code.

How it works...

While it is nice that we haven't really written any code, there is always a need to see what is going on in the XAML to have a better understanding of the page. What essentially happened was that it added the trigger node under the button to assign it to the button, as shown in the following code:

```
<phone:PhoneApplicationPage
  xmlns="http://schemas.microsoft.com/winfx/2006/xaml/presentation"
  xmlns:x="http://schemas.microsoft.com/winfx/2006/xaml"
  xmlns:phone="clr-
    namespace:Microsoft.Phone.Controls;assembly=Microsoft.Phone"
  xmlns:shell="clr-
    namespace:Microsoft.Phone.Shell;assembly=Microsoft.Phone"
  xmlns:d="http://schemas.microsoft.com/expression/blend/2008"
  xmlns:mc="http://schemas.openxmlformats.org/markup-
    compatibility/2006"
  xmlns:Custom="clr-namespace:System.Windows.
Interactivity;assembly=System.Windows.Interactivity" xmlns:ic="clr-
namespace:Microsoft.Expression.Interactivity.Core;assembly=Microsoft.
Expression.Interactions"
  mc:Ignorable="d" d:DesignWidth="480" d:DesignHeight="800"
  x:Class="BehavioursExample.MainPage"
  FontFamily="{StaticResource PhoneFontFamilyNormal}"
  FontSize="{StaticResource PhoneFontSizeNormal}"
  Foreground="{StaticResource PhoneForegroundBrush}"
  SupportedOrientations="Portrait" Orientation="Portrait"
  shell:SystemTray.IsVisible="True">

  <!--LayoutRoot is the root grid where all page content is placed-->
  <Grid x:Name="LayoutRoot" Background="Transparent">
    <Grid.RowDefinitions>
      <RowDefinition Height="Auto"/>
      <RowDefinition Height="*"/>
    </Grid.RowDefinitions>

    <!--TitlePanel contains the name of the application and page
        title-->
    <StackPanel x:Name="TitlePanel" Grid.Row="0" Margin="12,17,0,28">
      <TextBlock x:Name="ApplicationTitle" Text="MY APPLICATION"
      Style="{StaticResource PhoneTextNormalStyle}"/>
      <TextBlock x:Name="PageTitle" Text="page name" Margin="9,-
      7,0,0" Style="{StaticResource PhoneTextTitle1Style}"/>
    </StackPanel>

    <!--ContentPanel - place additional content here-->
    <Grid x:Name="ContentPanel" Grid.Row="1" Margin="12,0,12,0"/>
    <Button Content="Say Hello" VerticalAlignment="Top"
     Margin="132,171,146,0" Grid.Row="1">
```

```
          <Custom:Interaction.Triggers>
            <Custom:EventTrigger EventName="Click">
              <ic:ChangePropertyAction TargetName="textBlock"
               PropertyName="Text" Value="Hello from behavior"/>
            </Custom:EventTrigger>
          </Custom:Interaction.Triggers>
        </Button>
        <TextBlock x:Name="textBlock" TextWrapping="Wrap"
         Text="TextBlock" Margin="144,244,134,300" Grid.Row="1"/>
      </Grid>
    </phone:PhoneApplicationPage>
```

And from there you can see it sets the individual properties of the `ChangePropertyAction`. This action is actually very powerful because you can set any property of any control on your design surface without writing any code. So for example, you could hide and show a control if a button is clicked or change the background color of a control. In addition it adds the namespace at the top of the control for the Interactivity namespace.

With behaviors they are meant to be used for very basic types of functionality like this or navigating to a page. You can build custom behaviors to do more, but we will get into that later.

There's more...

Now that you have seen a very basic behavior, let's look at some of the other ones included in the SDK. It is good to have knowledge of these for the times you need them and when to use them. We will mention some of the most commonly-used ones in the following sections.

ControlStoryBoardAction

The `ControlStoryBoardAction` does exactly what it says—it allows you to control your animation storyboards, such as stopping, starting, or skipping to a specific point in your animation. By using this, you can create interactive animations that do much more than just play.

GoToStateAction

As we have covered in the previous recipes, the `GoToStateAction` allows you to jump between states. This is great for creating custom states of controls where you may need to have uncommon interaction or more complex interaction.

PlaySoundAction

Yet another very simple action, used to play a sound after a specific trigger. This is much easier than creating the code behind to do the same thing.

Custom behavior

One of the limitations with behaviors is that most of the time they are not really complex, which is great but sometimes you need to create a very reusable set of functionality that is an action. We can do this by creating a custom behavior. In our case, this example will be just to show a popup with a string that is passed in.

Getting ready

To get started, add an item to the project we've been working on and name it **ShowPopupBehavior**, as shown in the following screenshot:

How to do it...

As we have seen in the previous examples it is easy to implement the built in behaviors, but what if you want more functionality, this is how we do it.

1. From the **Projects** tab, we will want to open the file in Visual Studio by right-clicking the file and selecting **Edit in Visual Studio**.

    Luckily when creating a behavior in Blend like this, before going into Visual Studio, it creates a nice template for you to go by as follows:

    ```
    using System;
    using System.Collections.Generic;
    ```

```
using System.Text;
using System.Windows;
using System.Windows.Controls;
using System.Windows.Data;
using System.Windows.Documents;
using System.Windows.Input;
using System.Windows.Media;
using System.Windows.Media.Imaging;
using System.Windows.Shapes;
using System.Windows.Interactivity;
//using Microsoft.Expression.Interactivity.Core;

namespace BehavioursExample
{
  public class ShowPopupBehavior : Behavior<DependencyObject>
  {
    public ShowPopupBehavior()
    {
      // Insert code required on object creation below this point.

      //
      // The line of code below sets up the relationship between
         the command and the function
      // to call. Uncomment the below line and add a reference to
         Microsoft.Expression.Interactions
      // if you choose to use the commented out version of
         MyFunction and MyCommand instead of
      // creating your own implementation.
      //
      // The documentation will provide you with an example of a
         simple command implementation
      // you can use instead of using ActionCommand and
         referencing the Interactions assembly.
      //
      //this.MyCommand = new ActionCommand(this.MyFunction);
    }

    protectedoverridevoidOnAttached()
    {
      base.OnAttached();

      // Insert code that you would want run when the Behavior is
         attached to an object.
    }
```

```
protectedoverridevoidOnDetaching()
{
  base.OnDetaching();

  // Insert code that you would want run when the Behavior is
     removed from an object.
}

/*
public ICommand MyCommand
{
  get;
  private set;
}

private void MyFunction()
{
  // Insert code that defines what the behavior will do when
     invoked.
}
*/
  }
}
```

2. One of the things we will want to do with this behavior is allow a property for the string to show in the message box. We will need to do this by adding a `DependencyProperty` to this class. Below is the code needed to be added to a `DependencyProperty`.

   A `DependencyProperty` will allow us to use the property to bind to in XAML. The message `DependencyProperty` is in the following code snippet:

```
public static readonly DependencyProperty
DisplayMemberPathProperty =
    DependencyProperty.Register("Message", typeof(string),
    typeof(ShowPopupBehavior),
    new PropertyMetadata(string.Empty));

public string Message { get; set; }
```

3. Now that we have this defined, we want to uncomment the code that starts with /* and ends with */, by deleting these in the template that was created and adding one line to the `MyFunction` method. So the final code looks like this:

```
publicstaticreadonlyDependencyPropertyDisplayMemberPathProperty =
        DependencyProperty.Register("Message", typeof(string),
        typeof(ShowPopupBehavior),
        newPropertyMetadata(string.Empty));
```

```
        public string Message { get; set; }

    public ICommand MyCommand
    {
      get;
      private set;
    }

    private void MyFunction()
    {
            MessageBox.Show(Message);
    }


}
```

Let's build the project and reopen it in Blend. Delete the existing change property behavior and drag-and-drop our new behavior onto the button.

4. You will then need to add an `EventTrigger` under the MyCommand properties, giving it the button and click event. We then want to also set the message property to say **Hello**.

How it works...

Now let's run it and see what happens. What you see happen now is that you have encapsulated an action into a behavior that can be simply dragged-and-dropped onto the design surface like you did with the pre-existing behaviors.

What is going on under the covers is actually a little more complicated than the basic behavior because it has to add the event trigger and is actually using the `InvokeCommandAction` to fire your command. So if you examine the XAML below, you can see the results:

```
<phone:PhoneApplicationPage
    xmlns="http://schemas.microsoft.com/winfx/2006/xaml/presentation"
    xmlns:x="http://schemas.microsoft.com/winfx/2006/xaml"
    xmlns:phone="clr-
    namespace:Microsoft.Phone.Controls;assembly=Microsoft.Phone"
    xmlns:shell="clr-
    namespace:Microsoft.Phone.Shell;assembly=Microsoft.Phone"
    xmlns:d="http://schemas.microsoft.com/expression/blend/2008"
    xmlns:mc="http://schemas.openxmlformats.org/markup-
    compatibility/2006"
    xmlns:Custom="clr-namespace:System.Windows.
Interactivity;assembly=System.Windows.Interactivity" xmlns:local="clr-
namespace:BehavioursExample"
    mc:Ignorable="d" d:DesignWidth="480" d:DesignHeight="800"
```

```
x:Class="BehavioursExample.MainPage"
FontFamily="{StaticResource PhoneFontFamilyNormal}"
FontSize="{StaticResource PhoneFontSizeNormal}"
Foreground="{StaticResource PhoneForegroundBrush}"
SupportedOrientations="Portrait" Orientation="Portrait"
shell:SystemTray.IsVisible="True">

<!--LayoutRoot is the root grid where all page content is placed-->
<Grid x:Name="LayoutRoot" Background="Transparent">
  <Grid.RowDefinitions>
    <RowDefinition Height="Auto"/>
    <RowDefinition Height="*"/>
  </Grid.RowDefinitions>

  <!--TitlePanel contains the name of the application and page
      title-->
  <StackPanel x:Name="TitlePanel" Grid.Row="0" Margin="12,17,0,28">
    <TextBlock x:Name="ApplicationTitle" Text="MY APPLICATION"
       Style="{StaticResource PhoneTextNormalStyle}"/>
    <TextBlock x:Name="PageTitle" Text="page name" Margin="9,-7,0,0"
       Style="{StaticResource PhoneTextTitle1Style}"/>
  </StackPanel>

  <!--ContentPanel - place additional content here-->
  <Grid x:Name="ContentPanel" Grid.Row="1" Margin="12,0,12,0"/>
  <Button x:Name="button" Content="Say Hello"
   VerticalAlignment="Top" Margin="132,171,146,0" Grid.Row="1">
    <Custom:Interaction.Behaviors>
      <local:ShowPopupBehavior Message="Hello">
        <Custom:Interaction.Triggers>
          <Custom:EventTrigger SourceName="button"
           EventName="Click">
            <Custom:InvokeCommandAction CommandName="MyCommand"/>
          </Custom:EventTrigger>
        </Custom:Interaction.Triggers>
      </local:ShowPopupBehavior>
    </Custom:Interaction.Behaviors>
  </Button>
  <TextBlock x:Name="textBlock" TextWrapping="Wrap"
   Text="TextBlock" Margin="144,244,134,300" Grid.Row="1"/>
</Grid>
</phone:PhoneApplicationPage>
```

There's more...

By adding this level of customization, you can really begin to do a lot more with behaviors. There are also a number of existing behaviors on CodePlex and various other sites that people have written which are great for building games and other unique experiences. We will cover these in the next example.

Physics engine behavior

One of the coolest libraries out there is a Farseer Physics engine that was created for Silverlight, and which also works on Windows Phone 7. What does this do? Well this engine actually allows you to place things like a collision detection system with realistic physic responses on your objects. This opens up a lot of possibilities for creating various games such as the classic labyrinth balance game, pinball games, and many other types of games.

Getting ready

To get this library, you will need to download it from CodePlex at `http://physicshelper.codeplex.com/`. This will provide you with the Farseer Physics engine as well as the tools to add these behaviors to your project. Once we have installed the necessary tools, we will need to add a reference to the library items by right-clicking on the project and clicking on **Add Reference**, navigating to `C:\Program Files (x86)\Physics Helper\Physics Helper Library\WP7`, and selecting the `Farseer Physics 3.0 WinPhone.DLL`.

How to do it...

We will now create a little basic example to show how various objects collide on the phone:

1. To get started with our app, clear out the controls and convert our LayoutRoot to a canvas. Then add the `PhysicsControllerBehavior` to the canvas:

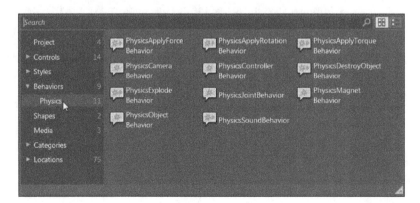

2. From there, draw four rectangles to act as a border around the canvas and then assign the `PhysicsObjectBehavior` and set the `IsStatic` property to `true`.

3. Let's add the snow. Draw a lot of ellipses on the screen and add a `PhysicsOjbectBehavior` to each. By doing this, we are creating objects that interact with each other and use physics to interact.

You should now have a layout that looks something like this:

While this isn't all that exciting on the screen in the editor, you could try running it to see the real magic. What happens now is that the balls fall due to the gravity level set in the `PhysicsEngineControl` behavior and the various `PhysicObjectBehavior`enabled objects.

How it works...

What actually happens in the XAML is very simple; it is just what we have learned in the previous recipes, but to provide interaction with each other. The majority of the sample is made of several ellipses that are defined like the code in the following XAML:

```
<Ellipse Fill="#FFF4F4F5" Height="9" Canvas.Left="149"
  Stroke="Black" Canvas.Top="141" Width="8">
  <Custom:Interaction.Behaviors>
    <pb:PhysicsObjectBehavior RestitutionCoefficient="1"/>
  </Custom:Interaction.Behaviors>
</Ellipse>
```

By using the behavior built into the physics engine, all that is required is the following XAML within your canvas:

```
<Custom:Interaction.Behaviors>
    <pb:PhysicsControllerBehavior GravityVertical="4"
        MousePickEnabled="True"/>
</Custom:Interaction.Behaviors>
```

This behavior provides much of the needed physics for things like games without having to write the complex code for determining how objects interact. You could use this for a pinball game or even in business applications to provide simple fluid animations.

There's more...

With the Farseer Physics engine, there is much more than just gravity that you can apply to objects, but you can also create things like joints, static objects, exploding objects, and much more. This allows you to create some of your favorite games that you have seen on other platforms with just Blend and almost no programming behind it.

4
DataBinding 101/MVVM

In this chapter, we will cover:

- ▸ Creating a simple model
- ▸ Creating a ViewModel
- ▸ Creating a view
- ▸ Element-to-element binding

Introduction

Throughout the previous chapters, we have learned various ways to layout and engage the user with animations while adding interactivity through behaviors. But as with many applications, you will need to create applications with data that comes from a database or web service. While traditionally databinding in applications has been just for placing simple lists or datagrids onto an application, with Silverlight binding can take on a whole new role. Binding in Silverlight contains both the traditional method of showing data on a form but also the ability to bind properties to properties of other controls in element-to-element binding, which we will demonstrate later in this chapter.

In this chapter, we will discuss at length the loose binding characteristics of Silverlight that enables us to maximize the code reuse for our application. Because of this loose binding, we will be able to demonstrate one of the more common architectures that has been made popular in Silverlight, **MVVM** which stands for **Model-View-View Model**. The foundation of MVVM is built on many common frameworks and has evolved only slightly with the evolution of Silverlight. Because of the years of this architecture being put through real world scenarios and the commonality of it in most Silverlight applications, Microsoft has decided to let you build MVVM applications directly on Windows Phone 7.

A case for MVVM

Before we get too deep into discussion about MVVM, let's first look at the need for MVVM and a little history to it. Traditionally in application development the lines of where logic for your application goes sometimes gets blurred. This blurring of lines causes applications to not optimize code re-usage that in turn leaves room for bugs and increases the maintenance of your application.

Separation of Concerns

The other case for MVVM is creating a true Separation of Concerns for parts of your application, with each part being completely independent from the other. It reminds me of my childhood; I always loved to have my dinner on a divided plate that would keep my peas away from my bread and my spaghetti sauce away from my peas and away from my dessert. Each part of MVVM is like a meal that isn't mixed together; while it is fine to mix your food, it does not allow you to enjoy each individual item. Architecting your application isn't that different; if you have been a programmer for very long, you know what I mean. You can mix your UI code with your business logic and your business logic with your data access but when something goes wrong in any of those areas, it becomes much harder to fix.

So with that said, the three core elements of MVVM create a fairly traditional three-tier architecture that many developers have become accustomed to but has a slight twist in it. The three tiers are:

1. **Model**: The model is probably the simplest part of your application. This is a single class file that represents the description of some data. In the simplest form, you may have a model for Person that has simple properties to represent First Name, Last Name, and E-mail.

2. **View**: The view is simply the user interface part of your application. This is what tells the application where to put the textboxes or how to display an animation.

3. **ViewModel**: The ViewModel is what brings the data and fills your model and is bound normally to your view. The majority of your logic will actually go in here. This is where you can also put the actions that can happen to your data.

Testability

By separating various pieces of your application into these main areas, you actually create a very testable application. When done correctly, it will allow you to create a unit test for the various pieces. Through these types of simplifications for testing, it allows you to find issues quicker while focusing on the business problem.

Reusability

By separating your code into a model, view, and controller, you will be able to maximize the reusability of your code. For example, you may start with an application wherein your MVVM architecture has a 1:1:1 pattern, meaning your model is only used by one ViewModel which is only used by one view. But with MVVM, you will have the flexibility to reuse pieces of your applications in multiple areas of your applications. For example, let's say you have a ViewModel for handling a customer's orders that handles business rules like order fulfillment and inventory and you originally start using it on a simple view that lets you enter just one customer at a time. But as your application grows in popularity, you will need to add more complex batch type entry views where a user can input multiple orders at a time. If you have structured an application as an MVVM application, then you can reuse the customer ViewModel instead of recreating your business logic.

Creating a simple model

Now that we have an understanding of why we need MVVM, let's start to dig into the implementation of how it actually works. In this first example, we will be creating a simple model, which for the most part really doesn't do a whole lot more than describe the data we want to present. In this case, we will be keeping track of venues for a band's concert tour. We will want to keep track of things such as the venue location, number of seats, date, opening act, and so on. We will carry this model through the next few examples to fill the data and allow you to simulate purchasing tickets. We will also create a model for the band information that will create the band name and their concert schedule.

Getting ready

To get started on this project, we will want to create a Windows Phone application in Silverlight for Windows Phone:

We will go ahead and name this project **BandTour**. Now let's go ahead and add a folder in the solution named Models which will contain our model for the Band and Concert models.

How to do it...

Now that we have our project structure, let's add our first class library:

1. Right-click on the **Views** folder and click on **Add | New Item**.

2. Then select file type class and name it **Band.cs**. This will create your band class.

3. Now repeat the process for the concert class. You should have two files in your **Views** folder, one named `Band.cs` and the other `Concert.cs`.

4. Double-click the **Concert.cs** file and add the properties for Venue, Date, and Opening Band. The code should look like the following:

```
namespace BandTour.Models
{
    public class Concert
    {
        public string Venue { get; set; }
        public DateTime Date { get; set; }
        public Band OpenBand { get; set; }
        public int NumberOfSeats { get; set; }
    }
}
```

5. Double-click the `Band.cs` and add the properties needed for it, which should create the following code:

```
namespace BandTour.Models
{
    public class Band
    {
        public string Name { get; set; }
        public System.Collections.ObjectModel.Collection<Concert>
        Concerts { get; set; }
    }
}
```

Congratulations! You have just created your first model in the MVVM architecture. From the looks of the code, this is about as simple as it can get. Although this application doesn't actually do anything, you have just set up the foundational pieces for your application. This foundation gives you a central point for managing the structure of the data you are creating that is completely independent from both your view and ViewModel.

There's more...

Before we move into a deeper discussion of the ViewModel, we need to introduce the `INotifyPropertyChanged` interface, which plays a very important role in how MVVM works. When a control in Silverlight has a property bound to it, it actually has to be notified that something has changed in the property. For example, if the property name of the Band changes, then you will need to let any control show that the data has changed. To implement this, you could simply implement the `INotifiyPropertyChanged` on each of the Model classes, but instead we will implement a base model class and call it ModelBase, which will provide the common logic for firing the events on the model. So let's add another class in the **Views** folder and call it ModelBase. Let's add the following code:

```
using System.ComponentModel;
namespace BandTour.Models
{
    public abstract class ModelBase : INotifyPropertyChanged
```

```
        {
            #region INotifyPropertyChanged Members

            public event PropertyChangedEventHandler PropertyChanged;

            #endregion

            protected virtual void RaisePropertyChanged(string
            propertyName)
            {
                var handler = PropertyChanged;

                if (handler != null)
                    handler(this, new
                    PropertyChangedEventArgs(propertyName));
            }
        }
    }
```

Now that we have our base class, let's implement it and set it to be called on both of our model classes. We will add the inheritance of the ModelBase on our band class and let's add some backing private fields to hold our variables since we cannot implement the defaults any more. In each of the sets, we will also need to call the `RaisePropertyChanged` method so that it will fire the event to let the view know something has changed. Now our band class will look more like this:

```
using System.Collections.ObjectModel;

namespace BandTour.Models
{
    public class Band : ModelBase
    {
        private Collection<Concert> _concerts;
        private string _name;

        public string Name
        {
            get { return _name; }
            set
            {
                _name = value;
                RaisePropertyChanged("Name");
            }
        }

        public Collection<Concert> Concerts
        {
            get { return _concerts; }
            set
            {
```

```
            _concerts = value;
            RaisePropertyChanged("Concerts");
        }
    }
    }
  }
}
```

And now let's do the same thing with our Concert class, which will cause it to look more like this:

```
using System;

namespace BandTour.Models
{
    public class Concert : ModelBase
    {
        private DateTime _date;
        private int _numberOfSeats;
        private Band _openBand;
        private string _venue;

        public string Venue
        {
            get { return _venue; }
            set
            {
                _venue = value;
                RaisePropertyChanged("Venue");
            }
        }

        public DateTime Date
        {
            get { return _date; }
            set
            {
                _date = value;
                RaisePropertyChanged("Date");
            }
        }

        public Band OpenBand
        {
            get { return _openBand; }
            set
            {
                _openBand = value;
                RaisePropertyChanged("OpenBand");
            }
        }
```

```
        public int NumberOfSeats
        {
            get { return _numberOfSeats; }
            set
            {
                _numberOfSeats = value;
                RaisePropertyChanged("NumberOfSeats");
            }
        }
    }
}
```

Now if you do not have the `RaisePropertyChanged` event, then your UI will not get updated when that data is changed. While for this exercise it is good to see how to create your own model, in the real world, it is very common for these to actually come from something like a WCF service or other types of generated class.

Creating a ViewModel

Now that we have our Model, it is time to do something with it. In the ViewModel, we will introduce several important concepts that are needed to begin implementing interactivity with our database and the UI. The key to the ViewModel is to think of it as the gatekeeper between your model, data, and your UI. It should be responsible for all interactions to get the data from your database or web service.

By creating a simple ViewModel, you will produce an easy to maintain layer of code for your application. It also gives you the ability to reuse the ViewModel with other views and keep the same functionality.

Getting ready

In our current BandTour project, we will create a folder called ViewModels. We will then create a class called `BandViewModel.cs`. This class will be responsible for creating the simple list of bands and concerts.

How to do it...

The first thing we want to add to our `BandViewModel.cs` is the initialization method that will create the data. For this example, it will just be creating random data, but in a real world example, this is where you could put the loading logic to pull data from a database. The following is our initialization code:

```
using System;

using BandTour.Models;
```

```
namespace BandTour.ViewModels
{
    public class BandViewModel : ModelBase
    {
        private Band _currentBand;

        public BandViewModel()
        {
            CurrentBand = new Band() { Name = "The Silver Lights" };
            CurrentBand.Concerts = new Collection<Concert>();

            for (int i = 0; i < 10; i++)
            {
                var newConcert = new Concert();
                newConcert.Date = DateTime.Now.AddDays(i * 7);
                newConcert.NumberOfSeats = 250 * i;
                newConcert.OpenBand = new Band { Name = "The Opening
                Band" };
                newConcert.Venue = i + "43 West Elem St., New York,
                NY";
                CurrentBand.Concerts.Add(newConcert);
            }

        }

        public Band CurrentBand
        {
            get { return _currentBand; }
            set
            {
                _currentBand = value;
                RaisePropertyChanged("CurrentBand");
            }
        }
    }
}
```

Through this simple ViewModel you can see just how easy it is to build. While this example is not very complex, it is important to get the concept we are going for here. It is not just merely filling a collection but also the underlying architecture that we will want to place in the system for maintainability. In the next section, we will cover the view and an example of how we start bringing everything together.

There's more...

One of the important things that you may want to do in production code is actually provide a way to have design time data. Design time data is data that is provided to your view when in the design surfaces of both Visual Studio and Expression Blend. Without design time data, you will not see an accurate rendering of the control in the view. In our current example, it is not accessing the database but if it was, that database may not be available at design time for various reasons. To handle the design time support, we will change our ViewModel slightly to use the `DesignerProperties.IsInDesignTool`. This property can actually verify if you are in the designer of Blend and Visual Studio. Now let's modify our ViewModel to show different data at design time versus runtime:

```
using System;
using System.ComponentModel;
using BandTour.Models;


namespace BandTour.ViewModels
{
    public class BandViewModel : ModelBase
    {
        private Band _currentBand;

        public BandViewModel()
        {
            if (DesignerProperties.IsInDesignTool)
            {
                CurrentBand = new Band() {Name = "The Silver
                Lights(Design)"};
                CurrentBand.Concerts = new Collection<Concert>();

                for (int i = 0; i < 10; i++)
                {
                    var newConcert = new Concert();
                    newConcert.Date = DateTime.Now.AddDays(i*7);
                    newConcert.NumberOfSeats = 250*i;
                    newConcert.OpenBand = new Band { Name = "The
                    Opening Band(Design)" };
                    newConcert.Venue = i + "43 West Elem St., New
                    York, NY(Design)";
                    CurrentBand.Concerts.Add(newConcert);
                }
            }
            else
            {
                CurrentBand = new Band() { Name = "The Silver Lights
                " };
                CurrentBand.Concerts = new Collection<Concert>();
```

```
            for (int i = 0; i < 10; i++)
            {
                var newConcert = new Concert();
                newConcert.Date = DateTime.Now.AddDays(i * 7);
                newConcert.NumberOfSeats = 250 * i;
                newConcert.OpenBand = new Band { Name = "The
                Opening Band" };
                newConcert.Venue = i + "43 West Elem St., New
                York, NY";
                CurrentBand.Concerts.Add(newConcert);
            }
        }
    }

    public Band CurrentBand
    {
        get { return _currentBand; }
        set
        {
            _currentBand = value;
            RaisePropertyChanged("CurrentBand");
        }
    }
}
}
```

What we are doing here is just adding the string (design) at the end of the strings during the design time version. In a real world application, we would use this to determine whether to get the data from the production environment or just give you something to work with in the designer.

Creating a view

Everything at this point has been pretty standalone with nothing to really see. With the view, we want to start bringing these elements together to give the user something they can actually see. Just like the ViewModel and the model, the view can actually stand completely independent from the others. This modularity helps provide simplicity in your application for testing and reuse.

Getting ready

We will be adding a view by using the `MainPage.xaml` page control that is at the start of your application. Let's go ahead and add the view for the concert details by creating a folder called **Views**, adding a **Windows Phone Portrait Page**, and naming it `Concert.xaml`:

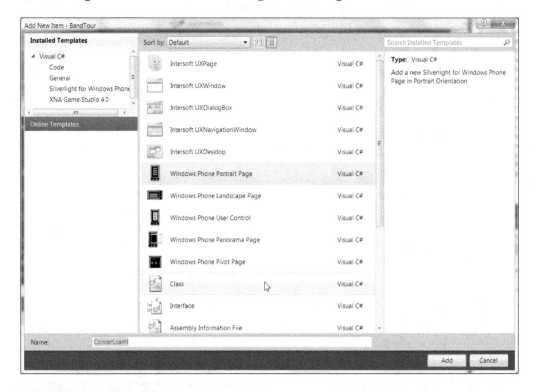

How to do it...

Swap over to Expression Blend to build the UI and the data sources. The reason for this is that Blend gives you a much better overview of the data sources in your project as well as an easier way to create them:

1. To switch to Blend, simply right-click on the `MainPage.xaml` and hit **Open in Expression Blend**.

2. Add an object data source by going to the data tab in Expression Blend, clicking the icon on the far right, and selecting **Create Object Data Source...**:

3. Once you have clicked that, you will get the following screenshot:

This screen can be a little overwhelming the first time you see it, but what you are looking for is the `BandViewModel` class. You can simply double-click it in the list to create your object data model. When done correctly, this will create a list of items you can bind to your view in your **Data** window and should look like the following screenshot:

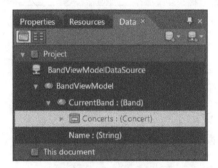

4. Drag the **Name** property to the textblock on the design surface that has the text Page Name. This will now bind the content property of the textblock to the name of the current band.

5. Now that we have the name of the band on the screen, provide the list of concerts also on this screen. This is simply done by dragging the **Concerts** from the data window to the main content area of the control. This will make your control look similar to the following screenshot:

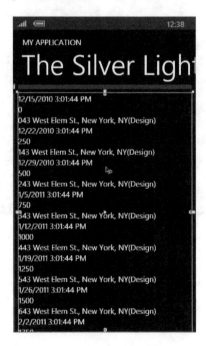

And from what you can see, this isn't very pretty. But what you have just done is bound your BandViewModel to your application as well as to your view, and also made it use design time data during the editing as you can tell by what is being rendered on the screen. Now when you run your application, you will not see the text (**Design**) on the list.

6. To make this look somewhat nicer, we are going to edit the current template, similar to how we have in the previous chapters. Right-click the list box and select **Edit Additional Templates | Edit Generated Items (ItemTemplate) | Edit Current**:

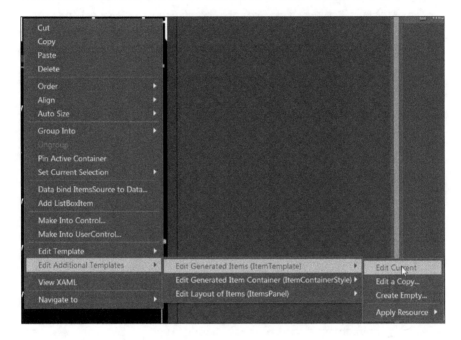

This will bring you to editing the ItemTemplate that was created based on the metadata from your Band class. This includes three textblocks for NumberOfSeats, Date, and Venue.

7. For now, delete the text blocks for NumberOfSeats and Date. Now when you run your application, it will show you a slightly more pleasant version of the listbox.

How it works...

When you first create your data source, you actually have the option to place it for the entire application to use or just the current control. In this case, we chose to do it at the application level so that we can reuse it on additional screens. What actually happened in the code when you created the data source is that Blend changed the XAML in the `app.xaml` to have the following:

```
<Application
    xmlns="http://schemas.microsoft.com/winfx/2006/xaml/presentation"
    xmlns:x="http://schemas.microsoft.com/winfx/2006/xaml"
    xmlns:phone="clr-namespace:Microsoft.Phone.
    Controls;assembly=Microsoft.Phone"
    xmlns:shell="clr-namespace:Microsoft.Phone.
Shell;assembly=Microsoft.Phone" xmlns:BandTour_ViewModels="clr-
namespace:BandTour.ViewModels" xmlns:d="http://schemas.microsoft.com/
expression/blend/2008" xmlns:mc="http://schemas.openxmlformats.org/
markup-compatibility/2006" mc:Ignorable="d"
    x:Class="BandTour.App"
    >

    <!--Application Resources-->
    <Application.Resources>
      <BandTour_ViewModels:BandViewModel
       x:Key="BandViewModelDataSource" d:IsDataSource="True"/>
    </Application.Resources>

    <Application.ApplicationLifetimeObjects>
        <!--Required object that handles lifetime events for the
        application-->
        <shell:PhoneApplicationService
            Launching="Application_Launching"
            Closing="Application_Closing"
            Activated="Application_Activated"
            Deactivated="Application_Deactivated"/>
    </Application.ApplicationLifetimeObjects>

</Application>
```

What you can see is that it added a resource to the `Application.Resources`. If you were doing this at the control level, it would have added to the XAML of the code you were working on.

In the next few steps, where we took the name property of the `CurrentBand` to the header textblock, it actually did two very important things. First it defined the `DateContext` for the entire control to the `BandViewModelDataSource`, which is defined in the `app.xaml`; it did this in the `LayoutRoot` definition as follows:

```
<Grid x:Name="LayoutRoot" Background="Transparent"
DataContext="{Binding Source={StaticResource
BandViewModelDataSource}}">
```

The second thing it did was set the binding of the textblock's content property as you can see in the XAML below:

```
<TextBlock x:Name="PageTitle" Text="{Binding CurrentBand.Name}"
Margin="9,-7,0,0" Style="{StaticResource PhoneTextTitle1Style}"/>
```

Then when we actually created the listbox by dragging and dropping the concerts on the main content, Blend created the listbox and set the `ItemsSource` property to the `Concerts` property of the `CurrentBand` as follows:

```
<ListBox ItemTemplate="{StaticResource ConcertTemplate}"
ItemsSource="{Binding CurrentBand.Concerts}"/></Grid>
```

This simple concept of binding gives you complete freedom to customize any part of your application. As you can see, there is also the ability to customize templates that provide you flexibility in the design of your application.

Element-to-element binding

While we have seen what happens when we bind to a ViewModel in order to get data, there is also the concept of having the ability to bind one control on a screen to another. One of the greatest and most overlooked features in Silverlight is element-to-element binding. This actually means that you can bind any property of any control to a property of another control. We will take a look at how to bind a few different controls to different properties of other controls.

Getting ready

In this example, we are going to stay in Blend the entire time, so let's create a new Windows Phone Application. On the Main Page, drag and drop both a textbox and a slider control. What we are going to do in this example is bind the value of the slider to the textblock.

We also want to go ahead and set the value of the SlideControl to 50 and the Maximum property to 100. This will make your slider control look 50 percent blue.

How to do it...

Now that we have the controls created, we need to bind them together. This is probably the simplest example in this chapter but gives you a lot of flexibility:

1. Select the textbox and find the text property in the property list, click on the little square to the right of the value, and then select the **Element Property Binding** menu:

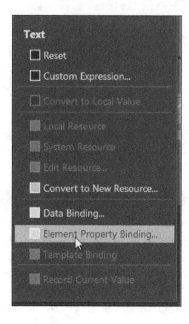

2. What happens next is Blend will change your pointer to select the control you want to bind to; simply click on the slider. This will bring up the binding property window.

3. We will want to set the property name to Value and expand the window to show the additional settings to set **TwoWay** binding, which should look as follows:

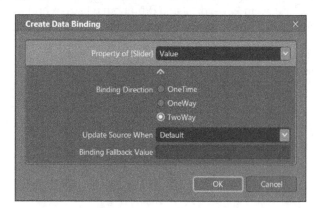

4. When you run your application, you will see that the text box is directly bound to the value of the slider and vice versa. If you move the slider, the value in the textbox automatically updates because of the binding, and if you change the value in the text box, the value of the slider changes.

How it works...

The simplicity of this example can be seen in the XAML that backs it up. The only thing that actually gets set is the text property of the textbox as follows:

```
<TextBox Height="76" Margin="133,135,161,0" TextWrapping="Wrap"
Text="{Binding Value, ElementName=slider, Mode=TwoWay}"
VerticalAlignment="Top"/>
```

Traditionally in applications, there would have been a need to create an event when the textbox or slider value changed, but with Silverlight you can simply bind the properties together. The other plus to this is that there is no code in your code behind, which illustrates that you can bind almost anything together through this simple binding.

5
Services, Data, and RSS

In this chapter, we will cover:

- ▸ Creating a WCF service to access a SQL database
- ▸ Using a WCF services in a Windows Phone application
- ▸ Building a simple RSS reader

Introduction

In the previous chapter, we covered the basics of databinding and using the pattern of MVVM to provide a solid foundation for your application. In this chapter, we will take this concept to the next level by building a few examples that can get data from the Web and bind them.

Creating a WCF service to access a SQL database

In the business world, you will find the need to get data from custom databases, specifically SQL databases in many applications. This example will walk you through getting data from a SQL Server database and displaying it on your Windows Phone application. We will take a break from the Windows Phone in the first part of this example to build the underlying Windows Communication Foundation Service to communicate to the SQL database.

Getting ready

To start this example, we will open Visual Studio and create an ASP.NET Web Application named WCFServer:

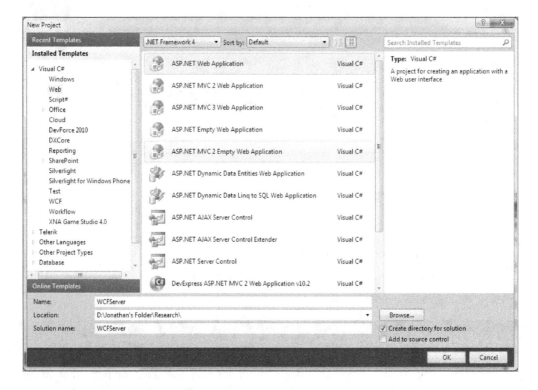

This will provide us with the server-side piece to access the data:

1. The next step is to add a SQL Database that we will use to populate the data. We do this by right-clicking the **App_Data** folder and selecting to add a new SQL Database under the **Data** section:

2. Now that we have a database, we will want to create a table in it. To do this, double-click the database file in your Solution Explorer. This will open up the server explorer on the left-hand side of your screen. From there, right-click the database in the server explorer and select **New Query**. Enter the following query and hit the execute button at the top:

```
CREATETABLE dbo.People
  (
  Id intNOTNULLIDENTITY (1, 1),
  FirstName varchar(50)NULL,
  LastName varchar(50)NULL,
  PhoneNumber varchar(50)NULL
  )ON [PRIMARY]
```

3. This will create our table in the database for us to use in this example. Now let's add some sample data by executing the following query:

```
InsertInto People(FirstName, LastName, PhoneNumber)values
('John','Doe','123-123-1234')
InsertInto People(FirstName, LastName, PhoneNumber)values
('Jane','Doe','123-223-1234')
InsertInto People(FirstName, LastName, PhoneNumber)values ('Bill',
'Smitherson','123-207-5234')
```

4. Now that we have a basic database to work with, we will want to add an Entity Framework model that will provide data access from our database to our web application. This is the main way for the server piece of our application to talk to the database so that it can pass it onto the Phone application.

5. To do this, right-click the web project and select **Add New Item**, select the **ADO.NET Entity Data Model**, and name it **MyModel**:

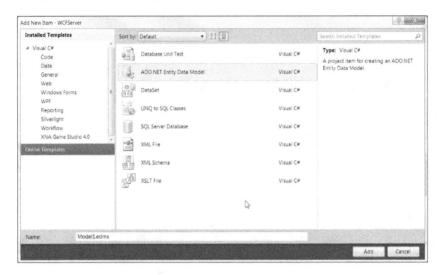

For the next few steps, there is a nice little wizard to help us along.

6. The first step asks how you want to generate the model. In this case, we will want to generate it from a database:

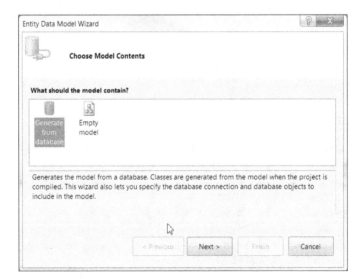

7. The next step will ask which database to use. In this case, we will select our `MyDatabase.mdf` database we just created:

8. And in the last step, it will ask you to select the objects you want to pull into your model. Select **tables**, which will select all the tables we have (which is only one).

9. Leave the default options and click on **Finish**.

This will create a very basic model for us to use in our web service.

How to do it...

Now that we have the database and entity framework model set up, we can get to building our service:

1. Navigate to **Add | New Item** again by right-clicking the WCFServer project and selecting the **Silverlight-enabled WCF Service** and name the service **MyService** option:

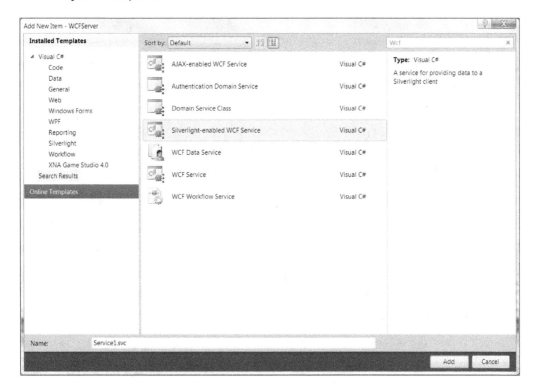

2. This will bring you to the following file:

```
using System;
using System.Linq;
using System.Runtime.Serialization;
using System.ServiceModel;
using System.ServiceModel.Activation;

namespace WCFServer
{
    [ServiceContract(Namespace = "")]
    [SilverlightFaultBehavior]
    [AspNetCompatibilityRequirements(RequirementsMode =
    AspNetCompatibilityRequirementsMode.Allowed)]
```

```
public class MyService
{
    [OperationContract]
    public void DoWork()
    {
        // Add your operation implementation here
        return;
    }

    // Add more operations here and mark them with
    [OperationContract]
}
}
```

As you can see, it gives you a basic template for providing functionality to your service.

3. Write the following code that will return a list of people in our database via a method called GetPeople:

```
using System;
using System.Collections.Generic;
using System.Linq;
using System.Runtime.Serialization;
using System.ServiceModel;
using System.ServiceModel.Activation;

namespace WCFServer
{
    [ServiceContract(Namespace = "")]
    [SilverlightFaultBehavior]
    [AspNetCompatibilityRequirements(RequirementsMode =
    AspNetCompatibilityRequirementsMode.Allowed)]
    public class MyService
    {
        [OperationContract]
        public List<Person> GetPeople()
        {
            var myModel = new MyDatabaseEntities();
            return myModel.People.ToList();
        }


    }
}
```

This is probably one of the most basic queries we could use but demonstrates how to make a simple call. But for now, this is all we need.

4. Now when you run this project, you will see an output similar to the following screenshot:

This is the service definition for the service we just created. Congratulations! You have just created your first WCF service. This service will be used in the next example to actually pull the data to the phone.

How it works...

WCF services actually are a semi open standard for applications to communicate from one server to another. This basic concept allows you to create simple controlled methods to access things from your server that you may need. This is ideal for placing data that needs to be secure or takes up large amounts of space that you couldn't distribute to the phone.

There's more...

Because of the scope of this book, we can't go into the extreme details of WCF services, as you could write an entire book just on this subject and there are already some from Packt:

----NOTE insert references to Packt books

Using a WCF service in a Windows Phone application

Now that we have a WCF service to work with, we need to build an application that can bind to it from the Windows Phone. To do this, add a project to this solution by right-clicking the solution root and selecting **Add New | Project**. We add this project as a Windows Phone application called WCFClient.

Getting ready

Now that we have our project created, we will want to add a reference to the service by right-clicking the references folder and selecting **Add Service Reference**:

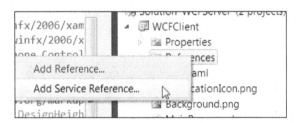

This will bring up the service reference tool, and we will hit the discover button to find the service that is in our other project:

Once you have seen this screen, simply change the NameSpace to MyServiceReference and then click **OK**.

How to do it...

Now to build a ViewModel that can get data from this data service:

1. Add a new class file to our project called `MyViewModel.cs`. This will provide the code in the client side to call the server.

2. Set up a reference to the service, make the call, and place the data in memory in a property called People. The completed ViewModel is as follows:

```
using System;
using System.Collections.ObjectModel;
using System.Net;
using System.Windows;
using System.Windows.Controls;
```

```csharp
using System;
using System.Collections.ObjectModel;
using System.ComponentModel;
using System.Net;
using System.Windows;
using System.Windows.Controls;
using System.Windows.Documents;
using System.Windows.Ink;
using System.Windows.Input;
using System.Windows.Media;
using System.Windows.Media.Animation;
using System.Windows.Shapes;
using WCFClient.MyServiceReference;

namespace WCFClient
{
    public class MyViewModel
    {
        private MyServiceReference.MyServiceClient myService =
        new MyServiceClient();
        public MyViewModel()
        {
            if (DesignerProperties.IsInDesignTool) return;
            People = new ObservableCollection<Person>();
            myService.GetPeopleAsync();
            myService.GetPeopleCompleted += myService_
            GetPeopleCompleted;
        }

        public System.Collections.ObjectModel.
        ObservableCollection<Person> People { get; set; }

        void myService_GetPeopleCompleted(object sender,
        GetPeopleCompletedEventArgs e)
        {
            People.Clear();
            foreach (var person in e.Result)
            {
                People.Add(person);
            }
        }
    }
}
```

When making ViewModels that you will bind in XAML and you want to keep design-time support, be sure to use the `DesignerProperties.IsInDesignTool` to determine that you are running in the designer and not make calls that will break Blend or Visual Studio.

3. Add reference to the ViewModel in our XAML for our `MainPage.xaml` as follows:

```
<phone:PhoneApplicationPage
    xmlns="http://schemas.microsoft.com/winfx/2006/xaml/
presentation"
    xmlns:x="http://schemas.microsoft.com/winfx/2006/xaml"
    xmlns:phone="clr-namespace:Microsoft.Phone.
Controls;assembly=Microsoft.Phone"
    xmlns:shell="clr-namespace:Microsoft.Phone.
Shell;assembly=Microsoft.Phone"
    xmlns:d="http://schemas.microsoft.com/expression/blend/2008"
    xmlns:mc="http://schemas.openxmlformats.org/markup-
compatibility/2006"
    xmlns:local="clr-namespace:WCFClient"
    x:Class="WCFClient.MainPage"
    mc:Ignorable="d" d:DesignWidth="480" d:DesignHeight="768"
    SupportedOrientations="Portrait" Orientation="Portrait"
    shell:SystemTray.IsVisible="True">

  <phone:PhoneApplicationPage.Resources>
    <local:MyViewModel x:Key="MyViewModelDataSource"
d:IsDataSource="True"/>
  </phone:PhoneApplicationPage.Resources>

    <Grid x:Name="LayoutRoot" Background="Transparent">
        <Grid.RowDefinitions>
            <RowDefinition Height="Auto"/>
            <RowDefinition Height="*"/>
        </Grid.RowDefinitions>

        <!--TitlePanel contains the name of the application and
page title-->
        <StackPanel x:Name="TitlePanel" Grid.Row="0"
Margin="12,17,0,28">
            <TextBlock x:Name="ApplicationTitle" Text="MY
APPLICATION" Style="{StaticResource PhoneTextNormalStyle}"/>
            <TextBlock x:Name="PageTitle" Text="page name"
Margin="9,-7,0,0" Style="{StaticResource PhoneTextTitle1Style}"/>
        </StackPanel>

        <!--ContentPanel - place additional content here-->
        <Grid x:Name="ContentPanel" Grid.Row="1"
Margin="12,0,12,0"/>
    </Grid>

</phone:PhoneApplicationPage>
```

4. In order to display the data coming back, add a listbox to the `MainPage.xaml` control. I actually prefer to show how to do this in Blend since it is a simple drag and drop. So let's open up the `MainPage.xaml` in Blend by right-clicking the `MainPage.xaml` or the project in Solution Explorer and selecting **Edit in Blend**.

5. Now that we have it opened in Blend, let's drag the **People** property from the **Data** tab to the design surface of Blend. This will create a list box with an `ItemTemplate` that matches the properties in your object:

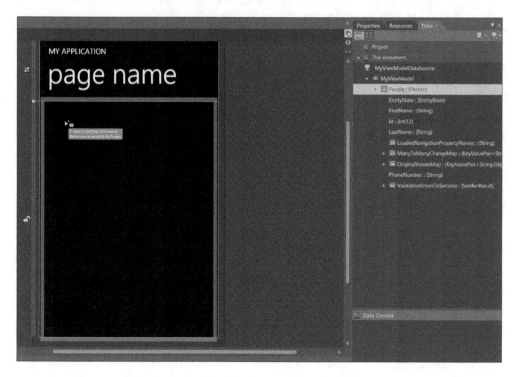

6. Now that you have added it to the page, save the file and go back to Visual Studio to run the project. Once the project runs, you should see a list of items from your database. This is actually making a call from the Windows Phone to your WCF service then to your database.

It seems like a lot of steps to get your data, but it gives you a simple way to reference the functionality on the server from you windows phone.

How it works...

When you dragged the list box over, it created an additional resource on your main page that is used for the item template, as shown in the following XAML:

```
<phone:PhoneApplicationPage
    xmlns="http://schemas.microsoft.com/winfx/2006/xaml/presentation"
```

```xml
    xmlns:x="http://schemas.microsoft.com/winfx/2006/xaml"
    xmlns:phone="clr-namespace:Microsoft.Phone.
Controls;assembly=Microsoft.Phone"
    xmlns:shell="clr-namespace:Microsoft.Phone.
Shell;assembly=Microsoft.Phone"
    xmlns:d="http://schemas.microsoft.com/expression/blend/2008"
    xmlns:mc="http://schemas.openxmlformats.org/markup-
compatibility/2006"
    xmlns:local="clr-namespace:WCFClient"
    x:Class="WCFClient.MainPage"
    mc:Ignorable="d" d:DesignWidth="480" d:DesignHeight="768"
    SupportedOrientations="Portrait" Orientation="Portrait"
    shell:SystemTray.IsVisible="True">

  <phone:PhoneApplicationPage.Resources>
    <local:MyViewModel x:Key="MyViewModelDataSource"
d:IsDataSource="True"/>
    <DataTemplate x:Key="PersonTemplate">
      <StackPanel>
        <TextBlock Text="{Binding EntityState}"/>
        <TextBlock Text="{Binding FirstName}"/>
        <TextBlock Text="{Binding Id}"/>
        <TextBlock Text="{Binding LastName}"/>
        <TextBlock Text="{Binding PhoneNumber}"/>
      </StackPanel>
    </DataTemplate>
  </phone:PhoneApplicationPage.Resources>
    <!--LayoutRoot is the root grid where all page content is
    placed-->
    <Grid x:Name="LayoutRoot" Background="Transparent"
DataContext="{Binding Source={StaticResource MyViewModelDataSource}}">
        <Grid.RowDefinitions>
            <RowDefinition Height="Auto"/>
            <RowDefinition Height="*"/>
        </Grid.RowDefinitions>

        <!--TitlePanel contains the name of the application and page
        title-->
        <StackPanel x:Name="TitlePanel" Grid.Row="0"
        Margin="12,17,0,28">
            <TextBlock x:Name="ApplicationTitle" Text="MY APPLICATION"
            Style="{StaticResource PhoneTextNormalStyle}"/>
            <TextBlock x:Name="PageTitle" Text="page name"
            Margin="9,-7,0,0" Style="{StaticResource
            PhoneTextTitle1Style}"/>
        </StackPanel>

        <!--ContentPanel - place additional content here-->
        <Grid x:Name="ContentPanel" Grid.Row="1" Margin="12,0,12,0">
          <ListBox ItemTemplate="{StaticResource PersonTemplate}"
```

```
ItemsSource="{Binding People}" Margin="8,44,8,8"/>
        </Grid>
    </Grid>

</phone:PhoneApplicationPage>
```

But with the power of databinding and a simple ViewModel, you can see that the design is completely separate, creating great isolation for functionality in your application. This simple service call will allow you do much more with little work.

Building a simple RSS reader

One of the more popular services out there, RSS is used on many blogs and other websites. This format is very standardized and can be used to create some great news reader type applications. In this example, we will create a very basic news reader application that can pull the new feed off the `developer.windowsphone.com` site.

Getting ready

To get started, we are going to create another basic Windows Phone Application called RSSReader. There will be several pieces to this application including a model and a ViewModel. Let's start by adding folders for both Models and ViewModels.

How to do it...

Now that we have our basic file structure set up, let's add our model for our articles:

1. This will be used to just give structure to the XML that is coming in from the RSS feed. Here is our model below:

```
using System;
using System.Collections.Generic;

namespace RSSReader.Models
{
    public class Article
    {
        public string Title { get; set; }
        public IEnumerable<string> Tags { get; set; }
        public string Author { get; set; }
        public string Intro { get; set; }
        public DateTime Published { get; set; }
        public string Url { get; set; }
        public string Description { get; set; }
        public string Category { get; set; }
    }
}
```

1. Now that we have a model that we can use to hold our data, we will need a ViewModel that can be used to get the data. Let's add a ViewModel called RSSViewModel and give it the following logic:

```csharp
using System;
using System.Collections.Generic;
using System.Diagnostics;
using System.Linq;
using System.Net;
using System.Xml.Linq;
using RSSReader.Models;

namespace RSSReader.ViewModels
{
    public class RSSReaderViewModel
    {
        public RSSReaderViewModel()
        {
            GetFeed("http://public.create.msdn.com/Feeds/CcoFeeds.
            svc/CmsFeed?group=News%20List");
        }

        public IEnumerable<Article> Posts { get; private set; }

        public void GetFeed(string url)
        {
            var client = new WebClient();
            client.DownloadStringCompleted +=
             HandleDownloadComplete;

            client.DownloadStringAsync(new Uri(url));

        }

        private void HandleDownloadComplete(object sender,
          DownloadStringCompletedEventArgs e)
        {
            try
            {
                var rssFeed = XDocument.Parse(e.Result);

                Posts = from item in rssFeed.Descendants("item")
                        select new Article
                               {
                                   Title = item.
                                    Element("title").Value,
                                   Published =
                                    DateTime.Parse(
                                    item.Element("pubDate").
```

```
                                            Value),
                                   Url = item.Element("link").
                                     Value,
                                   Description = item.
                                     Element("description").
                                     Value, Tags =
                                     (from category in item.
                                     Elements("category")
                                     orderby category.Value
                                     select category.Value).
                                     ToList()
                          };


        }
        catch (Exception ex)
        {
            Debug.WriteLine(ex.Message);
        }
    }



    }
}
```

2. Now that we have our model, we will need to associate it to the app by changing app.xaml to the following:

```
<!--Application Resources-->
<Application.Resources>
  <RSSReader_ViewModels:RSSReaderViewModel x:Key=
     "RSSReaderViewModelDataSource" d:IsDataSource="True"/>
</Application.Resources>

<Application.ApplicationLifetimeObjects>
    <!--Required object that handles lifetime events for the
        application-->
    <shell:PhoneApplicationService
        Launching="Application_Launching"
          Closing="Application_Closing"
        Activated="Application_Activated"
          Deactivated="Application_Deactivated"/>
</Application.ApplicationLifetimeObjects>
```

3. This will set the ViewModel as a static resource in the `app.xaml`. You will be able to bind to the list of news in your `mainpage.xaml` as follows:

```
<phone:PhoneApplicationPage
    x:Class="RSSReader.MainPage"
    xmlns="http://schemas.microsoft.com/winfx/2006/xaml/
          presentation"
    xmlns:x="http://schemas.microsoft.com/winfx/2006/xaml"
    xmlns:phone="clr-namespace:Microsoft.Phone.
          Controls;assembly=Microsoft.Phone"
    xmlns:shell="clr-namespace:Microsoft.Phone.
          Shell;assembly=Microsoft.Phone"
    xmlns:d="http://schemas.microsoft.com/expression/blend/2008"
    xmlns:mc="http://schemas.openxmlformats.org/
          markup-compatibility/2006"
    mc:Ignorable="d" d:DesignWidth="480" d:DesignHeight="768"
    FontFamily="{StaticResource PhoneFontFamilyNormal}"
    FontSize="{StaticResource PhoneFontSizeNormal}"
    Foreground="{StaticResource PhoneForegroundBrush}"
    SupportedOrientations="Portrait" Orientation="Portrait"
    shell:SystemTray.IsVisible="True">
<phone:PhoneApplicationPage.Resources>
    <DataTemplate x:Key="ArticleTemplate">
      <Grid>
        <TextBlock Margin="0,0,1,0" TextWrapping="Wrap"
          Text="{Binding Title}" d:LayoutOverrides="Width,
          Height"/>
      </Grid>
    </DataTemplate>
</phone:PhoneApplicationPage.Resources>

    <!--LayoutRoot is the root grid where all page content is
        placed-->
    <Grid x:Name="LayoutRoot" Background="Transparent"
        DataContext="{Binding Source={StaticResource
        RSSReaderViewModelDataSource}}">
        <Grid.RowDefinitions>
            <RowDefinition Height="Auto"/>
            <RowDefinition Height="*"/>
        </Grid.RowDefinitions>

        <!--TitlePanel contains the name of the application and
            page title-->
        <StackPanel x:Name="TitlePanel" Grid.Row="0"
            Margin="12,17,0,28">
            <TextBlock x:Name="ApplicationTitle" Text="RSS Reader"
                Style="{StaticResource PhoneTextNormalStyle}"/>
            <TextBlock x:Name="PageTitle" Text="WP7 News"
                Margin="9,-7,0,0" Style="{StaticResource
                PhoneTextTitle1Style}"/>
```

```
        </StackPanel>
        <!--ContentPanel - place additional content here-->
        <Grid x:Name="ContentPanel" Grid.Row="1"
            Margin="12,0,12,0" >
          <ListBox Margin="8" ItemsSource="{Binding Posts,
            Mode=OneWay}" ItemTemplate="{StaticResource
            ArticleTemplate}"/></Grid>
    </Grid>
  </phone:PhoneApplicationPage>
```

Now when you run the app, it should actually pull the news feed from the Windows Phone developer site.

How it works...

This is another simple example of how to use a ViewModel to get your data from an outside datasource and place it on your controls. We have taken what we have learned in this chapter and previous chapters to provide basic databinding in a very manageable format.

6
Location Services

In this chapter, we will cover:

- ▸ Tracking latitude and longitude
- ▸ Tracking altitude, speed, and course
- ▸ Saving battery by using a location wisely
- ▸ Using location services with the emulator
- ▸ Mapping your location

Introduction

One of the most powerful features of smartphones today is location awareness. Windows Phone 7 is no exception. The wide consumerization of GPS around 10 years ago brought handheld GPS receivers for consumers on the go, but few individuals could justify the expense or pocket space. Now that smartphones have GPS built in, developers have built incredibly powerful applications that are location-aware. For example, apps that help users track their jogging route, get real-time navigation assistance while driving, and map/analyze their golf game.

In this chapter, we will take a deep dive into the location API for Windows Phone 7 by building an application to help navigate during travel and another to map the user's location.

Tracking latitude and longitude

In this recipe, we will implement the most fundamental use of location services, tracking latitude and longitude. Our sample application will be a navigation helper which displays all the available location information. We will also review the different ways in which the phone gets its location information and their attributes.

Getting ready

We will be working in Visual Studio for this tutorial, so start by opening Studio and creating a new Windows Phone 7 application using the Windows Phone Application project template.

All the location/GPS-related methods and classes are found in the **System.Device** assembly, so add this reference next:

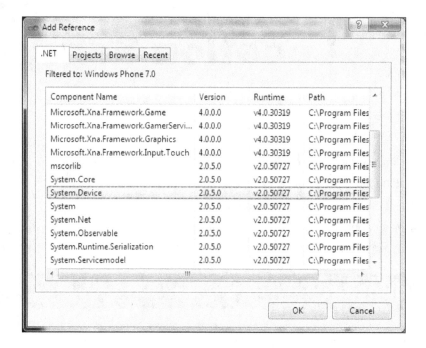

We will need some UI to start tracking and displaying the data, so go to the `MainPage.xaml` file, if it's not already open. Change the `ContentPanel` from a `Grid` to a `StackPanel`, then add a button to the designer, and set its `Content` property to `Start Tracking`. Next add four `TextBlocks`. Two of these will be Latitude and Longitude labels. We will use the others to display the latitude/longitude coordinates, so set their `x:Name` properties to `txtLatitude` and `txtLongitude` respectively. You can also set the application and page titles if you like. The resulting page should look similar to the following screenshot:

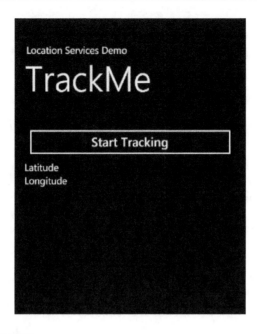

How to do it...

The core class used for tracking location is the GeoCoordinateWatcher. We subscribe to the events on the watcher to be notified when changes occur:

1   Double-click on your button in the designer to go to the click event handler for the button in the code behind file. This is where we will start watching for location changes.

2. Create a GeoCoordinateWatcher field variable named _watcher. Set this field variable inside your click event handler to a new GeoCoordinateWatcher. Next add a handler to the PositionChanged event named _watcher_PositionChanged. Then start watching for position changes by calling the Start method.

3. Next add a handler to the PositionChanged event named _watcher_ PositionChanged. Then start watching for position changes by calling the Start method.

4. In order to use the position information, create the void handler method with parameters named sender of type object and e of type GeoPositionChang edEventArgs<GeoCoordinate>. Inside this method set the Text properties on the txtLatitude and txtLongitude text boxes to the coordinate values e.Position.Location.Latitude and e.Position.Location.Longitude respectively.

Latitude and longitude as strings:

Latitude and longitude are of type `double` and can be converted to strings using the `ToString` method for display.

You should end up with a class that is similar to the following block of code:

```
public partial class MainPage : PhoneApplicationPage
{
    private IGeoPositionWatcher<GeoCoordinate> _watcher;

    public MainPage()
    {
        InitializeComponent();
    }

    private void butTrack_Click(object sender, RoutedEventArgs e)
    {
        _watcher = new GeoCoordinateWatcher();

        _watcher.PositionChanged += _watcher_PositionChanged;
        _watcher.Start();
    }

    void _watcher_PositionChanged(object sender,
        GeoPositionChangedEventArgs<GeoCoordinate> e)
    {
        txtLatitude.Text = e.Position.Location.Latitude.ToString();
        txtLongitude.Text = e.Position.Location.Longitude.ToString();
    }

}
```

That's it. You can now deploy this app to your phone, start tracking, and see the latitude and longitude changes on your screen.

How it works...

The watcher starts a new background thread to watch for position changes. Each change is passed to your event handler(s) for processing.

Window Phone 7 provides location services through the following three sources:

- ▶ **GPS**: Satellite based
- ▶ **Wi-Fi**: Known wireless network positions

- ▶ **Cellular**: Cellular tower triangulation

Each of these position providers has their strengths and weaknesses, but the combination of the three covers nearly any possible use case:

- ▶ GPS is the most accurate, but you must have an unobstructed view of the sky
- ▶ Wi-Fi can be accurate depending on how close you are to the access point, but you must be in the range of a known wireless network
- ▶ Cellular is the least accurate and only needs cell signal

So if you're in an urban area with tall buildings, GPS may be intermittent but Wi-Fi networks and cellular coverage should be plentiful. If you are in a rural area, GPS should work well and cellular triangulation might help where available.

See also

- ▶ *Tracking altitude, speed, and course*
- ▶ *Saving battery by using a location wisely*
- ▶ *Using location services with the emulator*

Tracking altitude, speed, and course

In this section, we will discuss the different types of location information that are provided by the GeoCoordinateWatcher and how they might be used. A quick look at the **Object Browser** shows us that the GeoCoordinate object has several interesting properties:

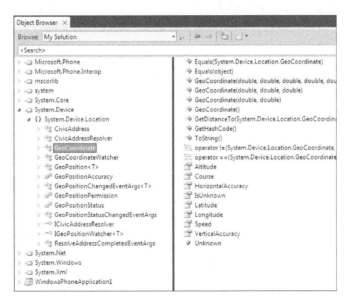

In addition to `Latitude` and `Longitude`, there is `Altitude`, `Speed`, and `Course`, among others. `Altitude` and `Speed` are pretty self-explanatory, but `Course` might not be as obvious. `Course` is your heading or the direction you are going, given two points. The following table shows each property and its unit of measurement:

Property	Unit of measure
Latitude	Degrees (-90.0 to 90.0)
Longitude	Degrees (-180.0 to 180.0)
Altitude	Meters
Speed	Meters per second
Course	Degrees (0.0 to 360.0)
Horizontal/Vertical Accuracy	Meters

Horizontal and Vertical Accuracy specifies the accuracy of `Latitude/Longitude` and `Altitude`, respectively, in meters. For example, this means your actual `Latitude` position is between the reported Latitude minus the accuracy value and the reported `Latitude` plus the accuracy value. The smaller the accuracy value, the more accurate but the longer it may take to get a position.

Now that we have reviewed all the information available to us, let's use it in our location app.

Getting ready

Add three more sets of `TextBlock` controls under the longitude control for each of the following properties: `Altitude`, `Speed`, and `Course`. Set the speed label `TextBlock Text` property to `Speed (mph)`. Name the `TextBlock` controls as you did for latitude/longitude so we can assign their `Text` properties from the code behind. The page should look similar to the following screenshot:

How to do it...

Perform the following steps to add altitude, speed, and course to the application:

1. Open the code behind file for the page, and in the `positionChanged` handler, set `Altitude` in the same way as we did for latitude/longitude before; simply set the `Text` property of the `txtAltitude TextBlock` to the `Altitude` property as a string.

2. For the `Speed` property, convert from meters per second to miles per hour. One meter/sec equals 2.2369363 miles per hour, so we can multiply the `Speed` property by 2.2369363 to get miles per hour.

3. Display `Course` so that the normal users can understand it, using the name of the direction (that is, North, South, East, West). The `Course` value is a degree value from 0 to 360, where 0/360 is north and the degrees go clock-wise with a compass.

4. Create a series of `if` statements that will provide the correct heading. Between 316 and 45 will be North, 46 and 135 will be East, 136 and 225 will be South, and between 226 and 315 will be West. Our `_watcher_PositionChanged` method is now as follows:

```
void _watcher_PositionChanged(object sender, GeoPositionChangedEve
ntArgs<GeoCoordinate> e)
        {
                txtLatitude.Text = e.Position.Location.Latitude.
                ToString();
```

```
txtLongitude.Text = e.Position.Location.Longitude.
ToString();
txtAltitude.Text = e.Position.Location.Altitude.
ToString();
txtSpeed.Text = (e.Position.Location.Speed *
2.2369363).
    ToString();

double course = e.Position.Location.Course;
string heading = string.Empty;
if (course >= 46 && course <= 135)
    heading = "East";
if (course >= 136 && course <= 225)
    heading = "South";
if (course >= 226 && course <= 315)
    heading = "West";
else
    heading = "North";

txtCourse.Text = heading;
}
```

How it works...

If you deploy the application to your phone now, you will see Speed display **NaN** (**Not a Number**), Altitude display zero, and Course is blank. This is because Altitude, Speed, and Course are only available when you specify that you want high accuracy location information. We do this by instantiating the GeoCoordinateWatcher with a GeoPositionAccuracy type of GeoPositionAccuracy.High in the constructor. By default, the accuracy is set to GeoPositionAccuracy.Default, which only uses cellular triangulation and is not accurate enough to calculate speed, altitude, or course. GeoPositionAccuracy.High uses GPS and Wi-Fi, when available, which provides more accurate positions. Although it is more accurate, it also uses more power and can take longer to get your position. This is why High is not the default. It is strongly recommended that you only use the higher accuracy when it is absolutely needed.

In this case, we need the Altitude, Speed, and Course, so it is necessary. Set the accuracy level to high in the GeoCoordinateWatcher constructor, like so:

```
_watcher = new GeoCoordinateWatcher(GeoPositionAccuracy.High);
```

If you redeploy the application to the phone, you may notice it still shows **NaN** for Speed. This may be because you are indoors and have an obstructed view of the sky or it may just take a few moments to get a good signal. Once you have a good GPS signal, you should see valid Speed, Altitude, and Course values. The best way to test this application is in the passenger seat of a driving vehicle so you can compare the vehicles, speedometer to the speed in the application.

There may be times, as well, when you lose GPS signal. When this occurs, the latitude and longitude values will also be set to **NaN**. In such cases, you may want to give the user a friendlier explanation of the problem. You can simply check the `IsUnknown` property in the position changed event and provide a better message. For example:

```
void _watcher_PositionChanged(object sender, GeoPositionChangedEventAr
gs<GeoCoordinate> e)
        {
            if (e.Position.Location.IsUnknown)
            {
                txtLatitude.Text = "Finding your position.
                    Please wait ...";
                txtLongitude.Text = "";
                txtAltitude.Text = "";
                txtSpeed.Text = "";
                txtCourse.Text = "";

                return;
            }

            txtLatitude.Text = e.Position.Location.Latitude.
            ToString();
            txtLongitude.Text = e.Position.Location.Longitude.
            ToString();
            txtAltitude.Text = e.Position.Location.Altitude.
            ToString();
            txtSpeed.Text = (e.Position.Location.Speed * 2.2369363).
            ToString();

            double course = e.Position.Location.Course;
            string heading = string.Empty;
            if (course >= 46 && course <= 135)
                heading = "East";
            if (course >= 136 && course <= 225)
                heading = "South";
            if (course >= 226 && course <= 315)
                heading = "West";
            else
                heading = "North";

            txtCourse.Text = heading;
        }
```

The last property we will cover in this recipe is the `Permission` property on the `GeoPositionWatcher`. Before submitting your app to the marketplace, you must define which phone capabilities your app requires. One of those capabilities is location. Before a user installs an application, he/she is informed of the capabilities the app requires and must accept them to install. Even though the user has given the app permission to use location services of the phone, the user can still turn off location services for all apps from the settings menu. The `Permission` property will help us check for this and tell the user why the app isn't working.

There is a slight trick though; the `Permission` property will be set to `Granted` when the watcher is first created, even if **Location services** are disabled in the **Settings** menu. It will be reset to `Denied` after the `Start` method is called. So we must check for a `Denied` permission value after calling the `Start` method. For instance:

```
private void butTrack_Click(object sender, RoutedEventArgs e)
{
  _watcher = newGeoCoordinateWatcher(GeoPositionAccuracy.High);

  _watcher.PositionChanged += _watcher_PositionChanged;
  _watcher.StatusChanged += _watcher_StatusChanged;
  _watcher.Start();
  if (_watcher.Permission == GeoPositionPermission.Denied)
    tbLatitude.Text = "Please enable location services and retry";
}
```

We can test this by turning off location services. From the start screen, flick left to the App list, tap **Settings**, and then tap **location**. Swipe the switch left to the **Off** position. Redeploy the application to your phone, click the **Start Tracking** button, and you will see our new message.

As mentioned previously, the user must accept the capabilities of the application before installing it. There may be future updates to the phone which allow the user to change the allowed capabilities of individual apps from the settings menu as well. The `Permission` property would also be useful in this scenario.

There's more...

You may have also noticed the `CivicAddressResolver` and `CivicAddress` classes in the `System.Device.Location` namespace. As its name implies, the `CivicAddressResolver` returns an address from a `GeoCoordinate`. Unfortunately, this is not yet implemented for Windows Phone. You can instantiate them and attempt to use them, but the returned `CivicAddress` will always be unknown. Hopefully, this will be implemented in the future updates of the operating system.

▸ *Tracking latitude and longitude*

▸ *Saving battery by using location wisely*

▸ *Using location services with the emulator*

Saving battery by using a location wisely

As was previously mentioned, when setting the `GeoPositionAccuracy` to high, location services can use more power than normal phone operations and thus drain the battery. Many mobile developers struggle to build location-aware applications that are power efficient, but the Windows Phone 7 platform has the necessary hooks to make it work. This section will give you the tips you need to get it right.

Let's take our sample application and add the code to use the location efficiently.

Getting ready

Add a second button under the track button with the text **Stop Tracking**. We also need to show the user what the current status of the watcher is, so add a set of `TextBlock` controls above latitude, labeled `Status`:

How to do it...

Perform the following steps starting in the `MainPage.xaml` file:

1. Double-click the **Stop Tracking** button in the designer windows to add a click event handler. Check to see if the `_watcher` field variable is null; if it isn't, stop it with the `Stop` method. This will allow the user to stop tracking:

```
private void butStopTracking_Click(object sender,
    RoutedEventArgs e)
{
        if (_watcher != null)
          _watcher.Stop();
}
```

    We can use the `StatusChanged` event to update the status `TextBlock` appropriately. This event is called when the watcher status changes. The `Status` property is a `GeoPositionStatus` enumeration, with the following values:

Status	Description
Disabled	Location services are disabled or unsupported, but in actual testing, this status has only ever been seen after removing the location capability from the `WMAppManifest`. This shouldn't be done if your app needs location services.
NoData	The watcher cannot get location data. This may be because the watcher has not been started, could not start, or lost a data connection.
Initializing	The watcher has been started and the location service is attempting to retrieve data.
Ready	The watcher has been started, is initialized, and is receiving data.

2. Add a `StatusChanged` event handler to the watcher under the assignment of the `PositionChanged` handler:

```
_watcher = new GeoCoordinateWatcher(GeoPositionAccuracy.High);
_watcher.PositionChanged += _watcher_PositionChanged;
_watcher.StatusChanged += _watcher_StatusChanged;
_watcher.Start();
```

3. In the handler method, update the status value `TextBlock` with the new status found in the `Status` property of the `GeoPositionStatusChangedEventArgs` parameter:

```
void _watcher_StatusChanged(object sender,
GeoPositionStatusChangedEventArgs e)
    {
tbStatus.Text = e.Status.ToString();
    }
```

4. Let's add another `Button` to the bottom of the page with the text `Get Last Position`. Double-click on the button in the designer to create and go to the click event handler in the code behind.

5. In the handler, we should check to see if the watcher is instantiated and then if the `Position` property is valid, by checking the watcher for `null` or the `IsUnknown` property on the `Location` property for false. If either is true, set the status value `TextBlock` to `No previous position` and `return`. Otherwise, display all the location information as we would for a position change and set the status value to the `Position Timestamp` property.

6. To avoid duplication, let's refactor the setting of the display fields from the `PositionChanged` method handler to a new method that can be called by the `PositionChanged` and get the previous position button click handlers:

```
void _watcher_PositionChanged(object sender,
    GeoPositionChangedEventArgs<GeoCoordinate> e)
{
    if (e.Position.Location.IsUnknown)
    {
        ClearUi();
        txtLatitude.Text = "Finding your position.
          Please wait ...";
        return;
    }
    DisplayPosition(e.Position.Location);
}


private void DisplayPosition(GeoCoordinate location)
{
    txtLatitude.Text = location.Latitude.ToString();
    txtLongitude.Text = location.Longitude.ToString();
    txtAltitude.Text = location.Altitude.ToString();
    txtSpeed.Text = (location.Speed * 2.2369363).ToString();

    double course = location.Course;
    string heading = string.Empty;
    if (course >= 46 && course <= 135)
        heading = "East";
    if (course >= 136 && course <= 225)
        heading = "South";
    if (course >= 226 && course <= 315)
        heading = "West";
    else
        heading = "North";
```

```
        txtCourse.Text = heading;
    }
    private void butGetLastPosition_Click(object sender,
    RoutedEventArgs e)
    {
        if (_watcher == null || _watcher.Position.Location.IsUnknown)
        {
            tbStatus.Text = "No previous position";
            return;
        }
        DisplayPosition(_watcher.Position.Location);
        tbStatus.Text = _watcher.Position.Timestamp.ToString();
    }
```

7. We also need to store the watcher in a field variable and check for `null` instead of creating a new watcher each time the **Start Tracking** button is clicked:

```
if (_watcher == null)
        {
            _watcher = new GeoCoordinateWatcher();
            _watcher.PositionChanged += _watcher_PositionChanged;
            _watcher.StatusChanged += _watcher_StatusChanged;
        }
```

8. Set the `MovementThreshold` to `40` for our sample app, during instantiation of the `GeoCoordinateWatcher`:

```
_watcher = new GeoCoordinateWatcher(GeoPositionAccuracy.High)
        {
            MovementThreshold = 40
        };
```

How it works...

When using location services, the first tip is to only watch for position changes when you need them. In this case, our sample app had partially taken that tip into account by only starting to watch for position changes after the user clicks the **Start Tracking** button. In this recipe, we also provided a way for the user to turn tracking off.

The next tip is to create as few watchers as possible, preferably one which you can reuse across the application. This will allow you to reuse the last known position from the watcher on any page. There is a `Position` property on `GeoCoordinateWatcher` which is set each time a new position is found; it is always the last known position. Few applications need to constantly track position changes. It is more likely that the application needs to only know a location occasionally. The `Position` property is a `GeoPosition<GeoCoordinate>` type which stores both the `GeoCoordinate` and the timestamp that is/was observed. If necessary, the application can determine if the coordinate is too old; in most cases it will not be.

So in this recipe we added a button for the user to get their last known position. We also refactored the start tracking button handler to use a single watcher instead of creating a new watcher each time the track button is clicked.

The last battery-saving tip is to adjust the accuracy of the watcher to your needs. We have already discussed setting the `GeoPositionAccuracy` to High only when needed. Using the default accuracy will help tremendously, but if high accuracy is necessary there is another setting that you should configure as well.

The `MovementThreshold` property on the `GeoCoordinateWatcher` allows you to set how often you wish to be notified of position changes. By default, it is set to zero, which notifies as often as there is a detected change in position. In fact, the `PositionChanged` event is fired with slightly different position values every second, even if you are standing still. This produces quite a bit of noise. It is common to set the threshold to at least 20 to get more meaningful position data. You should set the threshold according to the needs of your application.

In this recipe, we set the threshold to `40`.

Saving battery while using Location Services is all about configuring the watcher appropriately. Using the tips outlined in this recipe will help you make the best decisions for your application. The biggest mistake developers make with location services is not understanding how they are getting position data and not dialing down the accuracy for their needs. You will not make that mistake if you put these tips into practice.

See also

- ▶ *Tracking latitude and longitude*
- ▶ *Tracking altitude, speed, and course*
- ▶ *Using location services with the emulator*

Using location services with the emulator

Up to this point, we have only tested our sample application on a phone. If you run the application from the previous recipe in the emulator, you will find the status of the GeoCoordinateWatcher would be set to NoData when attempting to track position. This is because the emulator has no GPS receiver and does not support using location service natively.

There are several reasons you may need to use location services in the emulator. The most obvious is you do not have a Windows Phone. Although, there are many times during development of an application that it is just impractical to test location services on a phone. If, for instance, you are developing an informational bus route application, you cannot travel all over the city every time you wish to test a small feature. Or perhaps, if you are creating a national golf course locator, it's impractical to travel all over the country to test your app.

Fortunately, Location Services abstracts its API with the IGeoPositionWatcher interface. This interface defines the core of location services:

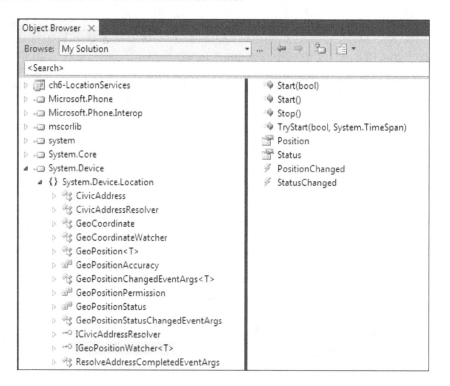

As you can see, it defines the methods, properties, and events we have been using up to this point. In this recipe, we will create our own fake implementation of this interface to use in the emulator.

Getting ready

We will continue using our navigation application in this recipe. Add a `Framework` folder in the root of the project and then add a class to that folder named `FakeGeoCoordinateWatcher`. This will be our new, fake implementation of the watcher. The `IGeoPositionWatcher` interface is generic, allowing you to define a location type. The `GeoCoordinateWatcher` implements `IGeoPositionWatcher` using a `GeoCoordinate` location type. Our fake watcher will implement the same interface and will be interchangeable with `GeoCoordinateWatcher`.

Add the necessary methods, events, and properties to implement the interface:

```
public class FakeGeoCoordinateWatcher :
        IGeoPositionWatcher<GeoCoordinate>
{
public void Start()
  {
        throw new NotImplementedException();
  }
public void Start(bool suppressPermissionPrompt)
  {
    throw new NotImplementedException();
  }
public bool TryStart(boolsuppressPermissionPrompt, TimeSpan timeout)
  {
        throw new NotImplementedException();
  }
public void Stop()
  {
        throw new NotImplementedException();
  }
public GeoPosition<GeoCoordinate> Position
  {
get { throw new NotImplementedException(); }
private set { throw new NotImplementedException(); }
  }
public GeoPositionStatus Status
  {
get { throw new NotImplementedException(); }
private set { throw new NotImplementedException(); }
  }
  publiceventEventHandler<GeoPositionChangedEventArgs
        <GeoCoordinate>>PositionChanged;
```

```
bliceventEventHandler<GeoPositionStatusChangedEventArgs>StatusChanged;
}
```

This satisfies the interface, but as you can see, it will only throw exceptions. There are many ways you could implement this. We will go with a very simple implementation that will allow us to start testing in the emulator quickly.

How to do it...

Our fake implementation will have a static set of coordinates that will be used to call the PositionChanged event at three second intervals:

1. First let's define our coordinates. For this we will use the coordinates from a small section of the Boston marathon, but any coordinates will do. Create a private `List<GeoCoordinate>` field variable named `_coordinates` and assign the coordinates as follows:

```
List<GeoCoordinate> _coordinates = newList<GeoCoordinate>
    {
newGeoCoordinate { Latitude = 42.248054, Longitude = -71.47439,
Altitude = 88.1, Course = 51, Speed = 2 },
newGeoCoordinate { Latitude = 42.248697, Longitude = -71.473961,
Altitude = 86.2, Course = 52, Speed = 4 },
newGeoCoordinate { Latitude = 42.249362, Longitude = -71.473403,
Altitude = 83.3, Course = 53, Speed = 3 },
newGeoCoordinate { Latitude = 42.24977, Longitude = -71.473017,
Altitude = 81.4, Course = 52, Speed = 5 },
newGeoCoordinate { Latitude = 42.250221, Longitude = -71.472695,
Altitude = 80.9, Course = 51, Speed = 2 },
newGeoCoordinate { Latitude = 42.250671, Longitude = -71.472394,
Altitude = 80.4, Course = 52, Speed = 4 },
newGeoCoordinate { Latitude = 42.251079, Longitude = -71.472094,
Altitude = 80.9, Course = 53, Speed = 3 },
newGeoCoordinate { Latitude = 42.25153, Longitude = -71.471815,
Altitude = 81.8, Course = 52, Speed = 2 },
newGeoCoordinate { Latitude = 42.251959, Longitude = -71.47145,
Altitude = 84.3, Course = 51, Speed = 3 },
newGeoCoordinate { Latitude = 42.252023, Longitude = -71.471386,
Altitude = 84.7, Course = 52, Speed = 4 },
newGeoCoordinate { Latitude = 42.252431, Longitude = -71.470807,
Altitude = 82.8, Course = 53, Speed = 3 },
newGeoCoordinate { Latitude = 42.252903, Longitude = -71.47012,
Altitude = 79.4, Course = 52, Speed = 2 }
        };
```

2. We will also need a timer to fire the `PositionChanged` event and pass the new coordinate. Declare another private field variable of type `System.Threading.Timer` named `_timer`:

```
privateTimer _timer;
```

The `Start` method is where all the logic begins.

3. First we will check to see if the timer is set. If it is not `null`, the timer has already been set and is ticking, so we just `return` out of the method because there is nothing to do. Otherwise, we will create the timer and set its properties in the constructor.

4. Set the first constructor parameter to `MyTimerCallback` for now and we will create it in a moment.

5. Set the second parameter to null.

6. Set the third parameter to a `TimeSpan` of 3 seconds.

7. Set the last parameter to a `Timespan` of `-1` millisecond to disable it.

8. Finally we will set the `Status` to `Initializing` if it is not already set to `Ready`:

```
public void Start()
    {
       if (_timer != null)
          return;

       _timer = new Timer(MyTimerCallback, null,
                new TimeSpan(0,0,3), new TimeSpan(-1));

       if (Status != GeoPositionStatus.Ready)
          Status = GeoPositionStatus.Initializing;

    }
```

9. Create the timer callback method which will return `void` and take an object parameter. In this method, find the next coordinate and update the `Position` property. The next coordinate will either be the first coordinate, if the `Position` has never been set, or the next coordinate in the list.

10. Find the current `Position` in the static list of coordinates and then use some LINQ methods (make sure to add `System.Linq` using the directive at the top of the page) to skip to the next coordinate.

11. Set the `Status` to `Ready` to mimic the real `GeoCoordinateWatcher` functionality and set the `Position` property to a new `GeoPosition<GeoCoordinate>` with the timestamp set to the current `DateTime` and the coordinate set to the next coordinate in the constructor.

12. Finally, reset the timer for the next coordinate. The simplest way to do this is to call `Dispose` on the timer, set it to null, and call the `Start` method again. This will reuse the code we have already written to create and reconfigure the timer:

```
private void MyTimerCallback(object state)
{
  GeoCoordinate position;
  if (Position == null)
    position = _coordinates.First();
  else
  {
    var index = _coordinates.IndexOf(Position.Location);
    position = _coordinates.Skip(index+1).FirstOrDefault() ?? _
    coordinates.First();
  }

  Status = GeoPositionStatus.Ready;

  Position = newGeoPosition<GeoCoordinate>
    (DateTime.Now, position);

  _timer.Dispose();
  _timer = null;
  Start();
}
```

13. For the other two start methods, we can simply call the first. In more complex scenarios, you can provide further logic where necessary:

```
public void Start(boolsuppressPermissionPrompt)
    {
      Start();
    }

    public bool TryStart(boolsuppressPermissionPrompt,
            TimeSpan timeout)
    {
      Start();
      Return true;
    }
```

14. All that is needed for the `Stop` method is to dispose the `timer` variable and set it to null. The timer controls when `PositionChanged` will be called again, so setting it to `null` will stop any further events from firing:

```
public void Stop()
```

```
        {
          _timer.Dispose();
          _timer = null;
        }
```

15. That handles all the methods. Now that we have the `Position` and `Status` properties, we will use the setter of these properties to call the `PositionChanged` and `StatusChanged` events, respectively. Both properties will need backing private fields which will be returned from the getters. The setters will set the backing field and then call the events.

16. There may be cases where the handlers aren't set before calling start, so we should make sure they aren't null before calling them as well:

```
private GeoPosition<GeoCoordinate> _position;
public GeoPosition<GeoCoordinate> Position
    {
      get { return _position; }
      private set
      {
        _position = value;

      Deployment.Current.Dispatcher.BeginInvoke(() =>
            {
              if (PositionChanged != null)
              PositionChanged(this, new GeoPositionChanged
              EventArgs<GeoCoordinate>(value));
            });
      }
    }

private GeoPositionStatus _status;
public GeoPositionStatus Status
    {
      get { return _status; }
      private set
      {
        _status = value;

      Deployment.Current.Dispatcher.BeginInvoke(
          () =>
            {
              if (StatusChanged != null)
              StatusChanged(this, new GeoPositionStatusChanged
              EventArgs(value));
            });
      }
    }
```

How it works...

Location services utilize a background thread for getting location information. This allows the UI to continue to be responsive while waiting on the next position. The `GeoCoordinateWatcher`, however, fires the `PositionChanged` and `StatusChanged` events on the UI thread to help developers avoid further complexity when working with Location Services. We have done the same in our `FakeGeoCoordinateWatcher` by wrapping the event calls with a `BeginInvoke` method on the UI thread.

If we do not fire the events on the UI thread, the sample application would throw the following error when using the `FakeGeoCoordinateWatcher`:

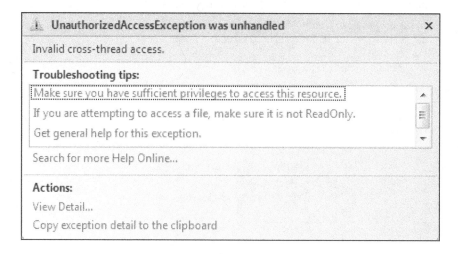

Now that we have finished with our fake watcher, we can update the sample application to use it, but we should not just replace the `GeoCoordinateWatcher`. It would be nice to avoid having to make a manual change every time we want to switch from the fake to the real watcher. First, let's change the declaration of our `_watcher` variable from:

```
GeoCoordinateWatcher _watcher;
```

to:

```
IGeoPositionWatcher<GeoCoordinate> _watcher;
```

This will allow us to use either a real `GeoCoordinateWatcher` or our fake implementation since they both implement the `IGeoPositionWatcher<GeoCoordinate>` interface. In most cases, we only need to use the fake watcher when in the emulator. Thankfully, we can check the `Microsoft.Devices.Environment.DeviceType` property and use the fake watcher if the DeviceType is Emulator:

```
if (Microsoft.Devices.Environment.DeviceType == DeviceType.Emulator)
        _watcher = new FakeGeoCoordinateWatcher();
```

```
else
        _watcher = new GeoCoordinateWatcher(GeoPositionAccuracy.
High) { MovementThreshold = 40 };
```

If you rebuild the application at this point, you will notice an error while checking
the watcher `Permission` property for a `Denied` status. This occurs because the
`IGeoPositionWatcher` interface doesn't define a `Permission` property. The `Permission`
property is only defined on the `GeoCoordinateWatcher`. To fix this, we can check that
the watcher is a `GeoCoordinateWatcher` and then cast the `_watcher` variable to a
`GeoCoordinateWatcher` and access the `Permission` property. This is not as clean as
before, but it is a small price to pay for adding the ability to get location information in
the emulator:

```
if (_watcher isGeoCoordinateWatcher&& ((GeoCoordinateWatcher)_
watcher).Permission == GeoPositionPermission.Denied)
    tbLatitude.Text = "Please enable location services and retry";
```

Now whether we are running the application in the emulator or on a phone, we will get
location information.

There's more...

We have successfully implemented the `IGeoPositionWatcher<GeoCoordinate>`
interface, but only in its simplest form. We attempted to have our fake implementation
mimic the `GeoCoordinateWatcher` in some areas, but it will not work exactly like a
`GeoCoordinateWatcher` at all times. You should always test your applications on a device
in the field to make sure location services will act as you expect them to. You will likely find
use cases or issues that you did not expect during development.

In addition, there are far more complex implementations that could be developed to more
closely match your needs.

See also

▸ *Tracking latitude and longitude*

▸ *Tracking altitude, speed, and course*

▸ *Saving battery by using a location wisely*

Mapping your location

One of the most common uses of location services is to display the user's position on a map.
This section will review the Map control for Windows Phone 7 and how to use it to display the
user's current position.

Getting ready

Create a new Windows Phone Application project in Visual Studio, open `MainPage.xaml`, and delete the default layout grid and its contents. Do not add any assembly references yet. Although the Map control is located in the `Microsoft.Phone.Controls.Maps` assembly, there is an easier way to add the assembly reference:

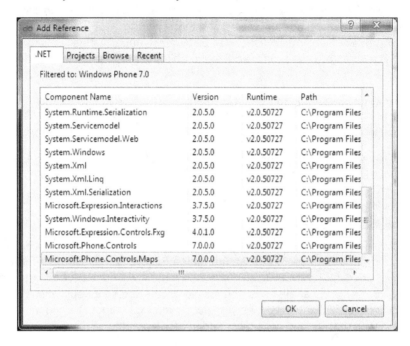

By dragging a `Map` control from the Toolbox to your page, you are also adding any of the assembly references you might need to use:

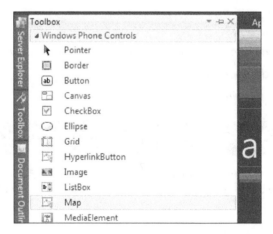

The added references include:

- ▸ `Microsoft.Phone.Controls.Maps`: Mapping controls
- ▸ `System.Device`: Location services
- ▸ `System.Runtime.Serialization`: General serialization classes
- ▸ `System.ServiceModel`: Windows Communication Foundation (WCF)

Now that we have all our references added, we can start working with the `Map` control. First expand the control to fill the page by deleting the width and height attributes. Notice the control is named `map1`.

If you run the app, you will see that the map displays the entire world by default. You will also notice a watermark that says **Invalid Credentials. Sign up for a developer account.** Ignore this for now.

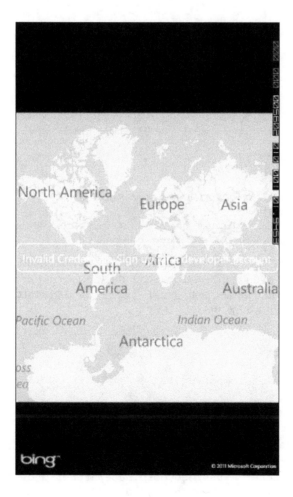

Viewing the map in landscape mode is preferable in many cases, so let's also allow landscape mode in the page header:

```
SupportedOrientations="PortraitOrLandscape" Orientation="Portrait"
```

Now we can rotate the phone (or emulator) to view the map in landscape mode as well:

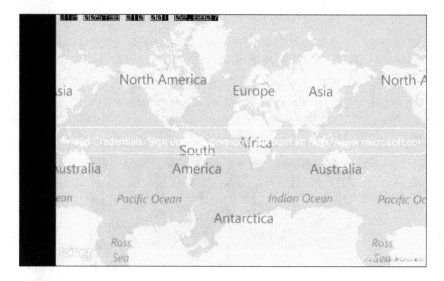

How to do it...

For this app, we will begin tracking a location at startup:

1. Create an `IGeoPositionWatcher<GeoCoordinate>` field variable and initialize it in the page constructor located in the code behind.

2. Copy the `FakeGeoCoordinateWatcher` from the navigation application to this project for use when in the emulator. Use the `GeoCoordinateWatcher` when on a device. Then add a handler to the `PositionChanged` event of the `watcher` and create the handler method:

```
private IGeoPositionWatcher<GeoCoordinate> _watcher;
public MainPage()
    {
        InitializeComponent();

        if (Microsoft.Devices.Environment.DeviceType ==
        DeviceType.Emulator)
          _watcher = new FakeGeoCoordinateWatcher();
        else
          _watcher = new GeoCoordinateWatcher(GeoPositionAccuracy.
          High) { MovementThreshold = 40 };
```

```
_watcher.PositionChanged          += _watcher_PositionChanged;
    }


Private void _watcher_PositionChanged(object sender, GeoPositionCh
angedEventArgs<GeoCoordinate> e)
    {
    }
```

There are several mapping classes that we will use with the map control. The first is the `Pushpin`, which highlights a specific point on the map.

3. Add a `Pushpin` as a child of the `Map` control in XAML, name it `pMyLocation`, and place a `TextBlock` inside the `Pushpin` with the text `Me`. This will be our marker on the map of the user's current position:

```xaml
<my:Map Name="map1" >
  <my:Pushpin x:Name="pMyLocation">
    <TextBlock>Me</TextBlock>
  </my:Pushpin>
</my:Map>
```

4. In the position changed handler, first make sure the location is known. If it is not, return out of the method; if it is, then set the pushpin's location to the new location. We can also have the map reposition to be centered on the user's position as it changes. Do this by setting the map's `Center` property to the new location:

```csharp
private void _watcher_PositionChanged(object sender, GeoPositionCh
angedEventArgs<GeoCoordinate> e)
    {
       var location = e.Position.Location;
       if (location.IsUnknown)
         return;

    pMyLocation.Location = location;
       map1.Center = location;
    }
```

5. Now, if you run the app in the emulator, you should see the `Me` pushpin in the Boston area moving slightly every few seconds. If you click on the map with your mouse, it will begin zooming in to more detail. We can also zoom the map by default to the street level by setting the `ZoomLevel` property to `18`:

```xaml
<my:Map Name="map1"ZoomLevel="18">
```

6. We will also add an indication of the accuracy of the position information using the `HorizontalAccuracy` value from the `GeoCoordinate`. We can use a `MapLayer` to add a red ellipse to the map around the user's position. Add a `MapLayer` node to the `Map` control just above the `Pushpin` in XAML. Give it a name so we can reference it in the code behind as well:

```
<my:MapLayer Name="accuracyLayer">
</my:MapLayer>
```

7. As you will recall, the `HorizontalAccuracy` value is in meters. We will need to convert the value from meters to the appropriate pixel size for the map.

Map Scale Information:

Map Scale is the ratio of inches on the map to inches on the ground. This ratio changes at each zoom level. Microsoft provides an in-depth description of the math behind the Bings Map Tile System, including the Map Scales for each zoom level at http://msdn.microsoft.com/en-us/library/bb259689.aspx.

At zoom level 18, the Map Scale is 1:2,257, meaning 1 inch on the map is equal to 2,257 inches on the ground. To get the correct pixel size, we first convert the accuracy value from meters to inches by multiplying the value by the number of inches in a meter (39.3700787). Next, divide the inches value by the Map Scale, 2,257. Finally we need to convert the map inches to pixels. The **DPI** (**Dots Per Inch**) for WP7 varies by phone screen size, but the estimated average DPI over all current Windows Phones on the market is 241.

8. Multiply the map inches value by 241. The result is the radius, in pixels, for our accuracy ellipse:

Phone	Screen Size	Pixel Height	Pixel Width	Diagonal Pixels	DPI
HTC Surround	3.8	800	480	933	246
Samsung Focus	4	800	480	933	233
LG Quantum	3.5	800	480	933	267
HTC HD7	4.3	800	480	933	217
Dell Venue Pro	4.1	800	480	933	228
HTC 7 Pro	3.6	800	480	933	259
				Average DPI	241

9. Create an ellipse, by setting the `Width` and `Height` properties to the pixel radius multiplied by two to get the diameter. Also set the `Fill` to a `SolidColorBrush` that is slightly transparent so you can see the map underneath it.

10. Unlike the standard Silverlight map control, the map control for Windows Phone does not yet have a `SetPosition` method. This means we will need to clear the `MapLayer` and recreate the ellipse on each position change:

    ❑ Call the `Clear` method on the layer's `Children` property to remove the old ellipse

    ❑ Call `AddChild` on the `Children` property passing the ellipse to recreate it

11. Along with the ellipse, you will pass the user's current location and an offset for the ellipse. The offset allows us to center the ellipse around the user's location, otherwise it would be displayed below and to the right of the `Pushpin`. We will create a new point with the x and y coordinates set to the negative radius to center it properly:

```
var radius = (e.Position.Location.HorizontalAccuracy * 39.3700787)
/ 2257 * 241;
var ellipse = new Ellipse { Width = radius * 2, Height = radius *
2, Fill = new SolidColorBrush(Color.FromArgb(125, 255, 0, 0)) };
accuracyLayer.Children.Clear();
accuracyLayer.AddChild(ellipse, location, new Point(-radius,
-radius));
```

12. We must also set the `HorizontalAccuracy` property of each `GeoCoordinate` in the `_coordinates` list in `FakeGeoCoordinateWatcher` to see the ellipse in the emulator. Set the `HorizontalAccuracy` to a value in the range from 5 to 60. Now if we deploy the app to the emulator, we can visually see the accuracy of the location information:

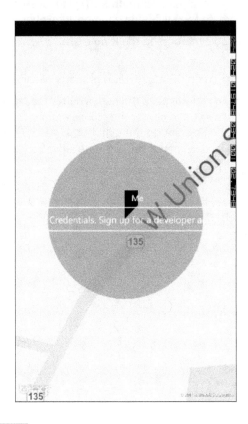

How it works...

The Windows Phone Map control is very similar to the Silverlight Map control. In many cases, code for the two is interchangeable. You will find many tutorials online for the Silverlight map control, which you can use to help you implement map features in your apps.

The Map control utilizes Bing Maps for obtaining map data. You will need Bing Maps Key to use the Map control in production, but we can use the Map without it for demonstration purposes. You can obtain a key after creating a Bing Maps Developer Account at `https://www.bingmapsportal.com`.

Creating an account and getting a key is a free and simple process that will take less than 15 minutes.

7
Push Notifications to the Phone

In this chapter, we will cover:

- ▶ Updating the tile background without push
- ▶ Creating a service to send notifications
- ▶ Registering for push notifications
- ▶ Creating a notifications helper
- ▶ Creating toast notifications

Introduction

The Push Notifications system is a unique approach to server-side communication with mobile applications. Other mobile platforms have similar capabilities, but developers are left to do most of the work, which can lead to varying implementations and potentially inefficient communication efforts. The Windows Phone platform has made this communication easier by defining a process and API for communication with the phone.

This chapter will focus on the ins and outs of using this API. We will explore the different types of notifications available and give real-world examples using them.

Updating the tile background without push

In this task, we will update the background of our application tile on a static schedule. This is the simplest form of push notification. The application will provide some eye candy for the user on the home screen by updating the tile background with the NASA daily image.

Getting ready

Create a new project in Visual Studio named **DailyTileBackground** using the **Windows Phone Application** template.

How to do it...

Scheduled tile background updates do not require a custom service component, only code on the phone to define the schedule and image source. So, the code for this task will be located in the `MainPage.xaml.cs` code-behind file:

1. Add the `using` statement for the `Microsoft.Phone.Shell` namespace.

2. Create a new `ShellTileSchedule` type and set its properties:

   - Recurrence: The type `UpdateRecurrence` has two options:

     - `OneTime`: used for single tile updates.

     - `Interval`: used for multiple updates at a given interval type.

   - `UpdateInterval`: Only used if `Recurrence` is set to `Interval`. The type `UpdateInterval` has several options such as `EveryHour`, `EveryDay`, `EveryWeek`, and `EveryMonth`.

   - `MaxUpdateCount`: The number of times to update the tile. A number less than one implies a never ending interval.

   - `StartTime`: The time to start updates.

   - `RemoteImageUri`: The `Uri` used to get the background image.

3. We will set up a recurring update on an hourly schedule starting now in the code-behind constructor:

```
var schedule = new ShellTileSchedule
                    {
                        Recurrence = UpdateRecurrence.Interval,
                        Interval = UpdateInterval.EveryHour,
                        MaxUpdateCount = 100,
                        StartTime = DateTime.Now,
                        RemoteImageUri = new Uri
                          ("http://localhost:31540/nasaImage.jpg")
                    };
schedule.Start();
```

The background image source can be a static `Uri` to any JPEG or PNG image on the Web.

4. Create a new website named `DailyTileBackground.Web` for providing the background image using the **ASP.NET Empty Web Application** project template in Visual Studio 2010.

5. Add a reference to the `System.ServiceModel` assembly.

6. Create an `HttpHandler` to dynamically provide a new image every day. We can use the NASA daily image feed as our image source. In the handler, read the RSS feed, get the image URL, fetch the image, and save the image to the response. This will provide a static URL for an image that changes daily:

```csharp
using System;
using System.Collections.Generic;
using System.Drawing;
using System.Drawing.Imaging;
using System.IO;
using System.Linq;
using System.Net;
using System.ServiceModel.Syndication;
using System.Web;
using System.Xml;

public classNasaImageHandler : IHttpHandler
    {
        public void ProcessRequest(HttpContext context)
        {
            XmlReader reader = XmlReader.Create("http://www.nasa.
              gov/rss/image_of_the_day.rss");
            SyndicationFeed feed = SyndicationFeed.Load(reader);
            var imageUri = feed.Items.First().Links.ElementAt(1).
              Uri;
            reader.Close();
            var requestPic = (HttpWebRequest)WebRequest.
              Create(imageUri);
            using (var response = requestPic.GetResponse().
              GetResponseStream())
            {
                using (Image img = Image.FromStream(response))
                {
                    img.Save(context.Response.OutputStream,
                        ImageFormat.Jpeg);
                }
            }
        }

        public bool IsReusable
        {
```

```
                      get { return true; }
           }
    }
```

7. Lastly, we need to register the `HttpHandler` in the `System.webServer` node of the `web.config` and run the application in the development web server. Ensure that the namespace and class name in the type attribute match what you created previously:

```
<configuration>
   . . .
   <system.webServer>
      . . .
   <handlers>
         <add name="nasa" verb="GET" path="*nasaImage*"
             type="DailyTileBackground.Web.NasaImageHandler,
             DailyTileBackground.Web" />
      </handlers>
```

Make sure to also update the `RemoteImageUri` property in your scheduler to match the development web server path.

How it works...

There are a couple scenarios that would remove the schedule we have created. The scheduler will attempt to update the tile three times, but if the update fails each time for any of the following three reasons, the scheduler will be removed:

▸ The image is larger than 80 KB in size

▸ The image takes longer than 15 seconds to download

▸ The image is not found

The scheduler will also be removed if the `Recurrence` is set to `Interval` and `MaxUpdateCount` is exceeded or the `Recurrence` is set to `OneTime`. If the scheduler is removed for any of the above reasons, you can recreate it by creating and starting a new `ShellTileSchedule`.

Testing this code is a bit frustrating. Although you might expect the tile background update to occur immediately, it usually takes an hour or more for the update to occur regardless of the scheduler's settings. There is not currently any way to debug tile updates or check the status of the scheduler either. Hopefully this will be easier in a later tool release.

There's more...

As mentioned previously, using the ShellTileSchedule is the simplest form of push notifications. It is so simple, in fact, that it does not use the Microsoft push notification services at all. Some may argue that it is not actually a push notification. If you consider there is no API for directly programming the application tile, it can be said the ShellTileSchedule is still *pushing* tile changes to the phone. The only difference really is that it's a pre-defined static schedule set of notifications.

The more common push notifications include:

▶ **Tile notifications**: Updates the application tile if pinned to the start screen:

▶ **Toast notifications**: Presents a message at the top of the phone which the user can click to open your application or disregard:

❑ **Raw notifications:** Sends notification to the running application

These notifications require an `HttpNotificationChannel` to be created on the phone. This channel provides a notification URI which is used to initiate a push notification. The typical push notification scenario involves three parties: the phone, an external application server, and the Microsoft notifications services:

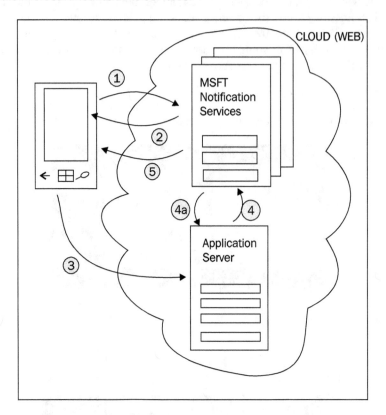

The typical workflow is explained as follows:

1. The phone application creates an `HttpNotificationChannel`.
2. A `ChannelUri` is returned to the phone.
3. The phone application passes the `ChannelUri` to an external application server.
4. At some point the application server sends a notification request to the Microsoft notification services via the provided `ChannelUri`:

    ❏   The notification status is returned to the application server.

5. The Microsoft notification servers pass the notification to the phone.

We will send some of these notification types in the following recipes.

Creating a service to send notifications

In this recipe, you will create the application server which will provide push notifications for a surf updates phone app. The service will allow users to register for notifications and periodically send updates which will update the phone applications start tile. The application start tile has three components which can be edited: background, title, and count. We will be editing the title and count. We will set the background statically.

Getting ready

We will use a WCF service project for the application server. Create a project named `SurfTileNotifications.Service` using the **WCF Service Library** project template.

How to do it...

The WCF service will have two service methods, namely, `GetIslandInfo` and `RegisterForNotifications`.

> We will be using the Surf Observations RSS feed from the National Weather Service website, `http://www.prh.noaa.gov/hnl/xml/Oahu.OMR.HFO.xml`, for live surf updates.
>
> The WCF service will read this data feed, parse it, and pass it to the phone in different ways. The `GetIslandInfo` method will be used when the phone application loads to fill the UI we built a moment ago. The service will also have a timer which gets the latest surf information once an hour from the feed and sends a tile notification to any phone that has registered for updates. The `RegisterForNotifications` method will register phones for these updates.

Perform the following steps to create the WCF service:

1. Rename the `IService1` interface in the WCF project to `ISurfService` using the refactor menu and delete the default service methods.

2. Add the `GetIslandInfo` method which takes no parameters and returns the IslandInfo type.

3. Add the `RegisterForNotifications` method which takes the `channelUri` and `beachName` as string parameters and returns void. Also make sure to add the `OperationContract` attribute to each method, otherwise the methods will not be available through the WCF service.

```
[OperationContract]
IslandInfo GetIslandInfo();
```

```
[OperationContract]
void RegisterForNotifications(string
   notificationChannelUri, string beach);
```

4. Next, create the `SurfInfo` and `IslandInfo` classes to hold the surf information for the application. These are just plain old C# classes with properties, nothing special:

```
public class SurfInfo
{
    public string BeachName { get; set; }
    public string Surf { get; set; }
    public string Wind { get; set; }

    public int? SurfMin { get; set; }
    public int? SurfMax { get; set; }
    public string Time { get; set; }
}
public class IslandInfo
{
    public SurfInfo[] Beaches { get; set; }
    public string Forecast { get; set; }
    public string Hazards { get; set; }
}
```

5. To implement the service, we will first need to rename the `Service1` class to `SurfService` and delete its contents. Create a basic implementation of the `ISurfService` implementation by adding the methods from the interface which throws `NotImplementedException` exceptions:

```
public IslandInfo GetIslandInfo()
{
  throw new NotImplementedException();
}


public void RegisterForNotifications
   (string notificationChannelUri, string beach)
{
  throw new NotImplementedException();
}
```

At this point, we should be compiling.

6. As mentioned previously, we will be using an RSS feed from the National Weather Service to get the surf data. Create a private string field named `_rssUri` and set it to be equal to `http://www.prh.noaa.gov/hnl/xml/Oahu.OMR.HFO.xml`.

7. Then create a private method named `RetrieveIslandInfo` which returns an `IslandInfo` type as follows:

```
private string _rssUri = "http://www.prh.noaa.gov/hnl/xml/
   Oahu.OMR.HFO.xml";
```

```
private IslandInfo RetrieveIslandInfo()
{
    using (XmlReader reader = XmlReader.Create(_rssUri))
    {
        var notAvailable = new IslandInfo { Forecast =
            "Not Available" };
        SyndicationFeed feed = SyndicationFeed.Load(reader);
        if (feed == null)
            return notAvailable;
        var islandInfo = new IslandInfo
                        {
                            Hazards = feed.Items.First(x =>
                            x.Title.Text.
                            Contains("Hazards")).Summary.Text,
                            Forecast = feed.Items.First(x =>
                            x.Title.Text.
                            Contains("Forecast")).Summary.Text,
                        };
        var nameRegex = new Regex("(.*)\\s*report");
        var surfReportRegex = new Regex("\\s*(\\d*)-(\\
            d*)\\D*\\s*ft\\s*at\\s*(.*)\\.");
        islandInfo.Beaches = feed.Items
            .Select(x => new { Item = x, BeachNameMatch =
            nameRegex.Match(x.Title.Text), SurfReportMatch =
            surfReportRegex.Match(x.Title.Text) })
            .Where(x => x.BeachNameMatch.Success)
            .Select(x =>
                    {
                        var beach = new SurfInfo
                                    {
                                        BeachName =
                                        x.BeachNameMatch.
                                        Groups[1].Value,
                                Surf = x.Item.Title.Text
                                    };
                        if (x.SurfReportMatch.Success)
                        {
                            if (x.Item.Content != null)
                                beach.Wind =
                                ((TextSyndicationContent)
                                 x.Item.Content).Text;
                            beach.SurfMin = int.Parse(x.
                            SurfReportMatch.Groups[1].Value);
                            beach.SurfMax = int.Parse(x.
                            SurfReportMatch.Groups[2].Value);
                            beach.Time = x.SurfReportMatch.
Groups[3].Value;
```

```
                                     }
                                  return beach;
                            })
                  .ToArray();
              return islandInfo;
          }
      }
```

 How we get this data is not pertinent to tile notification. Without getting into too many specifics, we are using WCF to open/read the RSS feed, Regex to parse the content of the feed items, and LINQ to create and iterate over the results and create our business entities.

8. Next create a private `IslandInfo` field named `_currentIslandInfo` and a private property named `CurrentIslandInfo`. Within the property getter, set `_currentIslandInfo` using the `RetrieveIslandInfo` method. If it is null, return `_currentIslandInfo`. Implement the `GetIslandInfo` method by returning the `CurrentIslandInfo` property:

```
private IslandInfo _currentIslandInfo;
private IslandInfo CurrentIslandInfo
{
    get
    {
        if (_currentIslandInfo == null)
            _currentIslandInfo = RetrieveIslandInfo();
        return _currentIslandInfo;
    }
}
public IslandInfo GetIslandInfo()
{
    return CurrentIslandInfo;
}
```

9. Now let's implement the `RegisterForNotifications` method. Create a private `Dictionary` of the `string, string` field named `_notificationUris` and initialize it to a new `Dictionary<string,string>`. Add the beachName to the dictionary using uri as the key. Next, we want to send the first tile notification for this registration. Call `NotifyPhoneOfSurf` by passing the uri and beachname:

```
public void RegisterForNotifications(string
notificationChannelUri, string beachName)
{
    _notificationUris[notificationChannelUri] = beach;
    NotifyPhoneOfSurf(notificationChannelUri, beach);
}
```

The private `NotifyPhoneOfSurf` method is where we will actually send the tile notification. First we must find the beach the user requested using LINQ; if it is null, we will return and not send a notification. Tile notifications are sent to the given channel URI as a post request with some custom headers and an XML payload. The XML allows you to specify the background image, count, and title for the tile update. We will set the count to the maximum surf level and the title to the beach name and time.

10. Create a `byte` array variable named `payload` to hold the XML payload in bytes. Convert the XML to bytes using the `Encoding.ASCII.GetBytes` method.

11. Next create an `HttpWebRequest` variable named `request` using the `channel` URI and the static `Create` method on the `WebRequest` type, cast to an `HttpWebRequest`.

12. Set the request `Method` to `POST`, the `ContentType` to `text/xml`, and the `ContentLength` to the payloads `Length` property.

13. There are two custom request headers required for tile notifications. Set `X-WindowsPhone-Target` to `token` to specify the notification as a tile notification and `X-NotificationClass` to `1` to specify that the notification is for immediate transmission.

14. After writing the payload to the request and calling `GetResponse` on the request, the completed code should look as follows:

```
private void NotifyPhoneOfSurf(string
    notificationChannelUri, string beachName)
{
    var surf = CurrentIslandInfo.Beaches.FirstOrDefault
        (x => x.BeachName == beachName);
    if (surf == null)
        return;

    string tileMessage = "<?xml version=\"1.0\"
encoding=\"utf-8\"?>" +
        "<wp:Notification xmlns:wp=\"WPNotification\">" +
            "<wp:Tile>" +
              "<wp:BackgroundImage></wp:BackgroundImage>" +
              "<wp:Count>" + surf.SurfMax + "</wp:Count>" +
                "<wp:Title>" + surf.BeachName + "-" +
                    surf.Time + "</wp:Title>" +
            "</wp:Tile> " +
        "</wp:Notification>";

    byte[] payload = Encoding.ASCII.GetBytes(tileMessage);
```

```
HttpWebRequest request = (HttpWebRequest)
    WebRequest.Create(notificationChannelUri);

request.Method = "POST";
request.ContentType = "text/xml";
request.ContentLength = payload.Length;

request.Headers.Add("X-WindowsPhone-Target", "token");
request.Headers.Add("X-NotificationClass", "1");

using (Stream requestStream = request.
        GetRequestStream())
    requestStream.Write(payload, 0, payload.Length);

var response = (HttpWebResponse)request.GetResponse();
}
```

15. The WCF service is complete. If you right-click on the service project in the Visual Studio **Solution Explorer** and click the **Debug/Start** new instance, the **WCF Test Client** should start and show the two service methods. You can click to open the GetIslandInfo service method and then click **Invoke** to see the data returned:

16. Remember the RSS feed will change throughout the day and we need to provide updates to the registered phones. So, we will add a `using` statement for the `System.Threading` namespace and a `private object` field named `_timer` to the `SurfService` class. Initiate the `_timer` field in the service constructor to a new `Timer` with a timer callback method, `null` state object, `0` due time, and `10` minute callback intervals.

17. Add the `TimerCallback` method with a single `object` parameter named `state` (this will not be used, but it is necessary).

18. Within the callback method, update the private `_currentIslandInfo` field and call `NotifyPhoneOfSurf` for each registered `Uri` passing the `Uri` and beach name:

```csharp
using System.Threading;

namespace SurfTileNotifications.Service
{
    public class SurfService : ISurfService
    {
        private Timer _timer;
        private Dictionary<string, string> _notificationUris =
                new Dictionary<string, string>();
        public SurfService()
        {
            _timer = new Timer(TimerCallback, null, 0,
                (long)TimeSpan.FromMinutes(10).TotalMilliseconds);
        }
        public void TimerCallback(object state)
        {
            _currentIslandInfo = RetrieveIslandInfo();
            foreach (var uri in _notificationUris)
            {
                NotifyPhoneOfSurf(uri.Key, uri.Value);
            }
        }
    }
```

How it works...

Each phone which registers for notifications will send its notification URI and the service will store it in a dictionary. The service has a timer which will periodically get the latest surf information and send it via a tile notification to each phone's URI.

An external web service which consolidates/aggregates other service calls and business logic is a common scenario in mobile development. In this recipe, we are calling out to the National Weather Service to get the surf information for the island of Oahu. In theory, each phone could make this call and get the data on some schedule, but this would require the user to run the app periodically and would use considerably more battery. By using tile notifications, the service is doing most of the work and pushing the data to the phones automatically. This will be a powerful pattern you can leverage in mobile development.

Registering for push notifications

Now we will learn how to register for push notifications with the application server we created in the last recipe (*Creating a service to send push notifications*). In this recipe, we will create a surf updates app for the Hawaiian island of Oahu. The application will provide surf information about the island and allow you to select a specific beach to send hourly surf updates to the application tile.

Getting ready

Create a new project in Visual Studio named `SurfTileNotifications` using the **Windows Phone Application** template for the phone application.

The phone application will display some general information about the surf conditions of the island and then list all the beach surf conditions on the `MainPage` of the phone project:

1. First set the `x:Name` attribute on the `PhoneApplicationPage` to `root`. Delete the `ApplicationTitle` TextBlock. Set the text property on the `PageTitle` `TextBlock` to `Oahu Surf Updates`.

2. Next create a `ScrollViewer` with an inner vertical `StackPanel`. Set the `ScrollViewer` control to `Grid.Row` one.

3. Within the `StackPanel`, create a `TextBlock` named `tbForecast` for general island surf forecast information and set its text property to `Loading`.

4. Create a `TextBlock` label with the text `Surf Hazards` in a larger font. Then another named `tbHazards` for displaying general surf hazards for the island and set its text property to `Surf hazard information`.

5. Add another `TextBlock` label with the text `Beaches` in a larger font.

6. Finally, add an `ItemsControl` named `icBeaches` and bind its `ItemsSource` property to the `Beaches` property on `ElementName` `root`. This is a standard data binding to a property in the code-behind. Also set the `ItemTemplate` to a `DataTemplate`, which defines the item to be a `RadioButton` control with a `GroupName` of beaches.

7. Then bind the `IsSelected` property to the `IsSelected` data context property. Add a `StackPanel` with two `TextBlock` controls inside the `RadioButton`. The first of which is bound to the `Surf` property and the second to the `Wind` property. Make the `Surf` `TextBlock` font a little larger as well to make it stand out a little more.

The `RadioButton` will allow the user to select a beach to receive tile updates for. They will register for updates using a button. Create a button with an inner `TextBlock` with text which reads `Register for Notifications`. To make the button always visible, you can create a new row to the `LayoutRoot` `Grid` with `Auto` height and set the `Grid.Row` property of the button to `2`.

Find an image of a wave or the ocean and add it to the project. In the **Properties** window, set its `BuildAction` to `Content`. Then set the background of the layout grid to an `ImageBrush`, with the `ImageSource` set to the image name and the `Opacity` set to `.4`.

You should end up with a page that looks similar to the following:

The page designer in Visual Studio often doesn't show background images or application bar images so don't worry if you don't see them. Try running the phone project and checking for the images in the emulator.

Review the `MainPage.xaml` file within the SurfUpdates solution packaged for *Chapter 7* to see a sample of this XAML code.

How to do it...

1. Add a Service Reference to the WCF service. Right-click the service project in the WCF Test Client and select **Copy Address**. Open the **Add Service Reference** dialog by right-clicking the **References** folder in the `SurfTileNotifications` project and clicking **Add Service Reference**.

2. Paste the address into the **Service** field, click **Go**, and then **OK**. This generates a proxy for the WCF service in the phone applications:

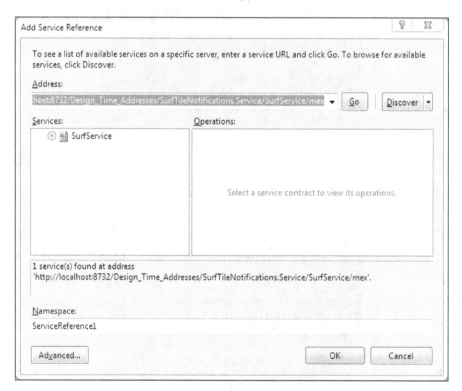

If you get an error generating the code for the service reference, then right-click on ServiceReference1 in Solution Explorer, and click **Configure Service Reference**. Change the Collection Type to `System.Collections.Generic.List` and uncheck **Reuse types in referenced assemblies** as these seem to be causing issues in some cases.

3. By default, the service reference is created using the `wsHttpBinding` binding which is not supported by Windows Phone. So, open the `ServiceReferences.ClientConfig` file and change the binding to `basicHttpBinding`:

```
<endpoint address="http://localhost:8732/Design_Time_Addresses/
SurfTileNotifications.Service/SurfService/"
              binding="basicHttpBinding" bindingConfiguration=
                 "BasicHttpBinding_ISurfService"
              contract="ServiceReference1.ISurfService"
              name="BasicHttpBinding_ISurfService" />
```

4. In the `MainPage` code behind, create four private fields:

   ❑ `HttpNotificationChannel` named `_channel`

   ❑ `String` named `_channelName` set to `SurfNotificationChannel`

   ❑ `ISurfService` named `_service`

   ❑ `Beach` name `_selectedBeach`

5. Create a public `ObservableCollection` of the `SurfInfo` property named `Beaches`:

```
private string _channelName = "SurfNotificationChannel";
private HttpNotificationChannel _channel;
private ISurfService _service;

public ObservableCollection<SurfInfo> Beaches { get; set; }
```

6. Initialize the `Beaches` property to a new `ObservableCollection` within the page constructor. Next create a string variable named `serviceNotAvailableMessage` and set it to be equal to the following:

```
The surf data service is currently not available. Please try again
later.
```

There are many reasons the WCF calls could fail, including:

- ▸ The phone cannot get an Internet connection
- ▸ The service server is offline
- ▸ The source RSS feed could be offline
- ▸ The source RSS feed could change its interface

To code defensively against these exceptions, we must wrap the WCF calls in try/catch blocks.

7. Create a `try catch` block at the bottom of the constructor. Initialize the `_service` field as a new `SurfServiceClient` within the `try` block.

8. Next create an `AsyncCallback` named `callback` and set it to a lambda with one parameter named `result`, which calls the `Dispatcher.BeginInvoke` method to ensure that the data is returned to the UI thread. Within the `BeginInvoke`, create another `try/catch` block. Set an `IslandInfo` variable using the `EndGetIslandInfo` method on the `_service` field, passing the resulting lambda parameter.

9. We can start displaying the island information with this result. Set the `tbHazards` and `tbForecast Textblock Text` properties, with the `Hazards` and `Forecast` properties from `islandInfo` respectively. Also add each beach from `islandInfo` to the `Beaches` property.

10. In the `catch` block of each `try/catch`, set the `tbForecast TextBlock Text` property to the `serviceNotAvailableMessage` and the `tbHazards TextBlock Text` property to an empty string:

```
public MainPage()
{
    InitializeComponent();

    Beaches = new ObservableCollection<SurfInfo>();

    var serviceNotAvailableMessage = "The surf data
        service is currently not available. Please try
        again later.";
    try
    {
        _service = new SurfServiceClient();
        AsyncCallback callback = result =>
            Deployment.Current.Dispatcher.BeginInvoke(() =>
{
try
{
```

```
var islandInfo = _service.EndGetIslandInfo(result);
tbHazards.Text = islandInfo.Hazards;
tbForecast.Text = islandInfo.Forecast;
foreach (var beach in islandInfo.Beaches)
{

Beaches.Add(beach);
}
}
catch(Exception e)
{
tbForecast.Text = serviceNotAvailableMessage;
tbHazards.Text = "";
}
});
        _service.BeginGetIslandInfo(callback, _service);
    }
    catch(Exception e)
    {
        tbForecast.Text = serviceNotAvailableMessage;
        tbHazards.Text = "";
    }
}
```

At this point, we should be able to start debugging in the emulator and see the data appear in the UI. Visual Studio should start the `SurfService` in debug as well:

 Notice that if you stop debugging and then go back to the emulator and run the surf application, you will see the not available message. This is because the surf service is no longer running. You can start the service in debug mode and then run the app in the emulator to avoid this error.

The user must have a way to choose the beach they would like to receive the tile notifications for:

11. Go back to `MainPage.xaml` and add a `Checked` event handler to the `RadioButton` control named `RadioButton_Checked`.

12. In the code-behind, create a handler method with the same name and two parameters, an `object` named `sender` and a `RoutedEventArgs` named `e`.

13. Create a `private SurfInfo` field named `_selectedBeach` at the top of the `MainPage` class.

14. Within the handler, set the `_selectedBeach` field to the `DataContext` property of the `OriginalSource` property on the event arguments parameter after it's been cast to a `RadioButton`. The `DataContext` will also need to be cast to the `SurfInfo` type:

```
private void RadioButton_Checked(object sender,
    RoutedEventArgs e)
{
    _selectedBeach = (SurfInfo)((RadioButton)
        e.OriginalSource).DataContext;
}
```

15. Double-click the **register for notifications** button in the designer to create a click handler in the code-behind.

We now have all the pieces in place to create a notification channel and register for notifications. Once a channel is created for an application, it typically exists until the phone is restarted. We should check for a pre-existing channel before creating a new one:

16. Set the `_channel` field using the `static Find` method on the `HttpNotificationChannel` class, passing the `_channelName` we defined earlier. Next check `_channel` to see if it's `null`. If it is, set `_channel` to a new `HttpNotificaitonChannel`, passing the `_channelName` into the constructor, add a handler to the `ChannelUriUpdated` event, and call the `Open` method. This will create a new channel and initialize it. If it is not `null`, call the `RegisterForNotifications` method which we will create in a moment.

17. Lastly, we must tell the application to accept the tile notifications by calling the `BindToShellTile` method, if it hasn't already been bound.

18. The completed click handler code should mimic the following:

```
private void Button_Click(object sender, RoutedEventArgs e)
{
    _channel = HttpNotificationChannel.Find(_channelName);
    if (_channel == null)
    {
        _channel = new HttpNotificationChannel
            (_channelName);
        _channel.ChannelUriUpdated +=
            _channel_ChannelUriUpdated;
        _channel.Open();
    }
    else
    {
        RegisterForNotifications(_channel.ChannelUri);
    }

    if (!_channel.IsShellTileBound)
    {
        _channel.BindToShellTile();
    }
}
void _channel_ChannelUriUpdated(object sender,
        NotificationChannelUriEventArgs e)
{
    RegisterForNotifications(e.ChannelUri);
}
```

Notice we only call `RegisterForNotifications` if the channel is pre-existing. This is because it may take a few moments for the `ChannelUri` to be set while first creating the channel. When it is finally set, the `ChannelUriUpdated` event will be called and our handler will register for notifications using the same method.

19. Add the `RegisterForNotifications` method with a `Uri` parameter. Call the `BeginRegisterForNotifications` method on the `_service` field passing the `AbsoluteUri` property of the passed in `uri` parameter, the `BeachName` property from the `_selectedBeach` field, and two nulls (we do not need the callback or state objects in this case):

```
void RegisterForNotifications(Uri uri)
{
    var beach = _selectedBeach;
    _service.BeginRegisterForNotifications
        (uri.AbsoluteUri, beach.BeachName, null, null);
}
```

How it works...

The Oahu Surf Update app can now register for surf update tile notifications by beach. Pin the application to your start page, run the application in debug mode, select a beach, register for notifications, and you should see the beach name/time in the title area of the tile and the maximum surf height in the count area:

 The wave image in the tile background in the previous screenshot is not set by the push notification, it is static. This requires further configuration, which was not covered in this recipe. For instructions on how to statically set the tile background, read the *First impressions* recipe in *Chapter 10*.

If you encounter exceptions, it may be helpful to stop debugging the application, start the service in debug mode, and run the application from the emulator. Visual Studio should break on any exceptions.

Keep in mind push notifications do not require a WCF service specifically, but they do need some way for an external source to obtain the channel URI and send notifications appropriately.

There's more...

You may have noticed we did not use the `HttpResponse` from the `SurfService`. `NotifyPhoneOfSurf` method in this application. The response contains valuable information about the notification request, including the HTTP response code, `NotificationStatus`, `SubscriptionStatus`, and `DeviceConnectionStatus`. You can use these within your service to intelligently retry requests if the phone is temporarily unavailable, for example. Or if the channel is permanently dropped, you can notify the application the next time it requests data.

The MSDN site (`http://msdn.microsoft.com/en-us/library/ff941100(VS.92).aspx`) provides descriptions of the various response information available and details about each error code.

See also

▶ *Creating a service to send notifications*

Creating a notifications helper

A notification helper can help to reduce the duplication involved with making different types of push notifications. As discussed, there are three types of push notifications you send: tile, toast, and raw. Each sends a binary payload to the Microsoft servers with some similar attributes. We will create a simple helper to abstract the calls and reduce duplication.

Getting ready

Create a folder named `Framework` in the `SurfTileNotifications.Service` project and a new class in the folder named `Wp7NotificationsHelper`. We will start by creating an enumeration of the push types called `NotificationType`:

```
public enumNotificationType
    {
        Tile,
        Toast,
        Raw
    }
```

Notifications also have a batch interval value which determines the immediacy of the notification. This value is different for each notification type:

	Immediate (0 milliseconds)	Delayed (7.5 minutes)	Delayed (15 minutes)
Tile	01	11	21
Toast	02	12	22
Raw	03	13	23

You can see that there is a pattern to the values. As a result, we can create the `NotificationType` and a `BatchingInterval` such that when combined produce the needed interval value by explicitly setting the integer value of each enumeration value. If we set the `NotificationType` values 1-indexed and the `BatchInterval` values 0-indexed in intervals of 10, the values can be added together to produce the correct value. Create the enums at the bottom of the helper file:

```
public enumNotificationType
    {
        Tile = 1,
        Toast = 2,
        Raw = 3
    }
public enumBatchingInterval
    {
        Immediately = 0,
        SevenMinutes = 10,
        FifteenMinutes = 20
    }
```

Next we will create a type to represent the result of the notification request. Create a class named `NotificationResult` with string properties named `NotificationStatus`, `SubscriptionStatus`, and `DeviceConnectionStatus`. We will also add a `bool` property named `NotificationSuccessful` that will only have a getter that reads the other statuses. If the `NotificationStatus` is `Received`, `DeviceConnectionStatus` is `Connected`, and `SubscriptionStatus` is `Active`, then that means there were no issues and the notification was successfully sent.

Also create an `HttpStatusCode` property named `HttpStatus` and a `bool` property named `SubscriptionNotFound`. The `SubscriptionNotFound` property will only have a getter as well. In the getter, return the result of `HttpStatus` equals `HttpStatusCode.NotFound`. The `NotFound` code encompasses several statuses from the notification status, all of which mean the notification subscription was not found:

```
public class NotificationResult
{
    public string NotificationStatus { get; set; }
```

```
public string SubscriptionStatus { get; set; }
public string DeviceConnectionStatus { get; set; }
public bool NotificationSuccessful { get {
    return NotificationStatus == "Received" && DeviceConnectionStatus
    == "Connected" && SubscriptionStatus == "Active"; } }
public HttpStatusCode StatusCode { get; set; }
public bool SubscriptionNotFound { get {
    return StatusCode == HttpStatusCode.NotFound; } }
}
```

How to do it...

Perform the following steps to create the helper class:

1. Add a `private` method named `SendNotification`, which will return the `NotificationResult` type and take the following parameters:

   - `uri`: string
   - `payload`: byte array
   - `type`: `NotificationType`
   - `interval`: `BatchingInterval`
   - `uniqueId`: string

   This method will handle the common functionality between notification types.

2. Within the method, create an `HttpWebRequest` variable named `request` using the static `WebRequest.Create` method passing the `uri` parameter. Cast the output as an `HttpWebRequest`. Set the `Method` property to `POST`, as we did when sending the tile notification:

   ```
   public NotificationResult SendNotification(string uri,
       byte[] payload, NotificationType type, BatchingInterval
       interval, string uniqueId)
   {
       HttpWebRequest request = (HttpWebRequest)WebRequest.
           Create(uri);
       request.Method = "POST";
   }
   ```

   Push notifications also support uniquely identifying a notification with a value that contains a `GUID`. This unique identifier is optional.

3. Create an `if` statement to check whether the `uniqueId` parameter is not `null`. If not, add it to the request header named `X-MessageID`:

   ```
   if (uniqueId != null)
       request.Headers.Add("X-MessageID", uniqueId);
   ```

You will remember setting the `ContentType` property on the request to text/xml and the `X-WindowsPhone-Target` header to token for the tile notification. The `ContentType` value is the same for toast notifications, but it is not required for raw notifications. Similarly, the `X-WindowsPhone-Target` header is set to toast for toast notifications but is not set for raw notifications.

4. Create two static `Dictionary` fields of `NotificationType` to `string`, each with two values for tile and toast notifications. The first will be named `_tokens` and the second `_contentTypes`:

```
static Dictionary<NotificationType, string> _tokens = new
   Dictionary<NotificationType, string>
             {
                {NotificationType.Tile, "token"},
                {NotificationType.Toast, "toast"}
             };
static Dictionary<NotificationType, string> _contentTypes
   = new Dictionary<NotificationType, string>
                  {
                     {NotificationType.Tile, "text/xml"},
                     {NotificationType.Toast, "text/xml"},
                  };
```

5. Check each dictionary for a matching `NotificationType` key and add the appropriate value, if found:

```
if (_contentTypes.ContainsKey(type))
    request.ContentType = _contentTypes[type];
if (_tokens.ContainsKey(type))
    request.Headers.Add("X-WindowsPhone-Target", _tokens[type]);
```

6. Next we will add the batching interval using the enumerations we created earlier. For the `X-NotificationClass` header, cast both the `type` and `interval` parameters to int, then add them together. Call `ToString()` on the result and set this as the value of the header:

```
request.Headers.Add("X-NotificationClass",
   ((int)type + (int)interval).ToString());
```

7. Moving on to the payload, we must set the `ContentLength` property on the request to the payloads `Length` property. Then open the request stream and write the payload to the stream:

```
request.ContentLength = payload.Length;
using (Stream requestStream =
   request.GetRequestStream())
   requestStream.Write(payload, 0, payload.Length);
```

8. Finally, create a `response` variable and set it to the output of the `GetResponse` method on the request. Then return a new `NotificationResult`, setting the status properties with the `X-NotificationStatus`, `X-SubscriptionStatus`, and `X-DeviceConnectionStatus` headers respectively. Set the `StatusCode` property to the `response.StatusCode` property:

```
var response = (HttpWebResponse)request.GetResponse();
    returnnewNotificationResult
{
    NotificationStatus = response.Headers ["X-NotificationStatus"],
    SubscriptionStatus = response.Headers ["X-SubscriptionStatus"],
    DeviceConnectionStatus = response.Headers
    ["X-DeviceConnectionStatus"] ,
    StatusCode = response.StatusCode
};
```

9. We will have three public methods, one for each notification type, in the helper that uses the `SendNotification` method. Name the method for tile notifications `SendTileNotification`. It will also return a `NotificationResult` and take the following parameters:

   ❑ uri: `string`

   ❑ interval: `BatchingInterval`

   ❑ number: `Nullable` int

   ❑ text: `string`

   ❑ background: `string`

   ❑ uniqueId: `string`

10. Within the method, build the XML payload using the number, text, and background parameters. Then convert the XML to a byte array and pass it to the private `SendNotification` method along with the `Tile NotificationType`, `uri`, `interval`, and `uniqueId` parameters:

```
public NotificationResult SendTileNotification(string
  uri, BatchingInterval interval, int? number, string
  text, string background, string uniqueId)
{
    string tileMessage = "<?xml version=\"1.0\"
      encoding=\"utf-8\"?>" +
        "<wp:Notification xmlns:wp=\"WPNotification\">" +
          "<wp:Tile>" +
            "<wp:BackgroundImage>" + background +
              "</wp:BackgroundImage>" +
```

```
                "<wp:Count>" + number + "</wp:Count>" +
                "<wp:Title>" + text + "</wp:Title>" +
            "</wp:Tile> " +
        "</wp:Notification>";

    byte[] payload = Encoding.ASCII.GetBytes(tileMessage);

    return SendNotification(uri, payload,
        NotificationType.Tile, interval, uniqueId);
}
```

11. The toast notification will be named `SendToastNotification` and be very similar to the tile method. The only real difference is instead of text, number, and background parameters, it will take two string text fields (`text1` and `text2`):

```
public NotificationResult SendToastNotification(string uri,
BatchingInterval interval, string text1, string text2, string
uniqueId)
{
    string tileMessage = "<?xml version=\"1.0\"
        encoding=\"utf-8\"?>" +
        "<wp:Notification xmlns:wp=\"WPNotification\">" +
            "<wp:Toast>" +
                "<wp:Text1>" + text1 + "</wp:Text1>" +
                "<wp:Text2>" + text2 + "</wp:Text2>" +
            "</wp:Toast>" +
        "</wp:Notification>";

    byte[] payload = Encoding.ASCII.GetBytes(tileMessage);

    return SendNotification(uri, payload,
        NotificationType.Toast, interval, uniqueId);
}
```

12. The last method is for raw notifications, which we will name `SendRawNotification`. It will take a `byte` array parameter named `payload`, which we will pass directly to the `SendNotification` method along with the other parameters:

```
public NotificationResult SendRawNotification(string uri,
    BatchingInterval interval, byte[] payload, string uniqueId)
{
    return SendNotification(uri, payload, NotificationType.Raw,
    interval, uniqueId);
}
```

How it works...

The helper does not send notifications all that differently from the implementation in the *Creating a service to send notifications* recipe. It does provide some enumerations and a result class to make notification calls easier. The `SendNotification` method provides the generic logic for all three notification types. Then we have a method for each notification type with specific parameters for each type. These methods set the differing parameters and then call the `SendNotification`. We have now abstracted the logic to send push notifications and can use this class many times, in many apps, with little duplicate code.

Let's update the Oahu Surf Updates application to use this helper. We had previously created very similar code in the `NotifyPhoneOfSurf` method of the `SurfService`:

```
private void NotifyPhoneOfSurf(string notificationChannelUri,
string beachName)
{
    var surf = CurrentIslandInfo.Beaches.FirstOrDefault
        (x => x.BeachName == beachName);
    if (surf == null)
        return;

    string tileMessage = "<?xml version=\"1.0\" encoding=\"utf-8\"?>" +
        "<wp:Notification xmlns:wp=\"WPNotification\">" +
            "<wp:Tile>" +
                "<wp:BackgroundImage></wp:BackgroundImage>" +
                "<wp:Count>" + surf.SurfMax + "</wp:Count>" +
                "<wp:Title>" + surf.BeachName + "-" + surf.Time
                    + "</wp:Title>" +
            "</wp:Tile> " +
        "</wp:Notification>";

    byte[] payload = Encoding.ASCII.GetBytes(tileMessage);

    HttpWebRequest request = (HttpWebRequest)WebRequest.Create(uri);

    request.Method = "POST";
    request.ContentType = "text/xml";
    request.ContentLength = payload.Length;

    request.Headers.Add("X-WindowsPhone-Target", "token");
    request.Headers.Add("X-NotificationClass", "10");

    using (Stream requestStream = request.GetRequestStream())
```

```
        requestStream.Write(payload, 0, payload.Length);

    var response = (HttpWebResponse)request.GetResponse();
}
```

Using the new helper, we can update it to the following:

```
private void NotifyPhoneOfSurf(string notificationChannelUri,
  string beachName)
{
    //if (CurrentIslandInfo.Beaches == null)
    //    return;
      (x => x.BeachName == beachName);
    if (surf == null)
        return;

    var response = _helper.SendTileNotification(notification
            ChannelUri, BatchingInterval.Immediately, surf.SurfMax,
            surf.BeachName + "-" + surf.Time, null, null);
            if (response.SubscriptionNotFound && _notificationUris.
                ContainsKey(notificationChannelUri))
                _notificationUris.Remove(notificationChannelUri);
    }
```

Notice that there is far less code. We have also added code to remove notifications registration if the subscription is not found.

Keep in mind this is a very basic helper class that does not take into account all the various intricacies of notifications, but it will get you started.

See also

- ▶ *Registering for push notifications*
- ▶ There are several helpers for Windows Phone 7 Push Notifications on the Internet, built by various individuals/organizations. Microsoft created a well-documented helper as well. You should check it out: `http://windowsteamblog.com/ windows_phone/b/wpdev/archive/2011/01/14/windows-push- notification-server-side-helper-library.aspx`

Creating toast notifications

In this recipe, we will create a simple **IM** (**Instant Message**) application that will allow the user to send a short message to another phone user. The message will be sent to other phone users as a Toast notification. We will again use a WCF service to act as the server component, which will register phones to receive notifications and accept messages to send to other users.

Getting ready

Create a new project in Visual Studio named **InstantMessenger** using the Windows Phone Application template. Also create a project named **InstantMessenger.Service** using the **WCF Service Library** project template.

Open `MainPage.xaml` in the phone application and set the `ApplicationTitle` header to `Chapter 7—Push Notifications` and the `PageTitle` to `instant messenger`. The UI for this application will be pretty simple. The user will need to provide the message, his/her name, and the recipient's name.

Add a new row to the `RowDefinitions` in the `LayoutRoot` Grid at the top of the page with a width of `Auto`. In the content area, delete the Grid in row 1 and replace it with a `TextBox` named `tbMessage`. Set its `Grid.Row` property to 1, `InputScope` property to `Chat`, and `Text` property to `Your message`. Next add a vertical `StackPanel` and set its `Grid.Row` property to 2. The rest of our input controls will be placed into this `StackPanel`.

Add another `TextBox` named `tbFrom` with the `Text` property set to `sender@acme.com`. Then another `TextBox` named `tbTo` with the `Text` property set to `recipient@acme.com`. Set the `InputScope` on both to `EmailSmtpAddress`.

We will also need a button to send the notification, so add a button which contains a `TextBlock` with the `Text` property set to `Send`.

Finally, we want to give the user some feedback to let them know whether the message was sent successfully or not. Create a `TextBlock` named `tbResult` with the `TextWrapping` property set to `Wrap`. This feedback will also need to stand out a little, so set its `Foreground` property to the `PhoneAccentBrush` static resource:

```
<Grid x:Name="LayoutRoot" Background="Transparent">
    <Grid.RowDefinitions>
        <RowDefinition Height="Auto"/>
        <RowDefinition Height="*"/>
        <RowDefinition Height="Auto"/>
    </Grid.RowDefinitions>
    <!--TitlePanel contains the name of the application and
        page title-->
    <StackPanel x:Name="TitlePanel" Grid.Row="0"
       Margin="12,17,0,28">
```

```xml
            <TextBlock x:Name="ApplicationTitle" Text="Chapter 7 -
                Push Notifications" Style="{StaticResource
                PhoneTextNormalStyle}"/>
            <TextBlock x:Name="PageTitle" Text="instant messenger"
                Margin="9,-7,0,0" Style="{StaticResource
                PhoneTextTitle1Style}"/>
        </StackPanel>

        <!--ContentPanel - place additional content here-->

        <TextBox x:Name="tbMessage" Grid.Row="1" InputScope="Chat"
                Text="Your message"></TextBox>
        <StackPanel Grid.Row="2">
            <TextBox x:Name="tbFrom" InputScope="EmailSmtpAddress"
                Text="sender@acme.com"></TextBox>
            <TextBox x:Name="tbTo" InputScope="EmailSmtpAddress"
                Text="recipient@acme.com"></TextBox>
            <Button Grid.Row="2" Click="Button_Click">
                <TextBlock>Send</TextBlock>
            </Button>
            <TextBlock x:Name="tbResult" TextWrapping="Wrap"
                Foreground="{StaticResource PhoneAccentBrush}"
                ></TextBlock>
        </StackPanel>
    </Grid>
```

The result should look like the following screenshot:

How to do it...

Perform the following steps to create a phone app that uses toast notifications:

1. In the service project, rename the `IService` interface to `IMessageService`. Delete its contents and replace it with a single method named `SendMessage` which takes the following parameters:

    ❏ `channelUri` (string)

    ❏ `recipient` (string)

    ❏ `sender` (string)

    ❏ `message` (string)

    This method will return a `string` that describes the status of the request. Make sure to add the `OperationContract` attribute to the method.

    This will be the only service method. By sending a message, the user is both registering to receive messages and sending a message.

2. Rename the `Service1` class to `MessageService`. The service will retain registrations via a static dictionary on the service, so create a private static `Dictionary<string, string>` field named `_phones` and initialize it to a new `Dictionary`.

3. Create a `SendMessage` method in the `MessageService` using the helper we created in the previous recipe to send the toast notifications. The method should match the method signature in `IMessageService`.

4. Within the method, register the sender and channel URI using the sender string. Create a static `string, string Dictionary` field named `_phones` to hold the registrations. Set the dictionary using the sender parameter as the key and the `channelUri` parameter as the value.

5. Copy the `Wp7NotificationsHelper` class from the last recipe into this project.

6. Next, create an instance of the `Wp7NotificationHelper` named `helper`. Before we can send the notification, we need to check to see if the recipient has previously registered with the service by calling the `ContainsKey` method on the `_phones` dictionary passing the recipient. If the key is not found, return the following string:

    `Recipient hasn't registered to receive messages.`

7. If the key is found, create a variable named `result` that accepts the result of the `SendToastNotification` helper method. For the first parameter, pass the `uri` in the `_phones` dictionary using the recipient as the key. Send the `BatchingInterval.Immediately` for the interval parameter. Set the `text1` parameter to `InstantMessenger` and the `text2` parameter to the message. We will not use the `uniqueId`, so set it to `null`.

8. If the result was successful, we will return the following message:

    ```
    Message sent successfully.
    ```

    Otherwise we will return the following:

    ```
    You message could not be sent. Try again later.
    ```

9. The previous steps should produce the following code:

    ```
    public string SendMessage(string channelUri, string
      sender, string recipient, string message)
    {
        _phones[sender] = channelUri;

        var helper = new Wp7NotificationsHelper();
        if (_phones.ContainsKey(recipient))
        {
            var result = helper.SendToastNotification
              (_phones[recipient], BatchingInterval.
              Immediately, "InstantMessenger", message, null);
            if (result.NotificationSuccessful)
                return "Message sent successfully.";
            else
                return "You message could not be sent.
                  Try again later.";
        }
        else
            return "Recipient hasn't registered to receive messages.";
    }
    ```

10. Add a service reference to the service you just created in the phone application. Remember to update the service binding to `BasicHttpBinding` in the `ServiceReferences.ClientConfig`.

11. Create a private `HttpNotificationChannel` field named `_channel`.

12. Create a private string field named `_channelName` and set it to `MessageChannel` in the `MainPage` code-behind.

    The last step is to call the service from the phone application. We will place all code within a click handler for the **Send** button.

13. Initialize the notification channel by checking if the channel has already been initialized with the `Find` method, otherwise set it to a new channel, add a `ChannelUriUpdated` handler, and open the channel. You must set this handler before opening the channel for it to be called.

Toast notifications are only displayed if the application is not running. If the application is running, you have to handle the toast notification manually. Handlers must be added for the `ShellToastNotificationReceived` and `HttpNotificationReceived` events after the channel has been opened, otherwise they will not be called.

14. Add a handler for the `ShellToastNotificationReceived` event and handle appropriately. In this case, we will show a `MessageBox`.

15. If the channel had been created previously, the `ChannelUriUpdated` event will not be called again. Call the `SendMessage` method by passing the `ChannelUri` if the channel is not null.

16. These steps produce the following:

```
private void Button_Click(object sender, RoutedEventArgs e)
{
    _channel = HttpNotificationChannel.Find(_channelName);
    if (_channel == null)
    {
        _channel = new HttpNotificationChannel (_channelName);
        _channel.ChannelUriUpdated += new EventHandler
            <NotificationChannelUriEventArgs>
            (_channel_ChannelUriUpdated);
        _channel.Open();
    }


    _channel.ShellToastNotificationReceived += new EventHandler<No
tificationEventArgs>(_channel_ShellToastNotificationReceived);

    if (_channel.ChannelUri != null)
        SendMessage(_channel.ChannelUri);
}

void _channel_ShellToastNotificationReceived
  (object sender, NotificationEventArgs e)
{
    Deployment.Current.Dispatcher.BeginInvoke(() =>
        MessageBox.Show(
            e.Collection.LastOrDefault().Value,
            e.Collection.FirstOrDefault().Value,
            MessageBoxButton.OK));
}
```

17. Create a private IMessageService field named _service at the top of the class.

18. Create the SendMessage method, returning void and taking the channel Uri as a parameter.

19. Within the method, initialize the _service field if it is null. Create a callback variable that will get the status from the EndSendMessage service method and display it in our rbResult TextBlock.

20. Lastly, call the BeginSendMessage method on _service, passing the uri as a string, the Text property from the tbFrom TextBox, the Text property from the tbTo TextBox, the Text property from the tbMessage TextBox, the callback, and null for the state parameter.

The previous steps should produce the following code:

```
void SendMessage(Uri uri)
{
    if (_service == null)
        _service = new MessageServiceClient();

    AsyncCallback callback = result =>
    {
        var status = _service.EndSendMessage(result);
        Deployment.Current.Dispatcher.BeginInvoke(() =>
            tbResult.Text = status);
    };
    _service.BeginSendMessage(uri.AbsoluteUri, tbFrom.
        Text, tbTo.Text, tbMessage.Text, callback, null);
}
```

21. Create the last handler method, ChannelUriUpdated, which will set up for receiving toast notifications and call the SendMessage method.

22. Check the channel IsShellToastBound property. If it is false, we call the BindToShellToast method. Then call the SendMessage method on the UI thread (using the current dispatcher), passing the ChannelUri property from the NotificationChannelUriEventArgs parameter:

```
void _channel_ChannelUriUpdated(object sender,
    NotificationChannelUriEventArgs e)
{
    if (!_channel.IsShellToastBound)
    {
        _channel.BindToShellToast();
    }

    Deployment.Current.Dispatcher.BeginInvoke(() =>
        SendMessage(e.ChannelUri));
}
```

How it works...

Run the phone application and send a message to yourself. The `MessageService` will register your sender address and then send the message back to you. The message will be displayed back to you as a `MessageBox` because you are running the application:

The UI presents the sender/receiver `TextBox` controls as e-mail addresses are sent. We simply need a unique identifier for the user. E-mail addresses are a good choice because everyone has one and they are unique. In a production application, you would have to confirm the e-mail address so users could not misrepresent themselves (steal other users' messages).

Verifying actual toast notifications in the emulator can be difficult. You could change the interval to 7 or 15 minutes, send the test message, close the application, and wait for the Toast Notification. You could also deploy the service to a local IIS server and send messages between the emulator and an actual device. The WCF Service Host used during debugging is only accessible locally by default. The service can be accessed outside the local machine if you set the port to 80 and open the firewall or you host it in IIS.

When you get it working, you will see the toast style notification appear at the top of the screen. If you click it, it will open the application for you to send another message:

There's more...

Authenticated Push Notifications

As you can imagine, users could use this application many times throughout the day and many notifications would be sent. One point to remember is that you are limited to 500 notifications per subscription per day by default. The only way around this limit is to use an authenticated notification service. This involves adding SSL to your server and registering the certificate with Microsoft. The MSDN site has documentation explaining the process:

```
http://msdn.microsoft.com/en-us/library/ff941099(v=VS.92).aspx
```

There are many good blog posts that describe the process and some of the gotchas as well.

8
Launchers and Choosers

In this chapter, we will cover:

- ▶ Automating e-mails
- ▶ Handling common About Us tasks
- ▶ Scanning barcodes
- ▶ Enabling photo extras
- ▶ Tombstoning

Introduction

Launchers and Choosers allow developers to interface with the phone's functions through a very simple API. Microsoft has not yet given lower level access to the phone operating system or hardware. Microsoft recently announced that 1500 new APIs will be included in their new Mango update. This will open up many more opportunities for developers. Until then, Launchers and Choosers provide access to many of the common tasks you might need, such as:

- ▶ Sending an e-mail
- ▶ Launching the media player
- ▶ Making a call
- ▶ Sending a text
- ▶ Opening the web browser
- ▶ Opening the marketplace hub to your application for purchasing
- ▶ Taking a picture
- ▶ Saving a phone number

These are just a few of the capabilities that Launchers and Choosers make available to us.

In this chapter, we will use some of these to develop real-world applications.

Automating e-mails

In this section, we will briefly discuss the differences between Launchers and Choosers and then utilize the `EmailAddressChooserTask` and `EmailComposeTask` tasks in a phone application. The Late for Work application will allow users to choose their boss' or colleague's e-mail address and then send a canned e-mail which explains why he/she is late for work. Let's face it; we don't have the time to write an e-mail about why we are late when we are late.

Getting ready

Launchers and Choosers are only slightly different; Choosers return something and Launchers do not. Choosers allow you to, for example, select an e-mail address, picture, or phone number and return it. Launchers perform tasks which do not return any items, in general, such as opening the marketplace hub or launching a web browser. Launchers and Choosers share a similar API which allows developers to very simply interface with the phone's core functions.

In this application, we will use the `EmailAddressChooserTask` to select an e-mail address from the phone contacts and then the `EmailComposeTask` to send an e-mail to the selected address.

Create a new phone application in Visual Studio named `LateForWork` using the **Windows Phone Application** template listed under the **Silverlight for Windows Phone** template group.

In the `MainPage.xaml` file, set the application title `TextBlock` to `Ch. 8 - Launchers and Choosers` and the page title `TextBlock` to `late for work`. Replace the content `Grid` in row 1 with a `StackPanel` and set its `Grid.Row` property to 1. Within the `StackPanel`, add a `Button` named `butChooseBoss` with an inner `TextBlock`. Set the `Text` property to `Select boss`. Add two more `TextBlocks` under the button. Set the `Text` property to `To:` for the first. Name the second `tbTo` and set its `Text` property to `boss@ acme.com`. Next add a `TextBlock` and set the `Text` property to `Body`. Then add another `TextBox` named `tbBody`. Set the height to 300 and the `TextWrapping` property to `Wrap`. Set the `Text` property to the following:

Good morning. I will be running a little late today due to a power outage last night which reset my alarm clock. Preparations are being made now for my immediate departure. Thank you for your understanding.

Add one more `Button` named `butSendEmail` with a `TextBlock`. Set the `Text` property to
`I'm Late!!!`. The resulting XAML should be similar to the following:

```
<StackPanel x:Name="TitlePanel" Grid.Row="0" Margin="12,17,0,28">
   <TextBlock x:Name="ApplicationTitle" Text="Ch. 8 - Launchers and
   Choosers" Style="{StaticResource PhoneTextNormalStyle}"/>
      <TextBlock x:Name="PageTitle" Text="late for work" Margin="9,-
      7,0,0" Style="{StaticResource PhoneTextTitle1Style}"/>
</StackPanel>

<StackPanel Grid.Row="1">
    <Button x:Name="butChooseBoss" Click="butChooseBoss_Click">
        <TextBlock Text="Select boss"></TextBlock>
    </Button>
    <TextBlock Text="To:" Style="{StaticResource
     PhoneTextNormalStyle}" />
    <TextBlock x:Name="tbTo" Text="boss@acme.com"
     Style="{StaticResource PhoneTextLargeStyle}" />
    <TextBlock Text="Body:" Style="{StaticResource
     PhoneTextNormalStyle}" Margin="0,20,0,0" />
    <TextBox x:Name="tbBody" Height="300" TextWrapping="Wrap"
        Text="Good morning.  I will be running a little late today
        due to a power outage last night which reset my alarm clock.
        Preparations are being made now for my immediate departure.
        Thank you for your understanding.">
    </TextBox>
    <Button x:Name="butSendEmail" Click="butSendEmail_Click">
        <TextBlock Text="I'm Late!!!"></TextBlock>
    </Button>
</StackPanel>
```

This should produce a page similar to the following screenshot:

How to do it...

All the code in this application will be placed in the click event handlers for the two buttons:

1. Double-click on each button in the designer to create click event handlers for them in the code-behind.

2. All the Launchers and Choosers are located in the `Microsoft.Phone.Tasks` namespace, so add a using statement to the top of the code-behind file.

3. We will start with the `butChooseBoss` click handler. Create a variable named `chooser` and set it to a new `EmailAddressChooserTask`.

4. This task will return an e-mail address in the Completed event, so create a handler for this event named `chooser_Completed`. Then call the `Show` method on the Chooser.

5. The `chooser_Completed` handler will have two parameters, namely, a sender object and `EmailResult`. Set the Text property on the `tbTo` TextBlock to the `Email` property of the result, if the `EmailResult` is equal to `TaskResult.OK`. If the user canceled the e-mail address selection, the result would be set to `Cancel` and nothing should be done.

6. In the `butSendEmail` click event handler, create a variable named `task` and set it to a new `EmailComposeTask`. Set the Body property to the `tbBody` TextBox Text property. Set the `Subject` property to `I'm running late`. Set the `To` property to the `tbTo` TextBlock Text property.

7. Then call the `Show` method on the task. Remember, most Launchers do not return any values so the task has no events and thus no event handlers are needed. The code behind should include the following:

```
private void butChooseBoss_Click(object sender, RoutedEventArgs e)
{
    var chooser = new EmailAddressChooserTask();
    chooser.Completed += new
    EventHandler<EmailResult>(chooser_Completed);
    chooser.Show();
}

void chooser_Completed(object sender, EmailResult e)
{
    if (e.TaskResult == TaskResult.OK)
        tbTo.Text = e.Email;
}

private void butSendEmail_Click(object sender, RoutedEventArgs e)
{
    var task = new EmailComposeTask
                {
                    Body = tbBody.Text,
                    Subject = "I'm running late",
                    To = tbTo.Text
                };
    task.Show();
}
```

How it works...

We used a Chooser and a Launcher in this application. As you can see, the APIs for these are very simple.

When you run this application in the emulator, you will see the e-mail address Chooser works great, but if you try to send the e-mail, you will be presented with an error because the emulator does not support setting up e-mail accounts:

When you run the application on a device and click the **Send** button, you will be presented with the option to select an e-mail account. The e-mail is then opened in the e-mail editor with the appropriate fields set. Click **Send** on the Application Bar to send the e-mail.

Handling common About Us tasks

This recipe will review a few tasks that are commonly used in the **About Us** section of phone applications.

A vital part to the success of an app is the reviews it gets in the marketplace. One popular way to increase the number of reviews your app gets is to make it easier for users to add reviews directly from within your application. The `MarketplaceReviewTask` task can help with this.

When you have multiple applications in the marketplace, there is also an opportunity for cross-marketing applications. If a user likes one of your applications, they are more likely to purchase another application you have developed. The `MarketplaceDetailTask` task allows you to open the details of another application for review and purchase.

Another common scenario is to have a button which opens your website on the phone for users to read more about your company or review privacy policies. The `WebBrowserTask` task makes this possible.

Getting ready

For this recipe, we will reuse the Late for Work application by adding an **about us** section with some buttons. We will leverage the `Pivot` control to create a simple design of two panels, one for the e-mail composition and the other for information about the application.

Reference the `Microsoft.Phone.Controls` assembly and add a namespace reference to the top of the page named `Controls`. The reference will mimic the following:

```
xmlns:Controls="clr-
namespace:Microsoft.Phone.Controls;assembly=Microsoft.Phone.Controls"
```

Add a `Pivot` control to the top of the page just before the `LayoutRoot` `StackPanel` with two inner `PivotItem` controls. Move the application title from the `ApplicationTitle` `TextBlock` to the `Pivot` `Title` property and the page title from the `PageTitle` `TextBlock` to the first `PivotItem` instance's `Header` property. Take the `StackPanel` in row 1 of the old content grid and move it to the first `PivotItem`. Remove the `Grid.Row` property:

```xml
<Controls:Pivot Title="Ch. 8 - Launchers and Choosers">
    <Controls:PivotItem Header="late for work">
            <StackPanel>
                <Button x:Name="butChooseBoss"
                 Click="butChooseBoss_Click">
                    <TextBlock Text="Select boss"></TextBlock>
                </Button>
                <TextBlock Text="To:" Style="{StaticResource
                 PhoneTextNormalStyle}" />
                <TextBlock x:Name="tbTo" Text="boss@acme.com"
                 Style="{StaticResource PhoneTextLargeStyle}" />
                <TextBlock Text="Body:" Style="{StaticResource
                 PhoneTextNormalStyle}" Margin="0,20,0,0" />
                <TextBox x:Name="tbBody" Height="300"
                 TextWrapping="Wrap"
                 Text="Good morning.  I will be running a little late
                 today due to a power outage last night which reset
                 my alarm clock.  Preparations are being made now for
                 my immediate departure.  Thank you for your
                 understanding.">
                </TextBox>
                <Button x:Name="butSendEmail"
                 Click="butSendEmail_Click">
                    <TextBlock Text="I'm Late!!!"></TextBlock>
                </Button>
            </StackPanel>
    </Controls:PivotItem>
</Controls:Pivot>
```

Set the second `PivotItem` instance's `Header` property to `about` and add a `StackPanel` to the item. Within the `StackPanel`, we will add three sets of a `TextBlock` and `Button` with a `TextBlock`. Set the following attributes:

- Set 1
  - `TextBlock`
    - Text: If you like this app, please add a review
  - `Button`
    - Name: `butAddReview`
    - `TextBlock.Text`: Add Review

- Set 2
  - `TextBlock`
    - Text: If you like this app, check out our other app
  - `Button`
    - Name: `butOtherApp`
    - `TextBlock.Text`: Other App

- Set 3
  - `TextBlock`
    - Text: Visit our website for more information about us
  - `Button`
    - Name: `butVisitWeb`
    - `TextBlock.Text`: Acme.com

The following is the resulting XAML:

```
<Controls:PivotItem Header="about">
    <StackPanel>
        <TextBlock TextAlignment="Center">If you like this app,
        please add a review.</TextBlock>
        <Button x:Name="butAddReview">
            <TextBlock>Add Review</TextBlock>
        </Button>
        <TextBlock TextAlignment="Center">If you like this app, check
        out our other app.</TextBlock>
        <Button x:Name="butOtherApp">
            <TextBlock>Other App</TextBlock>
        </Button>
```

```
    <TextBlock TextAlignment="Center">Visit our website for more
      information about us.</TextBlock>
    <Button x:Name="butVisitWeb">
        <TextBlock>Acme.com</TextBlock>
    </Button>
  </StackPanel>
</Controls:PivotItem>
```

This should complete the UI layout changes. The UI should look similar to the following screenshot. First the e-mail composition panel:

Second the about panel:

How to do it...

The following steps will guide you in writing the code to enable the about us functions:

1. Double-click each of the buttons on the about us panel from the designer to create click event handlers.

2. In the `butAddReview` click handler, create a new `MarketplaceReviewTask` and call the `Show` method. There are no properties to set on this task.

3. In the `butOtherApp` click handler, create a new `MarketplaceDetailTask`, setting the `ContentIdentifier` property to `5b425ecf-35e4-df11-a844-00237de2db9e`. There is another property on this task, `ContentType`, but it currently performs no function in this release of the OS; perhaps it will in a later update. Call the `Show` method on the task.

4. In the `butVisitWeb` click handler, create a new `WebBrowserTask` and set the `URL` property to `http://www.acme.com`. Call the `Show` method on the task.

5. The code-behind file should have these methods when you complete the steps:

    ```
    private void butAddReview_Click(object sender, RoutedEventArgs e)
    {
        var task = new MarketplaceReviewTask();
        task.Show();
    }
    ```

```
private void butOtherApp_Click(object sender, RoutedEventArgs e)
{
    var task = new MarketplaceDetailTask
            {
                    ContentIdentifier = "5b425ecf-35e4-df11-a844-
                    00237de2db9e"
            };
    task.Show();
}

private void butVisitWeb_Click(object sender, RoutedEventArgs e)
{
    var task = new WebBrowserTask {URL = "http://www.acme.com"};
    task.Show();
}
```

How it works...

When the `AddReview` button is clicked and the `Show` method on the
`MarketplaceReviewTask` is called, the phone will open the marketplace to the details page
for the currently running application at the review section. If the current application isn't in the
marketplace, you will receive the following message:

Can't get this info right now. Check back in a little while.

When the `OtherApp` button is clicked, the details for the application whose identifier matches
the `ContentIdentifier` property is displayed. You will receive the same error message
from above if a matching application cannot be found. Make sure the `ContentIdentifier`
property is set to a properly formatted `Guid`; otherwise you will receive a `FormatException`.

When the `VisitWeb` button is clicked, the browser will open to the specified URL.

Scanning barcodes

Data is stored all around us in this digital age. The problem is you need the right tools to
access it. In the case of barcodes, you traditionally needed expensive specialized scanners
that only retailers or distributers had access to. Now that we have smartphones in our pocket
with a camera and processor, many barcode reader applications have been developed.

In this recipe, we will utilize the `CameraCaptureTask`, `PhotoChooserTask`, and
`SearchTask` tasks to scan a barcode and search for the results with Bing.

This application will be standing on the shoulders of giants who have written algorithms and logic for scanning images for barcodes. The **Windows Phone 7 Silverlight ZXing Barcode Scanning Library** project on CodePlex contains a C# port of a scanner written in Java by Google. Check out all the details on the CodePlex site:

```
http://silverlightzxing.codeplex.com/
```

This project has Windows Phone code that abstracts away the barcode scanner specifics, but we will only be using the core barcode reader code in this example.

Getting ready

Create a new Windows Phone project named `BarCodeScanner` using the **Windows Phone Application** project template. Download the source code from CodePlex for the bar code reader, build the **debug** build configuration, and copy the **Silverlight_ZXing_Core.dll** from the `bin` directory of the `Silverlight_ZXing_Core` project. Paste it in the root directory of the `BarCodeScanner` project and add reference to the assembly.

Replace the content grid in row one of the `LayoutRoot` grid with a `StackPanel`. Add a `Button` named `butScanPicture` with a `TextBlock` set to `Scan Image`. Add another `Button` named `butCaptureBarcode` with a `TextBlock` set to `Scan with Camera`. Next add an image named `imgBarcode` and set the `Width` property to `400`. Then add a `TextBlock` with the Text Property set to `Results`. Lastly add a `Button` named `butSearchBarcode` with a `TextBlock` set to `Search`.

The XAML should resemble the following code:

```xml
<StackPanel x:Name="TitlePanel" Grid.Row="0" Margin="12,17,0,28">
    <TextBlock x:Name="ApplicationTitle" Text="Ch. 8 - Launchers
      and Choosers" Style="{StaticResource PhoneTextNormalStyle}"/>
    <TextBlock x:Name="PageTitle" Text="barcode scanner"
      Margin="9,-7,0,0" Style="{StaticResource
      PhoneTextTitle1Style}"/>
</StackPanel>
<StackPanel Grid.Row="1">
    <Button x:Name="butScanPicture" Click="butScanPicture_Click">
        <TextBlock>Scan Image</TextBlock>
    </Button>
    <Button x:Name="butCaptureBarcode"
     Click="butCaptureBarcode_Click">
        <TextBlock>Scan With Camera</TextBlock>
    </Button>
    <TextBlock>Results</TextBlock>
    <Image x:Name="imgBarcode" Width="400" ></Image>
    <TextBlock x:Name="results" x:Name="tbResults"
     TextAlignment="Center"></TextBlock>
```

```
<Button x:Name="butSearchBarcode" Click="butSearchBarcode_Click">
    <TextBlock>Search</TextBlock>
</Button>
</StackPanel>
```

The following screenshot shows what the UI is like on the phone:

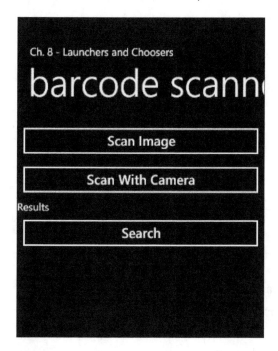

How to do it...

Perform the following steps to use the phone's camera to scan bar codes:

1. Add a `using` statement in the code-behind to the `Microsoft.Phone.Tasks` namespace.

2. Create two private fields, a `CameraCaptureTask` and `PhotoChooserTask` named `_cameraCaptureTask` and `_photoChooserTask`, respectively. Next initialize each in the `MainPage` constructor.

3. Set `_cameraCaptureTask` to a new `CameraCaptureTask` and the `_photoChooserTask` to a new `PhotoChooserTask`.

   Both tasks have the same signature for the Completed event handler so set them both to a handler named `_photoChooserTask_Completed`.

4. Create the handler method below the constructor with a return type of void and two parameters: object named `sender` and `PhotoResult` named e:

```
private CameraCaptureTask _cameraCaptureTask;
private PhotoChooserTask _photoPickerTask;


public MainPage()
{
    InitializeComponent();

    _cameraCaptureTask = new CameraCaptureTask();
    _photoPickerTask = new PhotoChooserTask();

    _cameraCaptureTask.Completed += new
      EventHandler<PhotoResult>(_photoChooserTask_Completed);
    _photoPickerTask.Completed += new
      EventHandler<PhotoResult>(_photoChooserTask_Completed);
}

void _photoChooserTask_Completed(object sender, PhotoResult e)
{
}
```

5. Add using statements for the following namespace:
   - `System.IO`
   - `System.Windows.Media.Imaging`
   - `com.google.zxing.oned`
   - `com.google.zxing`
   - `com.google.zxing.common`

6. Create a method named `ScanBarCode` which returns void and takes a `Stream` parameter named `photoStream`. Within the method, add a variable named `image` equal to a new `BitmapImage`.

7. Call the `SetSource` method on the image passing the `photoStream` parameter. We will use this image object to get the height/width of the image.

8. Since we have used the photo stream in creating the `BitmapImage`, we need to reset the position of the stream to zero by setting the `Position` property to zero. We also want to display the photo to the user. Set the Source property on the `imgBarcode` Image element to the `BitmapImage`.

9. Create a `WritableBitmap` named `bitmap` passing the `PixelWidth` and `PixelHeight` from the `BitmapImage` in the constructor. Then call the `LoadJpeg` method passing the photo stream. This `WritableBitmap` is required for the barcode reader.

10. Wrap the reader usage in a try/catch block because the barcode reader throws an exception if a barcode is not found when reading.

11. Create a `MultiFormatOneDReader` named `reader`, passing null for the hints parameter. Review the reader code for more details about hints.

12. Create a result variable set to the `decode` method on the reader. The `decode` method takes a `BinaryBitmap` type. The `BinaryBitmap` constructor takes a `Binarizer`. We will use a `HybridBinarizer`, which takes a `LuminanceSource` in the constructor. We will use a `RGBLuminanceSource` passing the `WritableBitmap` and `PixelWidth`/`PixelHeight` again from the `BitmapImage`.

> That is a lot of parameter chaining, which is exactly why the author of the scanning library created some WP7 wrappers. We did not use them in this project so we could highlight the use of standard Choosers. If you are going to use this barcode scanning library, you should probably use his Windows Phone 7 code as well for simplicity.

13. Display the results by setting the `Text` property on the `tbResults` TextBlock to the `Text` property of the result. If an exception is thrown, we want to notify the user that a barcode was not found in the image. Set the `tbResults` Text property to `Barcode not found.` in the catch block.

The `ScanBarcode` method is as follows:

```
void ScanBarcode(Stream photoStream)
{
    var image = new BitmapImage();
    image.SetSource(photoStream);
    photoStream.Position = 0;
    imgBarcode.Source = image;

    var bitmap = new WriteableBitmap(image.PixelWidth,
    image.PixelHeight);
    bitmap.LoadJpeg(photoStream);

    try
      {
        var reader = new MultiFormatOneDReader(null);
        var result = reader.decode(newBinaryBitmap(
```

```
            newHybridBinarizer(
                newRGBLuminanceSource(bitmap, image.PixelWidth,
                image.PixelHeight))));

            tbResults.Text = result.Text;
        }
        catch
        {
            tbResults.Text = "Barcode not  found.";
        }
    }
```

14. Now, go back to the completed handler. There are several states that can be returned from the Choosers. A photo stream is only returned if the state is set to OK.

15. Add an `if` statement that checks the `TaskResult` property on the `PhotoResult`. If it equals `TaskResult.OK`, call the `ScanBarcode` method passing the `ChosenPhoto` property on the `TaskResult`.

    The handler will be similar to the following code:

```
void _photoChooserTask_Completed(object sender, PhotoResult e)
{
    if (e.TaskResult == TaskResult.OK)
        ScanBarcode(e.ChosenPhoto);
}
```

16. Double-click each of the buttons in the designer window to create click handlers in the code-behind. Call the `Show` method on the `_cameraCaptureTask` in the click handler for the `butCaptureBarcode` button. Call the `Show` method on the `_photoPickerTask` in the click handler for the `butScanPicture` button.

17. Create a new `SearchTask` in the `butSearchBarcode` click handler, set its `SearchQuery` property to the `tbResults` TextBlock Text property, and call the `Show` method on the task.

    The handlers will resemble the following code:

```
private void butCaptureBarcode_Click(object sender,
RoutedEventArgs e)
{
    _cameraCaptureTask.Show();
}

private void butScanPicture_Click(object sender, RoutedEventArgs
e)
{
    _photoPickerTask.Show();
}
private void butSearchBarcode_Click(object sender,
RoutedEventArgs e)
```

```
    {
        var task = new SearchTask
                    {
                        SearchQuery = tbResults.Text
                    };
        task.Show();
    }
```

How it works...

The user will be able to capture a photo or select a photo from the pictures on their phone using the `CameraCaptureTask` and `PhotoChooserTask` tasks, respectively. The screenshot below shows the `PhotoChooserTask` in action:

Once the photo is captured or selected, the `Completed` event is called and the `ScanBarcode` method is called by passing the image to the barcode scanning library. If a barcode is found, the digits are displayed on the page. A screenshot of this follows:

The **Search** button searches for the found digits via the phone's built in Bing search capability. The search results are displayed as follows:

There's more...

Utilizing the camera sensor in a Windows Phone application can be tricky during development. Here are some tips that will help you along the way.

Debugging tips

Debugging the `CameraCapture` and `PhotoChooser` tasks can be tricky. The emulator does not support the `CameraCapture` task. The camera captured UI does show but no image is displayed, just black. You can use the `PhotoChooser` Chooser in the emulator, but there are only a few images to choose from by default. Those won't work for testing the `BarCodeScanner` application because they don't have barcodes. A simple work around is to programmatically add one or more images of barcodes to the photo collection. You could, for example, add some code to the constructor of the page to add a photo from the project. This requires a reference to the `Microsoft.Xna.Framework` assembly and use of the `MediaLibrary` class. Also remember to set the **Build Action** on the image to **Content** in the **Properties** window:

```
// Add sample barcode image to phone photo library
var uri = new Uri("Resources/barCodeSample.jpg", UriKind.Relative);
            var stream = Application.GetResourceStream(uri);
            var lib = new MediaLibrary();
            lib.SavePicture("barcodeSample.jpg", stream.Stream);
```

Debugging on a Windows Phone device may seem unsupported as well, by default. The problem is you can't access the media library while connected to the Zune software, but you have to be connected to debug. There is a workaround; Microsoft ships the `WpConnect.exe` utility with the development tools. It is usually installed in one of the following locations:

▸ `C:\Program Files (x86)\Microsoft SDKs\Windows Phone\v7.0\Tools\WPConnect`

▸ `C:\Program Files\Microsoft SDKs\Windows Phone\v7.0\Tools\WPConnect`

To connect with `WpConnect`, connect the device and let it connect to Zune. Then close the Zune software and run the `WpConnect.exe` utility. The utility should find and connect to your device after a few seconds. You should now be able to debug as before but also now use the `PhotoChooser` task and/or any other media-related areas of the phone.

Trigger happy Chooser

You may find an exception thrown if you click either the **Scan Image** or **Scan with Camera** buttons multiple times before the Chooser is shown.

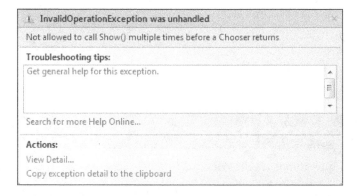

We can code defensively for this by disabling the buttons once one of them is clicked. Create a protected `bool` property named `ChooserEnabled` with a setter method only. Set the Chooser buttons' (`butScanPicture` and `butCaptureBarcode`) `IsEnabled` properties to the passed value in the setter method. The resulting code will resemble the following:

```
protected bool ChooserEnabled
{
    set
    {
        butScanPicture.IsEnabled = value;
        butCaptureBarcode.IsEnabled = value;
    }
}
```

Set the property to `true` in the `_photoChooserTask` complete handler. Set the property to `false` in the `butCaptureBarcode` and `butScanPicture` click handlers. The handlers should mimic the following code:

```
void _photoChooserTask_Completed(object sender, PhotoResult e)
{
    ChooserEnabled = true;
    if (e.TaskResult == TaskResult.OK)
        ScanBarcode(e.ChosenPhoto);
}

private void butCaptureBarcode_Click(object sender, RoutedEventArgs e)
{
    ChooserEnabled = false;
    _cameraCaptureTask.Show();
}

private void butScanPicture_Click(object sender, RoutedEventArgs e)
{
```

```
        ChooserEnabled = false;
        _photoPickerTask.Show();
    }
```

This will disable both buttons when either is clicked and re-enable them when the Chooser is complete.

Enabling photo extras

While developing applications for the Windows Phone is very rewarding, at times your application can still feel like a second-class citizen. One way to make it feel more integrated into the operating system in the case of a photo-related application is to integrate into the photo extras menu.

In this recipe, we will integrate the `BarCodeScanner` application into the photo extras menu.

How to do it...

Follow these steps to add a photo extra:

1. Open the `BarCodeScanner` project you created in the previous recipe.
2. Add an XML file named `Extras.xml` to the root of the project.
3. Set its **Copy to Output Directory** property in the **Properties** window to **Copy always**. A screenshot of this property follows:

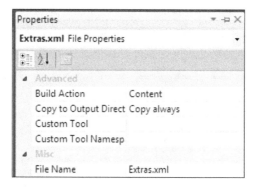

4. Open the XML file and add the following XML:

```xml
<Extras>
  <PhotosExtrasApplication>
    <Enabled>true</Enabled>
  </PhotosExtrasApplication>
</Extras>
```

5. Override the `OnNavigatedTo` method in the code-behind file, `MainPage.xaml.cs`. Create an `IDictionary` of string, named `querystrings` and set it to `NavigationContext.QueryString`.

6. Add a project reference to `Microsoft.Xna.Framework` if it isn't already referenced and a using statement at the top of the code-behind.

7. Create an `if` statement that checks that the `querystrings` dictionary contains a key named `token`. If it does, create a new `MediaLibrary` named `mediaLibrary`.

8. Create a new `Picture` variable named picture and set it to be equal to the `GetPictureFromToken` method, passing the `querystrings` dictionary item with the key `token`.

9. Lastly, call the `ScanBarcode` method passing the image stream by calling the `GetImage` method on the picture.

The handler will resemble the following code:

```
protected override void OnNavigatedTo(NavigationEventArgs e)
    {
        IDictionary<string, string> querystrings =
        NavigationContext.QueryString;

        if (querystrings.ContainsKey("token"))
        {
          var mediaLibrary = new MediaLibrary();
          Picture picture =
          mediaLibrary.GetPictureFromToken(querystrings["token"]);
          ScanBarcode(picture.GetImage());
        }
    }
```

How it works...

As you might have guessed, the `Extras.xml` file indicates to the device that the application provides photo extra functionality during installation. This file must be named `Extras.xml`. For packaging purposes, as noted before, it must always be copied to the output directory as well.

To test the code, deploy it to a device, take a photo of a barcode, view the photo in the viewer, select the ellipsis to see the available options, choose **extras**, and click **BarCodeScanner**. The **BarCodeScanner** application will start and the image will show under results, and if the barcode is found, the digits will be shown as well. Screenshots of this process follow. First the **extras** menu option:

Then the **EXTRAS** menu opens:

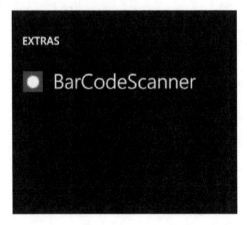

As you can see, the application name is used in the **extras** menu. Extras utilize a core tenant of Silverlight, Navigation. The photo viewer passes a token which identifies the selected photo over the `querystring` to the application. Once we override the `OnNavigatedTo` method and grab the token, we can get the image from the media library.

There's more...

At this time, photo extras are the only extras supported by the operating system. As you can imagine, there are many other areas of the user interface where extras could be utilized. The `Extras.xml` could easily be extended to support other types of extras. Look for them in the future. One addition to Extras that is coming in the Mango update is a Bing Search Extra.

Tombstoning

As you have seen in the previous sections, Launchers and Choosers are run outside of the applications that call them. So you ask, what happens to the application while the task is shown? It depends. Various Launchers/Choosers handle this differently. In some cases the application is closed completely and in others it is only suspended temporarily.

In this recipe, we will create an application to remind users of the websites that they should check every day. We will use the `WebBrowserTask` task to open the websites. The `WebBrowserTask` task causes the calling application to close completely so we will handle this by saving/restoring the state of the application through the Tombstoning process.

Tombstoning is the process by which Windows Phone applications are deactivated and restarted.

Getting ready

Create a new project named **CheckDaily** using the Windows Phone Application project template. Set the application title to `Ch. 8 Launchers and Choosers` and the page title to `check daily`. Replace the content Grid in row one of the `LayoutRoot` Grid with a StackPanel.

Add a `TextBox` named `tbUrlToAdd` to the `StackPanel` and set its `InputScope` to `Url`. Next add a `Button` named `btAddUrl` with a `TextBlock` whose `Text` property is set to `Add Url to List`. Add a `ListBox` named `lbUrls` and set the `ListBox.ItemTemplate` to a `DataTemplate` with a single `CheckBox` control. Bind the `IsChecked` property to `Checked` and set the `Binding Mode` to `TwoWay`. Add a `TextBlock` to the `CheckBox` and bind the `Text` property to `Url`. Set the `Click` event to `checkbox_Click` on the `CheckBox`.

The result will be similar to the following XAML:

```
<StackPanel x:Name="TitlePanel" Grid.Row="0" Margin="12,17,0,28">
    <TextBlock x:Name="ApplicationTitle" Text="Ch. 8 - Launchers and
    Choosers" Style="{StaticResource PhoneTextNormalStyle}"/>
    <TextBlock x:Name="PageTitle" Text="check daily" Margin="9,-
    7,0,0" Style="{StaticResource PhoneTextTitle1Style}"/>
</StackPanel>
<StackPanel Grid.Row="1">
    <TextBox x:Name="tbUrlToAdd" InputScope="Url" ></TextBox>
    <Button x:Name="btAddUrl" >
        <TextBlock>Add Url to List</TextBlock>
    </Button>
    <ListBox x:Name="lbUrls">
        <ListBox.ItemTemplate>
            <DataTemplate>
                <CheckBox Click="checkbox_Click" IsChecked="{Binding
                Checked, Mode=TwoWay}">
                    <TextBlock Text="{Binding Url}"></TextBlock>
                </CheckBox>
            </DataTemplate>
        </ListBox.ItemTemplate>
    </ListBox>
</StackPanel>
```

The page should look similar to the following screenshot:

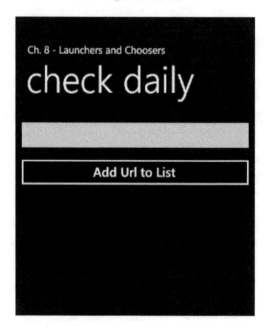

How to do it...

The following steps will define the tombstoning logic.

1. Create a class named `UrlToCheck` in the project with two properties: a `string` property named `Url` and a `bool` property named `Checked`. The resulting class follows:

```
public class UrlToCheck
{
    public bool Checked { get; set; }
    public string Url { get; set; }
}
```

2. Create an `ObservableCollection` of the `UrlToCheck` property in the **MainPage** code-behind named `UrlsToCheck`. Initialize the property to a new `ObservableCollection` with a single `UrlToCheck` type with the `Url` set to `http://www.weather.com`. Then set the `ItemSource` property on the `lbUrls` `ListBox` to the `UrlsToCheck` property in the XAML file. The `ObservableCollection` type will handle the dependency logic for binding to the user interface.

    These steps should produce the following code:

```
protected ObservableCollection<UrlToCheck> UrlsToCheck { get; set;
}

public MainPage()
{
    InitializeComponent();
    UrlsToCheck = new ObservableCollection<UrlToCheck> { new
    UrlToCheck { Url = "http://www.weather.com" } };
    lbUrls.ItemsSource = UrlsToCheck;
```

    There are different ways to persist the state of a Windows Phone application for tombstoning. This application will persist the state in `IsolatedStorage` using the `ApplicationSettings` property which is a `Dictionary`. The only state we need to persist for the **CheckDaily** application is the `UrlsToCheck` property.

3. Create two string field variables in the class named `_sitesToCheckKey` and `_timestampKey`. Set them to `sitesToCheck` and `timestamp`, respectively. These will be used as keys in the `ApplicationSettings` `IsolatedStorage` dictionary.

    The fields will resemble the following:

```
private string _sitesToCheckKey = "sitesToCheck";
private string _timestampKey = "timestamp";
```

4. Next create a method named `SaveState` which returns void.

5. Add a using statement to the `System.IO.IsolatedStorage` namespace.

6. Add the `UrlsToCheck` collection to the `IsolateStorageSettings. ApplicationSettings` dictionary at the `sitesToCheck` index.

7. Set the dictionary at the `timestamp` index to the current UTC `DateTime`.

8. Then call the `Save` method on `ApplicationSettings` to commit the changes.

   The resulting code is as follows:

```
void SaveState()
{
    IsolatedStorageSettings.ApplicationSettings[_sitesToCheckKey]
    = UrlsToCheck;
    IsolatedStorageSettings.ApplicationSettings[_timestampKey] =
    DateTime.UtcNow;
    IsolatedStorageSettings.ApplicationSettings.Save();
}
```

9. Create a method named `RestoreState` which also returns void. Before we can restore the application state, we must check to see if the state has previously been saved.

10. Create an `if` statement to see if the `ApplicationSettings` dictionary contains the `sitesToCheck` key. If not, call `return`.

11. Create a variable named `urls` equal to the `ApplicationSettings` at the `sitesToCheck` index cast as an `ObservableCollection` of `UrlToCheck`.

12. If the `urls` variable is not null, call the `Clear` method on the `UrlsToCheck` property, then add each URL in `urls` to the `UrlsToCheck` property.

13. Next create a `DateTime` variable named `timestamp`, equal to the item in the `ApplicationSettings` dictionary at the `timestamp` index cast as a `DateTime`.

14. If the `timestamp Date` property is not equal to the current Date, set the `Checked` property to `false` for each URL in the `UrlsToCheck` collection.

   These steps produce the following code:

```
void RestoreState()
{
    if
    (IsolatedStorageSettings.ApplicationSettings.Contains
    (_sitesToCheckKey) == false)
        return;

    var urls =
    IsolatedStorageSettings.ApplicationSettings[_sitesToCheckKey]
    as ObservableCollection<UrlToCheck>;
        if (urls != null)
```

```
        {
            UrlsToCheck.Clear();
            foreach (var urlToCheck in urls)
            {
                UrlsToCheck.Add(urlToCheck);
            }
        }

        DateTime timestamp =
        (DateTime)IsolatedStorageSettings.ApplicationSettings
        [_timestampKey];
        if (timestamp.Date != DateTime.UtcNow.Date)
            foreach (var urlToCheck in UrlsToCheck)
            {
                urlToCheck.Checked = false;
            }
    }
```

These two methods will handle persisting the state of the application.

15. Call the `Restore` method at the end of the constructor to restore state. This will handle restoring state when either the application is opened after being closed or re-activated after being tombstoned. We will need to save the application state whenever the `UrlsToCheck` collection changes.

16. Double-click the **btAddUrl** Button in the **MainPage** designer to create a click handler. In this handler, call the `Add` method on the `UrlsToCheck` property passing a new `UrlToCheck` with `Url` property set to the `tbUrlToAdd` `TextBox` instance's `Text` property.

17. Then call the `SaveState` method.

    The added URL click handler code is as follows:

```
private void btAddUrl_Click(object sender, RoutedEventArgs e)
{
    UrlsToCheck.Add(new UrlToCheck {Url = tbUrlToAdd.Text});

    SaveState();
}
```

18. Create a void method named `checkbox_Click` with an object parameter named `sender` and a `RoutedEventArgs` parameter named `e`.

19. Next create a variable named `urlToCheck` equal to the `DataContext` property cast as `UrlToCheck` on the sender parameter cast as a `CheckBox`.

20. Add a using statement to the `System.Phone.Tasks` namespace.

21. Add a `WebBrowserTask` task named `task` with the `Url` property set to the `Url` property of the `urlToCheck`.

22. Then call the `SaveState` method and finally call the `Show` method on the task.

23. The previous steps produce the following code:

```
void checkbox_Click(object sender, RoutedEventArgs e)
{
    var urlToCheck = ((CheckBox) sender).DataContext as
    UrlToCheck;
    var task = new WebBrowserTask { URL = urlToCheck.Url };
    SaveState();
    task.Show();
}
```

How it works...

If you debug the application, you will see that the `ListBox` lists `weather.com` by default and you can add additional URLs to the list by typing a URL in the `TextBox` and clicking the add button. If you click one of the URLs in the `ListBox`, the site will open in the browser. When you click the back button, you will return to the **CheckDaily** application and the URL you clicked will be checked. Each new day you run the application the URL list will remain, but the checks will be cleared for you to recheck the sites that day. The screenshot of a selected URL is as follows:

The URL list is persisted in the `IsolateStorage` settings when a URL is added to the list or clicked. The application is deactivated when the `WebBrowserTask` task is shown. When the user clicks back from the browser, the application is reopened and the URL list is restored from `IsolateStorage`. It will appear to the user that the application was only suspended. If back is clicked again, the application will actually close (remember the only way to close an application is to click back to the point before you started the application). When the application is restarted, the state is again restored in the constructor of the **MainPage** code-behind and it is as if the user never left.

As a test, you can comment out the `RestoreState` method call in the constructor, debug the application, and click the second URL. Click back and you will see the URL list reinitialized with only the default **weather.com** URL.

Tombstoning may seem complicated but is actually pretty simple. An application is closed when the user opens the application then clicks the back button. Any other redirection from the application will deactivate (tombstone) or suspend the application. This includes but is not limited to:

 ▸ Showing a Launcher/Chooser

 ▸ Answering a phone call

 ▸ Opening a toast notification

 ▸ Connecting to Wi-Fi

 ▸ Clicking the start button

When an application is deactivated, its current page name and navigation path is saved until reactivation but all other state is lost. It's up to the developer to save the state of their application. This typically means anything the user added or edited needs to be saved.

There's more...

Windows Phone does not currently allow third party applications to run in the background. Another way of saying this is it doesn't multi-task. The next version of the operating system (codename Mango) will allow multi-tasking but you will still need to handle the Tombstoning process for when the phone is running low on memory and must deactivate your app.

Methods of persisting state

The `ApplicationSettings` dictionary may not always be the best way to persist application state. The dictionary, for example, will throw an exception if you try to store a very large set of data. So, there are a couple of alternatives for persisting state.

You could use raw `IsolatedStorage` instead of the `ApplicationSettings` dictionary. The API for this is very similar to the **System.IO.File** API. Common usage involves serializing types for storage as a file. There are many helpers on the web for making this process easier.

Another alternative is to store the state externally via web services. This is much slower, but it makes the state available across many devices if the user has multiple devices. Or it could be shared with a complimenting website. This option is typically used when the state changes less often or as a backup to `IsolatedStorage` for redundancy.

Not all Launchers and Choosers are the same

In general, only Choosers do not cause an application to tombstone immediately. They defer tombstoning for as long as possible until the phone needs the utilized memory for other purposes. And in general, Launchers do cause an application to tombstone immediately. The `MediaPlayerLauncher` seems to be the exception to these rules. It also defers to tombstoning if possible.

Tombstone events

You may have noticed several event handlers in the `App.xaml.cs` file of a Windows Phone project. Four of these handlers are related to tombstoning and the application life cycle:

- `Application_Launching`
- `Application_Activated`
- `Application_Deactivated`
- `Application_Closing`

Another way to persist the state of an application is to utilize these handlers to save state just before the application closes or is deactivated. Then restore the state in the launched and activated handlers.

Be careful though, you must complete any operations in the deactivated handler within 10 seconds. Otherwise, the application will not be tombstoned and instead terminated. Microsoft suggests aiming for operations which complete within two seconds to be safe.

9
Sensing with Sensors

In this chapter, we will cover:

- ▸ Orienting your app
- ▸ That mic is hot
- ▸ Accelerating your apps
- ▸ Developing the touch
- ▸ Shaking it up
- ▸ Pinching with ease

Introduction

There are several interesting ways to interact with a Windows Phone. Sensors provide information from the user and outside world to the operating system and applications. In this chapter, we will explore the various sensors and learn how we can utilize them in our applications.

The most obvious interaction method, with a modern smartphone, is the touch interface. Many of the controls that ship with the development tools include support for the common touch interactions. Other interaction options include the microphone and accelerometer, which we will also review.

Orienting your app

Certain functions on a handheld device are better suited for viewing in landscape mode versus portrait mode. Windows Phone, like its competitors, can automatically change the display's orientation depending on the orientation of the phone. By default, a new Windows Phone project only supports portrait mode.

The automatic handling of orientation is a feature which is built into many of the standard phone controls. In most cases, the control will rotate to the proper orientation and resize to fit the screen. Many times, developers are not required to handle orientation changes at all. There are cases, however, when the UI would be more functional with a more drastic change in the layout. Windows Phone provides developers with the hooks they need to manually handle orientation changes when necessary.

In this recipe, we will create a simple web browser application which allows the user to enable automatic orientation handling or lock the orientation to portrait or landscape mode.

Getting ready

Create a new project named `OrientationChooser` using the Windows Phone Application project template.

We will be utilizing the `ProgressBar` control in this project. There is a `ProgressBar` control included in the first version of the standard tools for Windows Phone which works great in determinate mode. This mode is used when the developer updates the progress manually based on some calculated progress working to completion. It is more common to use the `ProgressBar` in indeterminate mode, which is just an animation that is shown until the work is complete. The standard control does support this, but it was found to be inefficient (as it overloads the UI thread causing the interface to be choppy).

The best alternative is the `PerformanceProgressBar` in the Silverlight for Windows Phone Toolkit. Download the toolkit source, build it, copy the `Microsoft.Phone.Controls.Toolkit` assembly to the `OrientationChooser` solution folder, and reference it.

`http://silverlight.codeplex.com/`

1. Open the `MainPage.xaml` designer. Add an XML namespace declaration for the toolkit to the top of the page in the root `PhoneApplicationPage` node. The declaration would match the following:

   ```
   xmlns:toolkit="clr-namespace:Microsoft.Phone.
   Controls;assembly=Microsoft.Phone.Controls.Toolkit"
   ```

2. Change the first `RowDefinition` to a height of 5 in the `LayoutRoot` Grid. Within the `Grid`, add a `PerformanceProgressBar` named `progressBar`. Set its `Visibility` property to `Collapsed` and its `IsIndeterminate` property to `True`. Next add a `WebBrowser` control named `webBrowser1`. Set its Source property to `http://m.bing.com` and `IsScriptEnabled` to `True` to allow JavaScript in the browser. The resulting grid should resemble the following:

```
<Grid x:Name="LayoutRoot">
    <Grid.RowDefinitions>
        <RowDefinition Height="5"/>
        <RowDefinition Height="*"/>
    </Grid.RowDefinitions>
    <toolkit:PerformanceProgressBar Grid.Row="0"
     x:Name="progressBar" Visibility="Collapsed"
     IsIndeterminate="True" />
    <phone:WebBrowser Grid.Row="1" x:Name="webBrowser1"
        Source="http://m.bing.com" IsScriptEnabled="True" />
</Grid>
```

3. We will utilize the `ApplicationBar` for buttons in this application so uncomment the `ApplicationBar` at the bottom of the page. Create three `ApplicationBarIconButton` instances: the first will allow the phone to handle orientation, while the second and third will statically set the orientation to Portrait and Landscape, respectively.

`ApplicationBarIconButton` instances display an icon and text value. Microsoft installs a set of icons with the development tools in one of the two locations, depending on your OS version:

▶ `C:\Program Files (x86)\Microsoft SDKs\Windows Phone\v7.0\Icons\dark`

▶ `C:\Program Files\Microsoft SDKs\Windows Phone\v7.0\Icons\dark`

The icon specified for an `ApplicationBarIconButton` should be 48 pixels in height/width and have a transparent background.

4. Set the `Name`, `IconUri`, `Text`, and `Click` properties on each button, as shown below:

```
<shell:ApplicationBarIconButton
    x:Name="butDynamic"
    IconUri="/Resources/dynamic.png"
    Text="Dynamic"
    Click="butDynamic_Click" />
<shell:ApplicationBarIconButton
    x:Name="butPortrait"
```

```
        IconUri="/Resources/portrait.png"
        Text="Portrait"
        Click="butPortrait_Click" />
<shell:ApplicationBarIconButton
        x:Name="butLandscape"
        IconUri="/Resources/landscape.png"
        Text="Landscape"
        Click="butLandscape_Click" />
```

5. Create a `Resources` folder in the project and copy the icons from this recipe's corresponding code sample to the folder. If the coding sample is not immediately available, you can skip this step and the icons will be set to the default **X** icon.

6. Also create an `ApplicationBarMenuItem` for redirecting the browser to Bing. Set its `Name`, `Text`, and `Click` properties as well. The items should resemble the following:

```
<shell:ApplicationBar.MenuItems>
    <shell:ApplicationBarMenuItem
        x:Name="butBing"
        Text="Back to Bing"
        Click="butBing_Click" />
</shell:ApplicationBar.MenuItems>
```

There isn't much to see in the designer, just the browser (shown as a box with the IE symbol) and the `ApplicationBar`. The Visual Studio designer window should now be similar to the following:

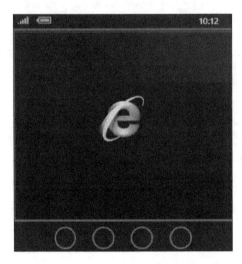

How to do it...

1. Set the `SupportedOrientations` property on the root `ApplicationPage` node to `PortraitOrLandscape`, like so:

```
SupportedOrientations="PortraitOrLandscape"
```

2. Create handlers for each of the `ApplicationBarIconButton` instances and the `ApplicationBarMenuItem` in the code-behind, each returning void and taking two parameters, an object named `sender` and `EventArgs` named e.

3. Perform the following:

   ❑ In the `butDynamic_Click` handler, set the `SupportedOrientations` property to `SupportedPageOrientation.PortraitOrLandscape`

   ❑ In the `butPortrait_Click` handler, set the `SupportedOrientations` property to `SupportedPageOrientation.Portrait`

   ❑ In the `butLandscape_Click` handler, set the `SupportedOrientations` property to `SupportedPageOrientation.Landscape`

The previous steps should result in the following code:

```
private void butDynamic_Click(object sender, EventArgs e)
{
    SupportedOrientations =
    SupportedPageOrientation.PortraitOrLandscape;
}
private void butPortrait_Click(object sender, EventArgs e)
{
    SupportedOrientations =
    SupportedPageOrientation.Portrait;
}
private void butLandscape_Click(object sender, EventArgs e)
{
    SupportedOrientations =
    SupportedPageOrientation.Landscape;
}
```

4. In the `butBing_Click` event handler, call the Navigate method on webBrowser1, passing a new `Uri` of `http://m.bing.com`. The handler should mimic the following:

```
private void butBing_Click(object sender, EventArgs e)
{
    webBrowser1.Navigate(new Uri("http://m.bing.com"));
}
```

5. Add a `using` statement at the top of the page for the `System.Windows.Navigation` namespace.

6. Next add handlers for the `Navigating` and `Navigated` events to the `webBrowser1` control in the constructor and create the corresponding handler methods.

7. Set the `Visibility` property on the progress bar to `Visible` in the navigating handler method and to `Collapsed` in the navigated handler method.

The handler code should resemble the following:

```
public MainPage()
{
    InitializeComponent();

    webBrowser1.Navigating += new
       EventHandler<NavigatingEventArgs>(webBrowser1_Navigating);
    webBrowser1.Navigated += new
       EventHandler<NavigationEventArgs>(webBrowser1_Navigated);
}

void webBrowser1_Navigating(object sender, NavigatingEventArgs e)
{
    progressBar.Visibility = Visibility.Visible;
}
void webBrowser1_Navigated(object sender, NavigationEventArgs e)
{
    progressBar.Visibility = Visibility.Collapsed;
}
```

How it works...

As mentioned previously, only portrait orientation is enabled by default in the application. Changing the `SupportedOrientations` property allows the application to display in landscape, portrait, or both. This property can also be set in the code-behind, as we have done in each of the `ApplicationBarIconButton` click handlers. Changing this property while the application is running will rotate the page/controls to the correct orientation and resize them accordingly.

We set the `SupportedOrientations` in the XAML to `PortraitOrLandscape`, so this is the new default. The application will initially start in Portrait mode in the debugger, but when we rotate the debugger to simulate rotating, the phone will change the application to landscape. In portrait mode, the app will display like the following screenshot:

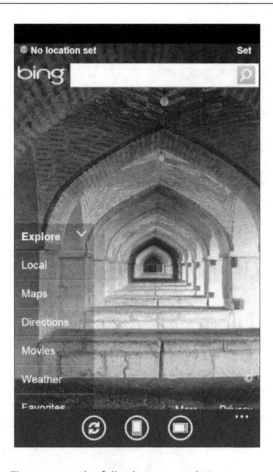

In landscape mode, it will appear as the following screenshot:

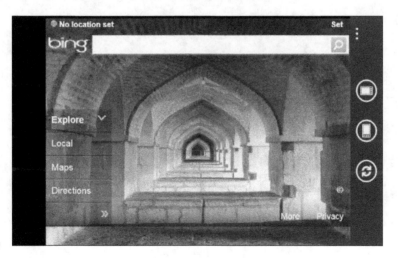

If we then click the portrait button, the application will go back to portrait orientation even though the phone is still rotated to landscape. Like so:

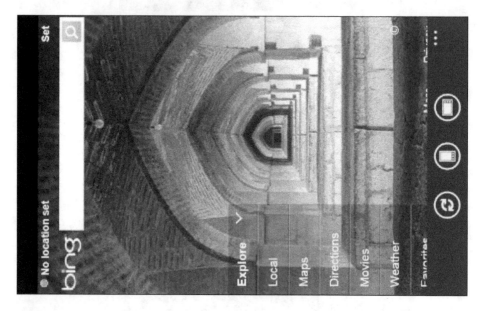

Notice how the application bar handles the orientation change. The icons and text simply rotate 90 degrees.

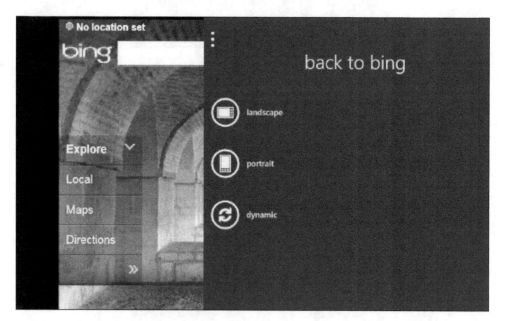

There's more...

Changing the `SupportedOrientations` property is the simplest method of working with orientations. In some cases, it may be beneficial to modify the layout of the page beyond the standard rotation/resizing which the phone handles. There is a way to perform more complex layout changes.

The `PhoneApplicationPage` class (the base class for the code-behind class) offers a virtual method which can be overridden to handle changes to the device's orientation. As an example, we can update the application to show a browser history panel in landscape mode only.

Add a `ColumnDefinition` to the `ColumnDefinitions` list of the layout grid and set its `Width` property to `Auto`. The `Auto` width will automatically adjust the size of the column based upon the width of its contents. Add a `ListBox` named `lbHistory` under the `WebBrowser` control. Set its `Grid.Column` property to 1 and its `Visibility` property to `Collapsed`. Set the `ItemTemplate` to a `DataTemplate` which contains a `Button` with a `Click` event handler named `History_Click`. Place a `TextBlock` inside the button and bind the `Text` property to the `Host` property.

The `ListBox` should resemble the following:

```
<ListBox x:Name="lbHistory" Grid.Row="1" Grid.Column="1"
  Visibility="Collapsed">
    <ListBox.ItemTemplate>
        <DataTemplate>
            <Button Click="History_Click">
                <TextBlock Text="{Binding Host}"/>
            </Button>
        </DataTemplate>
    </ListBox.ItemTemplate>
</ListBox>
```

Open the code-behind and create a `Stack` of the `Uri` field named `_history` and initialize it at the top of the class. This field will maintain the history list of `Uri`s. If you are not familiar with the `Stack` collection type, it is a **Last In, First Out (LIFO)** collection. In our case, we are using it to add new `Uri`s to the history list and when the back button is clicked, redirect the browser to the last `Uri`. The `Stack` field should mimic the following:

```
private Stack<Uri> _history= new Stack<Uri>();
```

We will add entries to the `_history` field in the `webBrowser1_Navigated` method by calling the `Push` method on the stack passing the `NavigationEventArgs Uri` property. Then set the `ItemSource` property on the history `ListBox` to the `_history` stack. Reverse the order of the stack by calling the `Reverse` method. The handler will resemble the following:

```
void webBrowser1_Navigated(object sender, NavigationEventArgs e)
{
    progressBar.Visibility = Visibility.Collapsed;
    _history.Push(e.Uri);
    lbHistory.ItemsSource = _history.Reverse();
}
```

We must handle traversing the history stack in two ways: by overriding the `OnBackKeyPress` method and in the `History_Click` handler.

If there are history entries we will traverse back through the `Uri`s for each Back click. Do this by checking that the `_history Stack` Count property is greater than 1. If it is, call the `Pop` method to remove the current `Uri` in the `_history Stack`. Next set the `WebBrowser` control's `Source` property to the `Pop` method to redirect to the previous `Uri`. Then set the `CancelEventArgs` parameter's `Cancel` property to true to keep the phone from closing the application.

The handler will resemble the following:

```
protected override void
    OnBackKeyPress(System.ComponentModel.CancelEventArgs e)
{
    if (_history.Count > 1)
    {
        _history.Pop();
        webBrowser1.Source = _history.Pop();
        e.Cancel = true;
    }
}
```

Now create the `History_Click` handler with an `object` parameter named `sender` and an `EventArgs` parameter named `e`. Within the method, create a variable named `uri` and set it from the `DataContext` property, of the `sender` parameter cast as a `Button`, cast as a `Uri`. Add an `if` statement that returns out of the method if the `uri` variable is `null`.

Next declare a `Uri` variable named `last`. Then a `do` loop which sets the `last` variable to the `Pop` method on `_history`. For the `while` statement, check if the `AbsoluteUri` property of the `last Uri` equals the `AbsoluteUri` property of the `uri` variable. This will loop through the history stack until the `Uri` that was clicked is found. Once it's found, the loop will end and you must call the `Navigate` method on `webBrowser1` passing the `uri` variable.

```
private void History_Click(object sender, EventArgs e)
{
    var uri = ((Button)sender).DataContext as Uri;
    if (uri == null)
        return;
    Uri last;
    do
    {
        last = _history.Pop();
    } while (last.AbsoluteUri != uri.AbsoluteUri);
    webBrowser1.Navigate(uri);
}
```

Lastly, we need to handle the orientation change. The virtual `OrientationChanged` method provides an extension point to handle the change. Override the method and set the `Visibility` property on the `lbHistory` `ListBox` control to `Visible` if the new orientation property is either `LandscapeLeft` or `LandscapeRight`. Otherwise, set the `Visibility` property to `Collapsed`. The orientation changed handler will mimic the following:

```
protected override void
  OnOrientationChanged(OrientationChangedEventArgs e)
{
    base.OnOrientationChanged(e);

    if (e.Orientation == PageOrientation.LandscapeLeft ||
        e.Orientation == PageOrientation.LandscapeRight)
        lbHistory.Visibility = Visibility.Visible;
    else
        lbHistory.Visibility = Visibility.Collapsed;
}
```

If you debug the application, search for CNN in the bing search and choose the first result. You will see the CNN mobile webpage, which looks the same in portrait mode as before:

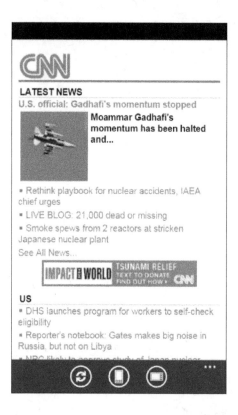

But if you rotate it to either landscape mode, it will show the history panel:

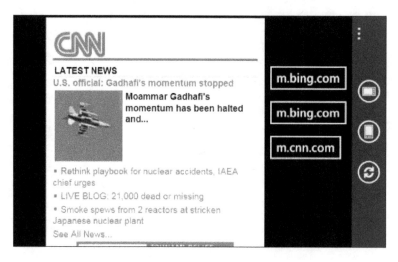

PortraitDown orientation

You may have noticed that nothing happens when you turn the phone upside down. You would expect the `PortraitDown` orientation to be used but it is not currently supported. Only the `PortraitUp`, `LandscapeLeft`, and `LandscapeRight` orientations are supported.

That mic is hot

The microphone is another sensor available to developers on Windows Phone. Some people may only think of using it for talking on the phone, but there are many interesting applications that can be built utilizing the microphone. In this recipe, we will create an app to record the user's voice and play it back at different pitches.

Getting ready

Create a new project named `VoicePitch` using the Windows Phone Application template and add a reference to the `Microsoft.Xna.Framework`. Open the `MainPage.xaml` file in the designer. Set the `ApplicationTitle` TextBox to `Ch.9 - Sensors` and the `PageTitle` to `voice pitch`. Replace the content panel `Grid` with a `StackPanel` in row one of the `LayoutRoot` grid. Add a `Button` to the `StackPanel` named `butStartStopRecording`. Add a `TextBlock` named `tbRecordButtonText` to the Button with the `Text` property set to `Start Recording` and the `Foreground` color property set to `#FF00FF00` (green). Next, add a `TextBlock` to the `StackPanel` and set its `Text` property to `Pitch`. Then add a `Slider` control with the following properties/values:

- `Maximum`: 10
- `Minimum`: (-10)
- `LargeChange`: 2
- `SmallChange`: 1
- `Value`: 0

Add another Button named `butPlay` with an inner `TextBlock` with the `Text` property set to `Play`. Finally, double-click each of the `Button` controls to create click event handlers. The resulting XAML should resemble the following:

```
<Grid x:Name="LayoutRoot" Background="Transparent">
    <Grid.RowDefinitions>
        <RowDefinition Height="Auto"/>
        <RowDefinition Height="*"/>
    </Grid.RowDefinitions>

    <StackPanel x:Name="TitlePanel" Grid.Row="0"
     Margin="12,17,0,28">
```

```
        <TextBlock x:Name="ApplicationTitle" Text="Ch. 9 -
        Sensors" Style="{StaticResource PhoneTextNormalStyle}"/>
        <TextBlock x:Name="PageTitle" Text="voice pitch"
        Margin="9,-7,0,0" Style="{StaticResource
        PhoneTextTitle1Style}"/>
    </StackPanel>

    <StackPanel Grid.Row="1">
        <Button x:Name="butStartStopRecording"
        Click="butStartStopRecording_Click">
            <TextBlock x:Name="tbRecordButtonText"
             Foreground="#FF00FF00">Start Recording</TextBlock>
        </Button>
        <TextBlock Text="Pitch"></TextBlock>
        <Slider x:Name="sPitch" Maximum="10" Minimum="-10"
        LargeChange="2" SmallChange="1" Value="0"></Slider>
        <Button x:Name="butPlay" Click="butPlay_Click">
            <TextBlock>Play</TextBlock>
        </Button>
    </StackPanel>
</Grid>
```

How to do it...

Perform the following steps in the code-behind file:

1. First add using statements for the following namespaces:
    - Microsoft.Xna.Framework
    - Microsoft.Xna.Framework.Audio
    - Color = System.Windows.Media.Color

2. We will also need several class-level fields for use across the methods. Create a Microphone field named _microphone, a byte array named _buffer, and a MemoryStream named _stream. In the constructor, initialize the _microphone field to the static Default property on the Microphone type.

3. Add a handler to the BufferReady event of the _microphone. Then add some XNA plumbing code which configures and starts a game loop.

    The fields and constructor code should mimic the following:

```
        private Microphone _microphone;
        private byte[] _buffer;
        private MemoryStream _stream;

        public MainPage()
```

```
        {
            InitializeComponent();

            _microphone = Microphone.Default;
            _microphone.BufferReady += new
               EventHandler<EventArgs>(_microphone_BufferReady);

            // Timer to simulate the XNA game loop (Microphone is
            from XNA)
            DispatcherTimer dt = new DispatcherTimer();
            dt.Interval = TimeSpan.FromMilliseconds(50);
            dt.Tick += delegate { try {
               FrameworkDispatcher.Update(); } catch { } };
            dt.Start();
        }
```

4. Create the `BufferReady` handler method which returns void and accepts an `object` named `sender` and an `EventArgs` named `e`.

5. Call the `GetData` method on the `_microphone` passing the `_buffer` field. Then write the buffer to the stream by calling the Write method on the `_stream` field passing the `_buffer`, 0 as the offset, and the Length property of the `_buffer` as the count.

   The buffer ready handler will resemble the following:

```
        void _microphone_BufferReady(object sender, EventArgs e)
        {
            _microphone.GetData(_buffer);
            _stream.Write(_buffer, 0, _buffer.Length);
        }
```

6. Move down to the click event handler for the start/stop button next. There are two obvious states for the button: started and stopped. Add an `if` statement that checks whether the `_microphone`'s State property is equal to `MicrophoneState.Stopped`.

7. If so, set the `_stream` field to a new `MemoryStream`. Set the microphone's `BufferDuration` property to a one second `TimeSpan` using the `FromSeconds` method.

8. Initialize the `_buffer` field to a new byte array setting the length with the `GetSampleSizeInBytes` method on the `_microphone` passing the `BufferDuration`. Then call the `Start` method on the microphone.

9. Next update the button visually by setting the `tbRecordButtonText` control's `Foreground` property to a new `SolidColorBrush`.

10. Call the `FromArgb` method on the `Color` type in the constructor of the brush passing the `255`, `255`, `0`, and `0`. Set the Text property on the TextBox to `Stop Recording`.

11. If the `_microphone` field's `State` property is not set to `Stopped`, call the `Stop` method on the `_microphone`. Then again set the `tbRecordButtonText` control's `Foreground` property to a new `SolidColorBrush`.

12. Call the `FromArgb` method on the `Color` type in the constructor of the brush by passing `255`, `0`, `255`, and `0`. Set the `Text` property on the `TextBox` to `Start Recording`.

The button click handler should resemble the following:

```
private void butStartStopRecording_Click(object sender,
RoutedEventArgs e)
{
    if (_microphone.State == MicrophoneState.Stopped)
    {
        _stream = new MemoryStream();

        _microphone.BufferDuration =
            TimeSpan.FromSeconds(1);
        _buffer = new
            byte[_microphone.GetSampleSizeInBytes
            (_microphone.BufferDuration)];
        _microphone.Start();

        tbRecordButtonText.Foreground = new
            SolidColorBrush(Color.FromArgb(255, 255, 0, 0));
        tbRecordButtonText.Text = "Stop Recording";
    }
    else
    {
        _microphone.Stop();
        tbRecordButtonText.Foreground = new
            SolidColorBrush(Color.FromArgb(255, 0, 255, 0));
        tbRecordButtonText.Text = "Start Recording";
    }
}
```

13. In the click handler for the `butPlay` button, create a variable named `soundEffect` and set it to a new `SoundEffect`. Pass the `ToArray` method on the `_stream` field, the `SampleRate` property on `_microphone`, and `AudioChannels.Mono` in the constructor.

14. Create a variable named `soundEffectInstance` and set it to be equal to the `CreateInstance` method on `soundEffect`. Then set the `Pitch` property on `soundEffectInstance` to the `Value` of the pitch slider cast as a float and divided by `10`. Finally, call the `Play` method on `soundEffectInstance`.

The play button click handler should mimic the following:

```
private void butPlay_Click(object sender, RoutedEventArgs e)
{
    var soundEffect = new SoundEffect(_stream.ToArray(),
    _microphone.SampleRate, AudioChannels.Mono);
    var soundEffectInstance = soundEffect.CreateInstance();
    soundEffectInstance.Pitch = (float)sPitch.Value / 10;
    soundEffectInstance.Play();
}
```

How it works...

The microphone API is offered through the XNA portion of the Windows Phone framework. This is why it is necessary to set up a game loop in the constructor of the code-behind. The following exception will be raised without it:

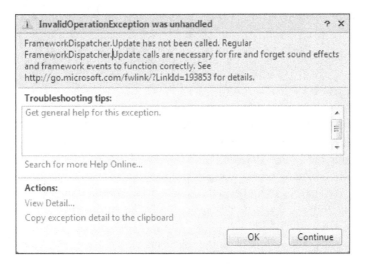

Once this setup is in place, the rest is pretty standard. When the start recording button is clicked the buffer is reset to a new byte array whose size is set according to the duration of the microphone buffer and the microphone is started. When the stop button is clicked the microphone is stopped. While the microphone is active, the buffer will start filling. Then the `BufferReady` event will be called and the audio data will be written to a `MemoryStream`.

The play button click handler creates a new sound from the `MemoryStream`, adjusts the pitch, and plays it. The `Pitch` property can be set to any value between -1 and 1 where 0 is normal. Remember we set the minimum and maximum on the slider to -10 and 10, respectively. So we divide the slider value by 10 to get a value based on 1.

At this point, you can debug the application in the emulator or on a device to record sounds, change the pitch, and play them back. The emulator will only work if you have a microphone on your computer. Note that you may need to configure the microphone levels for this to work well.

Accelerating your apps

The accelerometer is one of the most fun sensors to develop with on the Windows Phone. The immediate feedback from tilting the device is just neat. As you will see, the API is pretty simple as well.

In this recipe, we will use the accelerometer to scroll through results of a Bing images search. We will interface with Bing through their developer web service.

Getting ready

Create a new project named `BingSlideshow` using the Windows Phone Application project template.

1. Open the `MainPage.xaml` file and set the `x:Name` property on the root `PhoneApplicationPage` control to page. Next set the `ApplicationTitle` `TextBlock` to `Ch. 9 - Sensors` and the `PageTitle` `TextBlock` to `bing slideshow`. Add a `TextBox` named `tbSearch` under the `PageTitle` `TextBlock`. Then add a `Button` with an inner `TextBlock` and set the `Text` property to `Search`.

2. Next add a `ScrollViewer` named `svResults` and set the `Height` property to `480`. Within the `ScrollViewer`, add an `ItemsControl` and set its `ItemSource` property to a binding on the `Images` property with `ElementName` equal to page. Set the `ItemTemplate` property to a `DataTemplate` with an inner `Image` control. Set the `Image` contol's `Height` and `Width` properties to `300` and the `Source` property to `{Binding}`. Delete the `ContentPanel` Grid.

3. The previous setup will result in the following XAML:

```
<StackPanel x:Name="TitlePanel" Grid.Row="0"
 Margin="12,17,0,28">
    <TextBlock x:Name="ApplicationTitle" Text="Ch. 9 -
    Sensors" Style="{StaticResource
    PhoneTextNormalStyle}"/>
    <TextBlock x:Name="PageTitle" Text="bing slideshow"
     Margin="9,-7,0,0" Style="{StaticResource
     PhoneTextTitle1Style}"/>
    <TextBox x:Name="tbSearch"/>
    <Button Click="Button_Click">
```

```
            <TextBlock Text="Search"></TextBlock>
        </Button>
        <ScrollViewer x:Name="svResults" Height="480">
            <ItemsControl ItemsSource="{Binding Images,
              ElementName=page}">
                <ItemsControl.ItemTemplate>
                    <DataTemplate>
                        <Image Source="{Binding}" Height="300"
                          Width="300" />
                    </DataTemplate>
                </ItemsControl.ItemTemplate>
            </ItemsControl>
        </ScrollViewer>
    </StackPanel>
```

The `Images` property will be an `ObservableCollection` of `Uri` in the code-behind. The `Binding` on the `Source` property will bind the `Image` to each `Uri` directly.

As mentioned previously, we will be using the Bing API to retrieve results for the image search. To do so, you will need to sign up for a Bing API developer account and create an AppId by visiting the following website:

`http://www.bing.com/developers/createapp.aspx`

Once you have your AppId, go back to Visual Studio and add a Service Reference by right-clicking on the **References** item in the Solution Explorer:

Add a service reference to the Bing service metadata address (`http://api.search.live.net/search.wsdl?AppID=[YourAppId]`) by inserting your AppId into the query string. Use the default namespace of `ServiceReference1`:

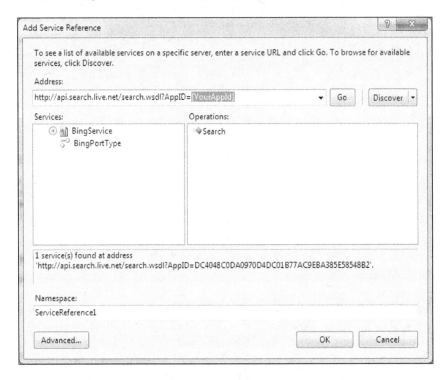

This service can be used to search all types of information. Most of the various Bing search types are available, including standard web, local, image, and video searches, to name a few. This application will use the image search.

Double-click on the search button in the designer to create a click handler in the code-behind. Within the handler create a `BingPortType` (this is the Bing service interface) variable named `client` and set it to be equal to a new `BingPortTypeClient`. Next create a `SearchRequest` variable named `request`. Auto initialize the request by setting the `AppId` property to your application ID, the `Sources` property to a new array of `SourceType` initialized with a `SourceType.Image`, and the `Query` property to the `Text` property of the search `TextBox`.

Next create an `AsyncCallback` variable named `callback` which we will be set with a lambda expression. The lambda will have one input named `response`. Create a variable named `response` and set it to be equal to the `EndSearch` method on the client passing the response parameters in the body of the lambda. Next call the `BeginInvoke` method on the current `Dispatcher`. Pass a parameter-less lambda to the method. Within the lambda body, create a variable named `images` and set it to be equal to a list of `Uri` objects created from the `MediaUrl` property of the `Results` property on the `Image` parameter. Then call the `Clear` method on the `ObservableCollection` `Images` property. Use a `foreach` loop to add each image `Uri` to the `Images` `ObservableCollection`.

Finally, call the `BeginSearch` method on a client by passing a new `SearchRequest1` with the `request` variable in the constructor, the `callback`, and null. The button click handler should resemble the following code:

```
private void Button_Click(object sender, RoutedEventArgs e)
{
    BingPortType client = new BingPortTypeClient();
    var request = new SearchRequest
                      {
                          AppId =
                          "DC4048C0DA0970D4DC01B77AC9EBA385E58548B2",
                          Sources = new[] {
                          SourceType.Image},
                          Query = tbSearch.Text
                      };
    AsyncCallback callback = response =>
                      {
                          var results =
                          client.EndSearch(response);
    Deployment.Current.Dispatcher.BeginInvoke(() =>
                      {
                          var images =
                          results.parameters.Image.Results.Select
                          (x => new Uri(x.MediaUrl));
                          Images.Clear();
                          foreach (var image in
                          images)
                          {
                              Images.Add(image);
                          }
                      });
                      };
    client.BeginSearch(new SearchRequest1(request), callback,
    null);
}
```

How to do it...

Perform the following steps in the MainPage code-behind file:

1. First we must add a reference to the `Microsoft.Devices.Sensors` assembly which contains the accelerometer-related classes:

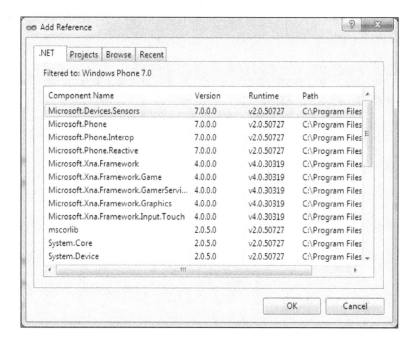

2. Then add a `using` statement to the top of the code-behind page using the following statement:

   ```
   using Microsoft.Devices.Sensors;
   ```

3. Create an `ObservableCollection` of `Uri` property on the class named `Images`. Initialize this property to a new `ObservableCollection` of `Uri` in the class constructor.

4. Create a variable named `accelerometer` and set it to a new `Accelerometer`. Add an event handler to the `ReadingChanged` event named `accelerometer_ReadingChanged`. Then call the `Start` method on the accelerometer.

   The images property and constructor should resemble the following:

   ```
   public ObservableCollection<Uri> Images { get; set; }

   public MainPage()
   {
       InitializeComponent();
   ```

```
Images = new ObservableCollection<Uri>();
var accelerometer = new Accelerometer();
accelerometer.ReadingChanged += new
   EventHandler<AccelerometerReadingEventArgs>
   (accelerometer_ReadingChanged);
accelerometer.Start();
```

}

5. Create the handler method with two parameters: an `object` named `sender` and an `AccelerometerReadingEventArgs` named e.

6. Call the `BeginInvoke` method on the current `Dispatcher` with a parameter-less lambda.

7. Within the lambda body:

   ❑ Create a variable named `scrollChange` and set it to be equal to the `Y` property on the event arguments parameter multiplied by the `svResults` `ScrollViewer` `ViewportHeight` property, and then divide by 10.

   ❑ Call the `ScrollToVerticalOffset` method on the `ScrollViewer`, passing the `VerticalOffset` property plus the `scrollChange` variable.

   ❑ Call the `UpdateLayout` method on the `ScrollViewer`.

The accelerometer reading changed handler should mimic the following:

```
void accelerometer_ReadingChanged(object sender,
AccelerometerReadingEventArgs e)
{
    Deployment.Current.Dispatcher.BeginInvoke(() =>
    {
      var scrollChange = e.Y * svResults.ViewportHeight / 10;
      svResults.ScrollToVerticalOffset(svResults.VerticalOffset +
        scrollChange);
      svResults.UpdateLayout();
    });
}
```

How it works...

To see this application in action, you will need a Windows Phone device. The emulator does not currently support accelerometer testing. When the user runs this application, they will be able to enter a search term in the search box, click the search button, and then image results will be shown below. They can then tilt the phone forward and backward to scroll through the images.

We only utilized the Y-axis information from the accelerometer in this example but the X-axis and Z-axis changes are also available. Be careful not to put too much logic in the `ReadingChanged` handler. The `Accelerometer` sensor is very sensitive, so it often calls this handler constantly. Any long running code would degrade the performance of the application.

Developing the touch

As you have seen, Windows Phone 7 is all about touch. Touch is the primary interface for the phone so it is built into all the controls. But what if you want to read raw touch data and handle it in a custom way? That is available too.

In this recipe, we will create a finger painting application which uses the touch API to read raw touch data and draw to the screen. The application will also let you change the paint color and size.

Getting ready

Create a new project named FingerPaint using the Window Phone Application project template. The XAML on this app will be very simple. We need a Canvas to draw on and some buttons. Open the MainPage.xaml file and delete the LayoutGrid. Replace it with a Canvas named canvas1. Uncomment the ApplicationBar at the bottom of the page. Delete the ApplicationBarMenuItem controls.

Create two ApplicationBarIconButton controls. Name the first butSize, add a Click handler, set the IconUri property to /Resources/size0.png, and set the Text property to size. Name the second butColor, add a Click handler, set the IconUri property to /Resources/color0.png, and set the Text property to color.

The resulting XAML should mimic the following:

```
<Canvas x:Name="canvas1"></Canvas>

<phone:PhoneApplicationPage.ApplicationBar>
    <shell:ApplicationBar IsVisible="True" IsMenuEnabled="True">
        <shell:ApplicationBarIconButton x:Name="butSize"
          Click="butSize_Click" IconUri="/Resources/size0.png"
          Text="size"/>
        <shell:ApplicationBarIconButton x:Name="butColor"
          Click="butColor_Click" IconUri="/Resources/color0.png"
          Text="color"/>
    </shell:ApplicationBar>
</phone:PhoneApplicationPage.ApplicationBar>
```

The buttons will allow you to flip through different colors and sizes. You will either need to use the icons from the code that accompanies this chapter or create them yourself. If you would like to create them, you will need three size icons and five color icons. Each icon should be 48 pixels in height and width, have a transparent background, and be saved as a PNG file with an alpha channel. These are not technically necessary, but they do add a nice interface for the user. Create a folder in the project named Resources. Place the images in the folder and add them to the solution.

Select them all and go to the **Properties** window to set the **Build Action** property to **Content** and the **Copy to Output Directory** property to **Copy Always**. This will ensure that they can be accessed by the application.

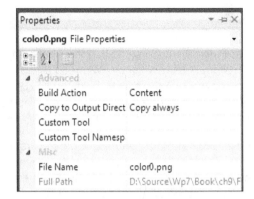

Open the code-behind file and create a private array of the `int` field named `_sizes`. Initialize the field to a new array with the values `25`, `50`, and `100`. Create an array of the `Color` field named `_colors` and initialize it to a new array with five color values. Use the static `FromArgb` method on the `Color` type to create the colors. Create the following values:

- Red: 255, 255, 0, 0
- Yellow: 255, 255, 255, 0
- Green: 255, 0, 255, 0
- Aqua: 255, 0, 255, 255
- Blue: 255, 0, 0, 255

The class variables should resemble the following:

```
private int[] _sizes = new[] { 25, 50, 100 };
private Color[] _colors = new[] {
    Color.FromArgb(255,255,0,0),
    Color.FromArgb(255,255,255,0),
    Color.FromArgb(255,0,255,0),
    Color.FromArgb(255,0,255,255),
    Color.FromArgb(255,0,0,255),
};
```

Then create two `int` fields named `_selectedSizeIndex` and `_selectedColorIndex` to maintain the state of the currently selected size/color, like so:

```
private int _selectedSizeIndex;
private int _selectedColorIndex;
```

Create the two click handler methods for the `ApplicationBarIconButton` controls, each with two parameters, an `object` named `sender` and an `EventArgs` named `e`. In the `butSize_Click` handler, increment the `_selectedSizeIndex` field. Then set it to the modulus (remainder) of itself and the length of the `_sizes` array. This will ensure the `_selectedSizeIndex` is always in the range of the array.

Next, create a variable named `button` and set it to be equal to the `sender` parameter cast to the `ApplicationBarIconButton` type (this will require a using statement for the `Microsoft.Phone.Shell` namespace at the top of the page). Then set the button's `IconUri` property to a new `Uri` passing a format string expression and `UriKind.RelativeOrAbsolute` in the constructor. Set the format expression to `Resources/size{0}.png` and the first argument to `_selectedSizeIndex`.

In the `butColor_Click` handler, do the same by exchanging `_selectedSizeIndex` for `_selectedColorIndex`, `_sizes` for `_colors`, and the filename portion `size` of the string expression for `color`.

The click handlers should be coded as follows:

```
private void butSize_Click(object sender, EventArgs e)
{
    _selectedSizeIndex++;
    _selectedSizeIndex = _selectedSizeIndex % _sizes.Length;

    var button = (ApplicationBarIconButton)sender;
    button.IconUri = new
      Uri(string.Format("Resources/size{0}.png",
      _selectedSizeIndex), UriKind.RelativeOrAbsolute);
}

private void butColor_Click(object sender, EventArgs e)
{
    _selectedColorIndex++;
    _selectedColorIndex = _selectedColorIndex %
    _colors.Length;

    var button = (ApplicationBarIconButton)sender;
    button.IconUri = new
      Uri(string.Format("Resources/color{0}.png",
      _selectedColorIndex), UriKind.RelativeOrAbsolute);
}
```

How to do it...

In the constructor for the code-behind do the following:

1. Add a handler named `Touch_Reported` for the static `FrameReported` event on the `Touch` type.

2. Create the method with an object parameter named `sender` and a `TouchFrameEventArgs` parameter named e. Within the handler, create a variable named `touchPoints` and set it by using the `GetTouchPoints` method on the `TouchEventArgs` parameter passing the `canvas1` control.

3. Next, create a `ForEach` loop that loops through each `touchPoint`.

4. Within the loop, add an `if` statement which checks whether the `Action` property on the `touchPoint` is equal to `TouchAction.Move`. Inside the `if` block, create a variable named `ellipse` and set it to a new `ellipse`.

5. Auto initialize the `ellipse` by setting the `Height/Width` properties to the `_sizes` array at the `_selectedSizeIndex` and the `Fill` property to a new `SolidColorBrush` passing the `_colors` array at the `_selectedColorIndex`.

6. Call the static `SetLeft` method on the `Canvas` type passing the `ellipse` variable and the `X` property on the `Position` property of the `touchPoint`, minus the ellipse `Width` property divided by two.

7. Also call the static `SetTop` method on the `Canvas` type by passing the `ellipse` variable and the `Y` property on the `Position` property of the `touchPoint`, minus the `ellipse` `Width` property divided by two.

8. Finally, add the `ellipse` to the `Children` property of the `canvas`.

    The following code should be produced:

```
public MainPage()
    {
        InitializeComponent();
        Touch.FrameReported += Touch_FrameReported;
        }
void Touch_FrameReported(object sender, TouchFrameEventArgs e)
    {
        var touchPoints = e.GetTouchPoints(canvas1);
        foreach (var touchPoint in touchPoints)
            if (touchPoint.Action == TouchAction.Move)
                {
                    var ellipse = new Ellipse
                        {
                            Width =
                        _sizes[_selectedSizeIndex],
```

```
                                              Height =
                          _sizes[_selectedSizeIndex],
                                             Fill = new
            SolidColorBrush(_colors[_selectedColorIndex])
                                                };
                      Canvas.SetLeft(ellipse,
             touchPoint.Position.X - ellipse.Width / 2);
                        Canvas.SetTop(ellipse,
             touchPoint.Position.Y - ellipse.Height / 2);
                      canvas1.Children.Add(ellipse);
                }
        }
```

How it works...

We now have a finger painting application. If you run the application in the emulator, you will see that you can draw with the mouse changing the colors and sizes of the paint. On a device, you can use your finger.

Within the `FrameReported` event handler, we are first getting the touch points. For each touch point, we are creating an ellipse in the appropriate size and color, then setting its position on the canvas, and adding it to the canvas as a child object. We also take the X/Y positions and adjust them by subtracting half the width/height of the paint point so the touch point position will be centered on the user's finger.

You may be wondering why there are multiple touch points. The current Windows Phones in the market today support up to four simultaneous touch points. By handling the touch points in a loop, we are supporting multiple fingers painting at the same time. The emulator does not currently support multi-touch, so you will need to test this on a device.

The Windows Phone specification supports up to 10 simultaneous touch points, so we may see phones in the future which can handle more than four simultaneous touches.

There are a few other interesting properties on the `TouchPoint` type. The `Id` property identifies each touch in the order in which it was added. This allows you, for example, to handle the first touch differently from the last. There is also a `TouchDevice` property which has properties for identifying which control the `TouchPoint` is directly over. This is very useful when modifying other controls on the page with touch in a custom way.

Shaking it up

You have seen how we can handle the `Accelerometer` sensor manually with the raw X/Y/Z data, but there may be more complex movements which you wish to handle as well. An example of a more complex movement is shaking the phone. Some smartphone games have used this movement to roll dice or shuffle cards. You could, of course, analyze the raw accelerometer data for these complex movements yourself, but helpers have been developed by various organizations/individuals to do this.

One such helper is the Shake Gesture Library from Microsoft on the Windows Phone App Hub site:

```
http://create.msdn.com/en-us/education/catalog/article/Recipe_Shake_
Gesture_Library
```

In this recipe, we will utilize this small library to erase the user's work in the FingerPaint application by shaking the phone.

Getting ready

Download the Shake Gesture Library, open it in Visual Studio, and build it. Open the FingerPaint solution, copy the `ShakeGestures.dll` to the solution folder, and add a reference to the library.

How to do it...

Open the `MainPage.xaml.cs` file and perform the following steps:

1. Add a `using` statement at the top of the page for the `ShakeGestures` namespace. For example:

    ```
    using ShakeGestures;
    ```

2. In the constructor, add a handler named `Instance_ShakeGesture` to the `ShakeGesture` event on the static `Instance` property of the `ShakeGestureHelper` class.

3. Set the `MinimumRequiredMovesForShake` property on the `Instance` to 5. Also set the `Active` property to `true`.

    The constructor should resemble the following:

    ```
    public MainPage()
    {
        InitializeComponent();

        Touch.FrameReported += new
        TouchFrameEventHandler(Touch_FrameReported);

        ShakeGesturesHelper.Instance.ShakeGesture += new
          EventHandler<ShakeGestureEventArgs>
          (Instance_ShakeGesture);
    ShakeGesturesHelper.Instance.MinimumRequiredMovesForShake = 5;
        ShakeGesturesHelper.Instance.Active = true;
    }
    ```

4. Add the `ShakeGesture` handler method with two parameters: an `object` named `sender` and a `ShakeGestureEventArgs` named `e`.

5. Within the method, create an `if` statement to check the `ShakeType` property on the event arguments parameter for either `ShakeType.X` or `ShakeType.Y`.

6. Then call the `BeginInvoke` method on the current `Dispatcher` by passing a parameterless lambda. Within the lambda body, call the `Clear` method on the `Children` property of `canvas1`.

    The shake handler should resemble the following:

    ```
    void Instance_ShakeGesture(object sender, ShakeGestureEventArgs e)
        {
            if (e.ShakeType == ShakeType.X || e.ShakeType ==
            ShakeType.Y)
                Deployment.Current.Dispatcher.BeginInvoke(() =>
                canvas1.Children.Clear());
        }
    ```

How it works...

The ShakeGesture library makes identifying shake gestures much easier. All you do is add an event handler, configure the gesture Instance with some properties, and set it as active. The properties define the type of shaking you want to handle. For the FingerPaint app, we are setting the `MinimumRequiredMovesToShake` property to 5, which seems to work well. Any less and any slight movement by the user may be interpreted as a shake. Any more, and the user's arm might get tired from shaking to erase a drawing. There are several other properties to explore on the Instance if this doesn't meet your needs.

In the handler, we are simply checking for an up/down or left/right shake, ignoring the Z-index or depth shake. Lastly, we clear the children on the canvas on the UI thread.

Pinching with ease

There are several standard touch gestures that consumers expect with touch screens, for example, click, double-click, flick, pan, pinch, and stretch. As you have seen, the Windows Phone operating system builds many of these into the controls. There may be opportunities for you to utilize these same touch gestures in custom controls or non-traditional pages. It is possible to capture and analyze raw touch data for patterns which match the touch gestures, but there are helper libraries which have already done this work.

The Silverlight for Windows Phone Toolkit includes a library which makes identifying and handling touch gestures easier:

```
http://silverlight.codeplex.com/
```

In this recipe, we will add pinch/stretch gestures to the image results of the `BingSlideshow` application.

Getting ready

Download the Silverlight for Windows Phone Toolkit source, and then open and build it in Visual Studio. Copy the `Microsoft.Phone.Controls.Toolkit.dll` from the `bin` folder of the project with the same name. Open the `BingSlideshow` project, copy the toolkit assembly to the solution folder, and reference it.

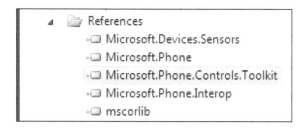

How to do it...

Open the `MainPage.xaml` file and perform the following steps:

1. Add an XML namespace declaration in the root `PhoneApplicationPage` node named `toolkit`, which references the `Microsoft.Phone.Controls` assembly and the `Microsoft.Phone.Controls.Toolkit` namespace.

   The namespace should mimic the following:

   ```
   xmlns:toolkit="clr-namespace:Microsoft.Phone.
   Controls;assembly=Microsoft.Phone.Controls.Toolkit"
   ```

2. Find the `Image` control within the `DataTemplate` for the `ItemsControl` and break it up into a node with a start and end tag.

3. Within the `Image` node, create a `GestureService.GestureListener` control with an inner `GestureListener` named `glImage`.

4. Also add a handler for the `PinchDelta` event named `glImage_PinchDelta`.

   The image control should resemble the following:

   ```
   <Image Source="{Binding}" Height="300" Width="300" >
       <toolkit:GestureService.GestureListener>
           <toolkit:GestureListener x:Name="glImage"
           PinchDelta="glImage_PinchDelta" />
       </toolkit:GestureService.GestureListener>
   </Image>
   ```

5. Open the code-behind file and create the `PinchDelta` handler method with two parameters: an `object` named `sender` and a `PinchGestureEventArgs` named `e`.

6. Within the handler, create a variable named `image` and set it to be equal to the `sender` parameter cast as an `Image`. Then create a variable named `delta` and set it to be equal to the `Math.Pow` method by passing the `DistanceRatio` property from the event args parameter and `.5`.

7. Create a variable named `newSize` and set it to be equal to the `Height` property on the image multiplied by the delta.

8. Add an `if` statement to check if `newSize` is less than `150` or greater than `450`, and if it is, return out of the method. Otherwise, set the `Height` and `Width` image properties on the `image` to the new size.

   The handler should mimic the following:

   ```
   private void glImage_PinchDelta(object sender,
   PinchGestureEventArgs e)
   {
       var image = (Image)sender;
       var delta = Math.Pow(e.DistanceRatio, .5);
   ```

```
var newSize = image.Height*(delta);
if (newSize < 150 || newSize > 450)
    return;
image.Height = newSize;
image.Width = newSize;
}
```

How it works...

You will need to test this code on a device because the emulator doesn't support multi-touch. This code will allow the user to pinch and stretch individual images in the result to resize them within the allowed space. The listener controls add handlers to the Image behind the scenes which watch for raw touch events that are directly over the Image control. When touch points are captured, they are analyzed to find a matching gesture. If the matched gesture is a Pinch/Stretch, our PinchDelta handler is called.

In the code-behind, we are getting a reference to the image via the sender parameter first. Then we adjust the delta measurement from the event arguments because the reported delta is too large to directly apply to the image size. If we didn't adjust the delta, a pinch would instantly set it to a width of 150 and a stretch would instantly set it to 450. We want to smoothly show variable widths, so we adjust the delta to a lower ratio. Then calculate the new size, check that it is within the page size constraints, and if it is, set the new image size.

There's more...

Adding the Pinch gesture was pretty simple. While we have this project open, we can add another gesture as well.

Open the XAML file again, find the GestureListener control, and add another event handler for the Hold event named glImage_Hold, like so:

```
<toolkit:GestureListener x:Name="glImage" PinchDelta="glImage_
PinchDelta" Hold="glImage_Hold" />
```

Create the handler method in the code behind with two parameters: an object named sender and a GestureEventArgs named e. Again, create a variable that references the image from the sender parameter. Call the static Show method on MessageBox, passing the text as Would you like to delete this image?, the caption as Delete?, and the button type as MessageBoxButton.OKCancel. Store the response in a variable named result. If the result is equal to MessageBoxResult.OK, call the Remove method on the Images property passing the image's DataContext property cast as a Uri.

The handler should resemble the following:

```
private void glImage_Hold(object sender, GestureEventArgs e)
{
    var image = (Image)sender;
```

```
var result = MessageBox.Show("Would you like to delete
this image?", "Delete?", MessageBoxButton.OKCancel);
if (result == MessageBoxResult.OK)
    Images.Remove((Uri)image.DataContext);
}
```

Now we can touch and hold onto an image to get the option to delete it:

If the user chooses **Cancel**, nothing happens, but if he/she chooses **OK**, the image will be removed from the results.

10
Preparing Apps for the Marketplace

In this chapter, we will cover:

- ▶ Configuring capabilities
- ▶ Maintaining responsiveness
- ▶ Adding trial support
- ▶ Creating iconography
- ▶ Submitting an app

Introduction

Are you ready to share your code with the world? The Windows Phone Marketplace is ready to take your applications and do just that. Although there are some hoops to jump through, it is by no means difficult. Many developers say it is easier to work with than some of the other *stores* on competing platforms. In this chapter, we will discuss the app submission process in detail, discussing each step and some of the caveats.

Before we can do that, we must cover some of the common tasks that accompany preparation for marketplace submission. There are coding tasks which are, many times, forgotten about until the app is ready for submission. Some of these changes may be required to successfully pass the application certification process. Others are just good practice or will help your app get more downloads.

All Windows Phone applications are certified during the Marketplace submission process to be reliable, efficient, and free of harmful code. Microsoft provides the Windows Phone 7 Application Certification Requirements document, which is a must read (along with this book) for anyone considering marketplace submission.

```
http://msdn.microsoft.com/en-us/library/hh184843(v=VS.92).aspx
```

Configuring capabilities

Through the various chapters of this book, you have seen the different capabilities of Windows Phone. Some of these capabilities are considered potentially sensitive such as the GPS and other location services, the microphone, push notifications, and so on. Microsoft has provided a recognition and approval system of these capabilities for end users. The goal of which is to properly inform users of the capabilities of the app and if they do not approve, allow them to cancel installation or close the app.

In this recipe, we will cover how to configure the application's declared phone capabilities and handle some of the certification requirements for using the push notifications capability.

Getting ready

Open the Oahu Surf Updates solution from *Chapter 7*.

How to do it...

Open the `WMAppManifest.xml` file located in the properties folder of the Windows Phone Application project:

1. Find the `Capabilities` node. Comment out all the child nodes except `ID_CAP_NETWORKING` and `ID_CAP_PUSH_NOTIFICATION`, like so:

```
<Capabilities>
  <!--<Capability Name="ID_CAP_GAMERSERVICES"/>
  <Capability Name="ID_CAP_IDENTITY_DEVICE"/>
  <Capability Name="ID_CAP_IDENTITY_USER"/>
  <Capability Name="ID_CAP_LOCATION"/>
  <Capability Name="ID_CAP_MEDIALIB"/>
  <Capability Name="ID_CAP_MICROPHONE"/>-->
  <Capability Name="ID_CAP_NETWORKING"/>
  <!--<Capability Name="ID_CAP_PHONEDIALER"/>-->
  <Capability Name="ID_CAP_PUSH_NOTIFICATION"/>
  <!--<Capability Name="ID_CAP_SENSORS"/>
  <Capability Name="ID_CAP_WEBBROWSERCOMPONENT"/>-->
</Capabilities>
```

2. Next, we must provide a way for the user to turn off push notifications. Open the `MainPage.xaml` file and find the `RegisterForPushNotifications` button at the bottom of the page.

3. Set the `Name` attribute to `butRegisterForNotifications` and the `IsEnabled` attribute to `false`. Set the `Name` attribute on the inner `TextBlock` to `tbRegisterButtonText`.

The button should mimic the following:

```
<Button x:Name="butRegisterForNotifications" IsEnabled="False"
  Grid.Row="2"
  Click="Button_Click">
    <TextBlock Name="tbRegisterButtonText">Register for
        Notifications</TextBlock>
</Button>
```

4. In the code-behind, create a new method named `SetRegisterButtonText` with no parameters, which returns `void`. Within the method, set the `_channel` field using the static `Find` method on the `HttpNotificationChannel` type passing the `_channelName` field. If the channel is not null and the `IsShellTileBound` property is true, then set the `tbRegisterButtonText` TextBox Text property to `Disable Notifications`. Otherwise set the property to `Register for Notifications`.

The method should resemble the following:

```
void SetRegisterButtonText()
{
    _channel = HttpNotificationChannel.Find(_channelName);
    if (_channel != null && _channel.IsShellTileBound)
        tbRegisterButtonText.Text = "Disable Notifications";
    else
        tbRegisterButtonText.Text = "Register for Notifications";
}
```

5. Call this method at the bottom of the page constructor as well as the bottom of the `Button_Click` method.

6. We will handle the unregistration in the `Button_Click` handler method after the `_channel` field has been set. Again, check if the `_channel` is not `null` and the `IsShellTileBound` property is `true`. If so, call the `UnbindToShellTile` method on the channel and call `return`.

The top of the click handler should mimic the following:

```
private void Button_Click(object sender, RoutedEventArgs e)
{
    _channel = HttpNotificationChannel.Find(_channelName);
    if (_channel != null && _channel.IsShellTileBound)
    {
        _channel.UnbindToShellTile();
        SetRegisterButtonText();
        return;
    }
```

7. Next, enable the register button once the data has been received. Find the code (around line 55) which adds beaches to the `Beaches ObservableCollection`. This is in the callback for the call to the WCF service to get the latest beach information. Within this `foreach` loop, set the `IsEnabled` property on the `butRegisterForNotifications Button` to `true`.

The loop should be coded as follows:

```
foreach (var beach in islandInfo.Beaches)
{
    if (beach.BeachName == selectedBeach.BeachName)
        beach.IsSelected = true;
        Beaches.Add(beach);
        butRegisterForNotifications.IsEnabled = true;
}
```

We also need to explain surf notifications to the user and allow them to cancel the registration.

8. Create a `string` variable named `key` equal to `pushNotificationsApproved` at the top of the `Button_Click` method.

9. Next, add an `if` statement that checks whether the `Contains` method on the static `ApplicationSettings` property of the `IsolatedStorageSettings` type returns `false`. If so, create a variable named `result` and set it to be equal to the static `Show` method on the `MessageBox` type. Pass the following for the `MessageBox Text` parameter:

Surf notifications utilize the Push Notifications feature of Windows Phone to send current surf information to the application start tile. Click OK to proceed or Cancel to cancel. You can turn off notifications in the future with the Disable Notifications button on the main screen.

10. Pass `Surf Notifications Approval` for the second parameter and `MessageBox.OKCancel` for the third.

11. Next, check if the result equals `MessageBoxResult.OK`, and if so set the `ApplicationSettings` at the `key` index equal to true. If not, call `return`. The final notifications approval code should resemble the following:

```
string key = "pushNotificationsApproved";
if
    (IsolatedStorageSettings.
    ApplicationSettings.Contains(key) == false)
{
    var result = MessageBox.Show("Surf notifications
    ...", "Surf Notifications Approval",
    MessageBoxButton.OKCancel);
    if (result == MessageBoxResult.OK)
```

```
        IsolatedStorageSettings.ApplicationSettings[key] = true;
    else
        return;
}
```

How it works...

The `WMAppManifest.xml` file controls which capabilities an application has access to. As a developer, you must define the capabilities your application will require. The user is notified of these capabilities before they install the application. You should comment out or delete any capabilities from the manifest which you do not require. This will:

▸ Ensure a user is not misinformed about the capabilities your app uses

▸ Probably shorten the testing time during submission

The Oahu Surf Updates application uses two capabilities: networking and push notifications; so we comment out the other capabilities in the `WMAppManifest` file. If you were to also comment/delete the networking capability, the application would not have access to the cellular or Wi-Fi connection and would show the **service unavailable** message.

In addition to configuring the manifest file, the Application Policies section of the Windows Phone 7 Application Certification Requirements document specifies other requirements for several capabilities. For example:

▸ 2.13 If your application uses the **Microsoft Push Notification Service** (**PNS**), the application and the use of the PNS must comply with the following requirements:

  ❑ 2.13.1 The application must first describe the notifications to be provided and obtain the user's express permission (opt-in), and must provide a mechanism through which the user can opt out of receiving push notifications. All notifications provided using PNS must be consistent with the description provided to the user and must comply with all applicable 2.0 Application Policies and 3.0 Content Policies.

So an application must explain to the user how the push notifications will be utilized, allow them to cancel turning them on, and provide a way to turn them off later. This is why we also altered the register for the notifications button above. The button now enables and disables notifications. If after enabling notifications, the user clicks the button again to disable them, we call the `UnbindToShellTile` method on the channel, which will invalidate the notification subscription. Once invalidated, any requests to the notification servers for notifications to this phone will return a *subscription not found* error code.

The first time the user enables the notifications, a message box will be shown which explains that notification services will be used to provide the latest surf information to the application tile on the start screen. If the user clicks **Cancel**, notifications will not be set up for the user.

There's more...

Obtaining express permission from the user is also required for using Location Services and sending *personal information* to external services. Microsoft is taking user privacy very seriously and you can tell. You can employ a similar method as we did in this section to handle this. In the case of Location Services, you must also make a privacy policy statement available to further document details of how the location information will be used. Ignoring these requirements and not implementing these measures will result in marketplace certification failure.

Automated capabilities detection

Instead of relying on the Marketplace application submission process to check whether you have allowed only the correct capabilities, Microsoft has provided a command line tool that you can run locally before submitting the app. The `CapabilityDetection.exe` tool is installed along with the developer tools and when run, it analyzes a Windows Phone application then outputs which capabilities it uses. This makes setting the capabilities in the `WMAppManifest.xml` file much easier. You no longer have to guess what capabilities are needed, as this command line tool will tell you what capabilities to specify.

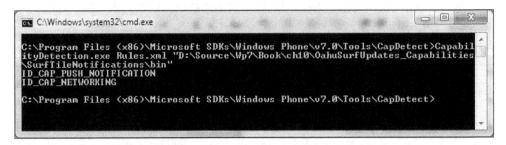

This utility searches through the scanned application's code for CLR Types which are known to facilitate each capability. Note that it would not typically find the underlying types if they are created and utilized via reflection.

You can get more details on MSDN at `http://msdn.microsoft.com/en-us/library/gg180730(VS.92).aspx`.

Maintaining responsiveness

Many smartphone applications rely on external web services to retrieve data. This offloads processing from the phone and makes a far broader range of data available. Since connectivity is never assured, developers must code for times when no connection is available. During the certification process, Microsoft specifically tests applications for errors or unresponsiveness when a connection is not available. In this recipe, we will add code to ensure that the Oahu Surf Updates application remains responsive during times of low or no cellular or Wi-Fi service.

Getting ready

Open the Oahu Surf Updates application and add a reference to the Silverlight for Windows Phone Toolkit in the `SurfTileNotifications` project:

`http://silverlight.codeplex.com/`

In the `MainPage.xaml` file, add a namespace named `Toolkit` to the root `PhoneApplicationPage` node. Set the namespace to `Microsoft.Phone.Controls` and the assembly to `Microsoft.Phone.Controls.Toolkit`, like so:

```
xmlns:Toolkit="clr-namespace:Microsoft.Phone.
Controls;assembly=Microsoft.Phone.Controls.Toolkit"
```

Add a `PerformanceProgressBar` named `progressBar` under the `tbForecast` TextBlock. Set its `Visibility` property to `Collapsed` and the `IsIndeterminate` property to `True`:

```
<Toolkit:PerformanceProgressBar x:Name="progressBar"
Visibility="Collapsed" IsIndeterminate="True" />
```

How to do it...

Open the `MainPage.xaml.cs` file and perform the following steps:

1. Add a using statement for the `Microsoft.Phone.Net.NetworkInformation` namespace.

2. Next, add an `if` block at the top of the constructor just below the `IntializeComponent` call, which checks if the static `NetworkInterfaceType` property on the `NetworkInterface` type is equal to `NetworkInterfaceType.None`.

3. Within the `if` block, set the `Text` property on the `tbForecast` TextBlock to A data connection is not currently available. Please try later. Set the `Text` property on the `tbHazards` TextBlock to an empty string. Then call `return`.

   The previous two steps should produce the following code:

```
if (NetworkInterface.NetworkInterfaceType ==
    NetworkInterfaceType.None)
{
    tbForecast.Text = "A data connection is not
     currently available.  Please try later.";
    tbHazards.Text = "";
    return;
}
```

4. Set the `Visibility` property on the `progressBar` to `Visibility.Visible` at the top of the first `try` block just above the creation of the `SurfServiceClient.`, like so:

    ```
    progressBar.Visibility = Visibility.Visible;
    ```

5. Add a `finally` block on the inner `try` block and set the `Visibility` property to `Visible.Collapsed`, like so:

    ```
    finally
    {
        progressBar.Visibility = Visibility.Collapsed;
    }
    ```

How it works...

The Application Certification Requirements document specifies the requirements for application responsiveness in recipe 5.1 Application Reliability and 5.2 Performance and Resource Management. The key points are:

▶ 5.1.2: The application must handle exceptions raised by the .NET framework and not terminate unexpectedly

▶ 5.1.3: The application must not become unresponsive to user input because of an operation within the application

▶ 5.2.1.a: The application must render the first screen within five seconds after launch

▶ 5.2.1.b: The application must be responsive to user input within 20 seconds after launch

The Oahu Surf Updates application did provide a shotgun approach to handling any data retrieval issues with try/catch blocks around the web service call. There are many exceptions which can be thrown during a service call so some type of handling is necessary. Exceptions could be caused by losing connectivity after the data transfer has started, the service host rebooting, or some type of serialization issue with the data, for example.

The first change above checks explicitly for a data connection. If it isn't available, we show a message in the `TextBlock` which explains that they do not currently have a data connection so they should retry the app later. Users appreciate a simple explanation of errors, when possible. We will continue to use the try/catches around the service method calls to catch any exceptions from the service call. If exceptions are caught, a message is displayed explaining the service is down.

You can see the **A data connection is not currently available. Please try later.** message by running the application in the emulator after disabling your computer's Internet connection:

It is not uncommon for smartphone users to experience poor data reception at times. As a result, the call to retrieve island info may take a while. Per recipe 5.1.3 of the certification requirements, we added a progress bar which is shown once the service call begins and hides when the call completes or when an exception is caught. Now, in addition to the **Loading ...** message, you will also see a progress indicator while the surf data is being retrieved:

Regarding loading the application for the first time or restarting the application, the best approach is to do as little as possible in the `App.xaml.cs` and `MainPage.xaml.cs` constructors. If possible, execute any long running processes on a background thread. This also applies to the TombStoning events. The Oahu Surf Updates app does have a lot of code in the `MainPage.cs` file, but it is basically just some property initialization and then calls the web service asynchronously (on a background thread) so no improvement is needed.

Adding trial support

Windows Phone has a unique Trial API which developers can use to create trials of their application. The developer is free to code the trial limitations as they see fit. Other smartphone development platforms lack this and must resort to submitting two versions of applications to the market, one with trial limitations and the other without. Regarding the effectiveness of the Windows Phone Trial API, a director at Microsoft has reported the following:

Nearly 1 out of 10 trial apps downloaded convert to a purchase and generate 10 times more revenue, on average, than paid apps that don't include trial functionality.

In this recipe, we will update the InstantMessenger application from *Chapter 7* to enable a trial which will only allow them to use the application for a specific number of days and notify the user of their trial status when the app starts.

Getting ready

Open the InstantMessenger project from *Chapter 7*. In the `MainPage.xaml` file, find the send button around line 36 and cut it out. Replace it with a `Grid`. Add a `Grid.ColumnDefinitions` node with two inner `ColumnDefinitions`. Set the first's `Width` property to `*` and the second's to `Auto`. Then paste the button which you cut out above. Add a `x:Name` attribute and set it to `butSend`. Remove the `Grid.Row` attribute.

Add a second `Button` named `butPurchase` below the first. Set its `Grid.Column` property to 1 and its `Visibility` to `Collapsed`. Add a `TextBlock` inside the `Button` tags and set its `Text` property to `Purchase`. Lastly, double-click the button in the designer to create a `Click` handler.

The grid XAML should resemble the following:

```
<Grid>
            <Grid.ColumnDefinitions>
                <ColumnDefinition Width="*"></ColumnDefinition>
                <ColumnDefinition
                 Width="Auto"></ColumnDefinition>
            </Grid.ColumnDefinitions>
            <Button x:Name="butSend" Click="Button_Click">
                <TextBlock>Send</TextBlock>
            </Button>
            <Button x:Name="butPurchase" Grid.Column="1"
             Visibility="Collapsed" Click="butPurchase_Click">
                <TextBlock>Purchase</TextBlock>
            </Button>
    </Grid>
```

How to do it...

Open the code-behind for the `MainPage` and perform the following steps:

1. Add a using directive at the top of the page for the `Microsoft.Phone.Marketplace` namespace as follows:

   ```
   using Microsoft.Phone.Marketplace;
   ```

2. At the bottom of the constructor, create a variable named `license` and set it to be equal to a new `LicenseInformation`.

3. Next, create an `if` statement which checks the `IsTrial` method on the license. All of the remaining code for this recipe will be placed inside this `if` statement.

   The license variable and the `if` statement should be coded as follows:

```
var license = new LicenseInformation();
        if (license.IsTrial())
        {

        }
```

4. In the body of the `if` statement, set the `Visibility` property on the `butPurchase` button to `Visibility.Visible`. Then create a variable named `trialStartDateKey` and set it to be equal to `TrialStartDate`.

   This step should produce the following code:

```
butPurchase.Visibility = Visibility.Visible;
   var trialStartDateKey = "TrialStartDate";
```

5. Create another `if` statement and check whether the `Contains` method on the static `ApplicationSettings` property of the `IsolatedStorageSettings` type is `false`, passing the `trialStartDateKey`.

6. In the body of the `if` statement, set the `ApplicationSettings` at the `trialStartDateKey` index to `DateTime.Now`.

   The previous two steps should produce the following code:

```
if (IsolatedStorageSettings.ApplicationSettings.
   Contains(trialStartDateKey) == false)
   IsolatedStorageSettings.ApplicationSettings[trialStartDateKey] =
   DateTime.Now;
```

7. Create a variable named `startDate` under the last `if` statement and set it to be equal to the `ApplicationSettings` at the `trialStartDateKey` index casted to a `DateTime`.

8. Create another variable named `trialLimit` and set it to be equal to `10`.

9. Next create a variable named `currentTrial` and set it to be equal to the `Subtract` method on the static Now property of the `DateTime` type passing the `startDate` variable then select the `Days` property off the result.

   The code from the previous steps should mimic the following:

```
var startDate =
    (DateTime)IsolatedStorageSettings.ApplicationSettings
    [trialStartDateKey];
var trialLimit = 10;
```

```
var currentTrial =
  DateTime.Now.Subtract(startDate).Days;
```

10. Add another `if` statement which checks whether the `currentTrial` is greater than or equal to the `trialLimit`.

11. Inside the `if` statement body, set the `IsEnabled` property on the `butSend Button` to `false`. Then set the `Text` property on the `tbResult TextBlock` to a message which explains that the trial has expired. For example:

```
if (currentTrial >= trialLimit)
            {
                butSend.IsEnabled = false;
                tbResult.Text = "Your trial has expired.  If
                  you would like to continue using this
                  application please purchase it.";
            }
```

12. Next add an `else` statement. In the body, set a variable named `result` to the static `Show` method on the `MessageBox` type. We will use the overload which takes the following three parameters:

   ❑ For the first, call the static `Format` method on the `string` type passing a `string` which describes how many days remain in the trial (with an argument) and asks if they would like to purchase the application. Set the format argument to the `trialLimit` variable minus the `currentTrial` variable.

   ❑ The second parameter on the `Show` method is the caption which we will set to `Trial Status`.

   ❑ The third is the button type for the message box. Set this to `MessageBoxButton.OKCancel`.

13. Lastly, we must check the `MessageBox` result with an `if` statement. If the result is equal to `MessageBoxResult.OK`, then create a new `MarketplaceDetailTask` and call the `Show` method.

The last `else` statement should resemble the following:

```
else
{
    var result = MessageBox.Show(
        string.Format("You have {0} days remaining
          in this trial.  Would you like to purchase
          this application? Click OK to purchase or
          Cancel to continue your trial.",
          trialLimit - currentTrial),
        "Trial Status",
        MessageBoxButton.OKCancel);
      if (result == MessageBoxResult.OK)
        new MarketplaceDetailTask().Show();
}
```

How it works...

In the XAML file, we added a purchase button and named the send button so that we could alter the user interface for the application if it is in trial mode. There isn't much to the Trial API; either the user is in trial mode or not. If they are, we display the purchase button in the UI and check how long they've been in trial mode. If it is their first time to run the application, we set the trial start date in application settings.

The `trialLimit` variable sets how many days we will allow for the trial. If the user exceeds the limit, we disable the send button and add a message explaining that the trial has ended. Otherwise, we show a message box which notifies them how many more days are left in the trial and provide an option to purchase the application.

You can test this in the debugger with some tweaks. The `IsTrial` method will always return `false` in the emulator, so for testing purposes, you can replace it with `true`:

If you debug the application in the emulator now, the application will act as if the application is always in trial mode. This will allow you to see the message boxes with the number of days left in the trial. Over time, you may need to clear out the start date to refresh the testing scenario. That can be done by simply commenting out the `if` statement which checks to see if the application setting exists, like so:

```
//if (_license.IsTrial())
if (true)
```

Lastly, you will need to test what the application does when the trial has expired. It is ridiculous to wait for 10 days just to test this. You can, instead, set the `trialLimit` to 0 to see the send button disabled and the expire message on the next run.

For example:

```
//var trialLimit = 10;
var trialLimit = 0;
```

Obviously, you will want to be careful to reset all these tweaks before submitting the application to the marketplace.

As you will see in a later recipe, you must specify that the application supports trials during marketplace submission for the Trial option to be shown in the marketplace for your app.

There's more...

Expiring a trial based on time is a common approach, but the Trial API for Windows Phone supports any expiration method. For instance, we could instead expire the trial based on the number of messages sent. This could be accomplished by storing the messages sent count in `ApplicationSettings` instead of the first run date and incrementing the count in the click handler for the send button. Rather than checking if the `currentTrial` is greater than `trialLimit`, you would compare the messages sent count to the limit.

You could even implement some combination of the two. The possibilities really are endless.

Creating iconography

Many developers work tireless hours on the code and UI in their applications but cut corners on their iconography. An application's first impressions are made by its icons. Given two applications with the same functionality and price, users will always select the app whose icon looks nicer. This doesn't mean icons have to be works of art or be outsourced to a professional artist (although it can't hurt). But at least make sure the icon is saved appropriately and is not blurred.

In this recipe, we will create the icons for the Oahu Surf Updates application and App Hub submission process.

Getting ready

You will need a graphic editing program to create icons. There are several free applications which will do the job, for example Paint.NET and GIMP. Even the Paint program in Windows will work. We will use Paint in this section.

Icons can be custom creations, photos, or some combination of the two. Search for a photo of a wave on the royalty-free image site `http://www.sxc.hu`. Look for a photo that is clear, sharp, with nice colors, and whose height and width is larger than 200 px. Copy the image to your clipboard (right-click and select copy).

How to do it...

Perform the following steps to create the application icons:

1. Open the Windows Paint program. Paste the photo you selected from the photo exchange site to the art board:

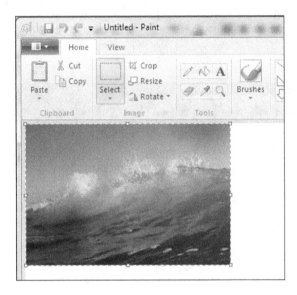

2. Next, click the **Crop** button in the **Home** ribbon to crop the image down to the pasted portion. Then use the selection tool to select a 200 by 200 pixel square and crop again or use the cropping draggers:

After cropping, the image should resemble the following screenshot:

3. Now we can start saving the icon in all the sizes we will need. Select the file menu button and choose **Save as/PNG picture**. Name the file wave_200.png and save it in the resources folder of the Oahu Surf Updates project:

4. Next, click on the **Resize** button on the ribbon menu, choose **resize by Pixels**, set the **Horizontal** field to **173**, make sure the **Maintain aspect ratio** checkbox is checked, and click **OK**. Save the photo again with the filename `wave_173.png`. Repeat this process for the following sizes: 99 px and 62 px.

5. Open the Oahu Surf Updates project in Visual Studio. Move the 173 px and 62 px icon files to the root project directory. Next, shift select all of the icon files and open the properties window to set the **Build Action** to **Content** and the **Copy to Output Directory** to **Copy always**:

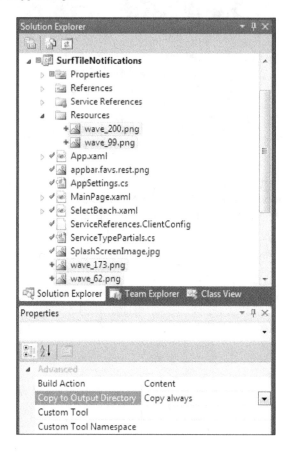

6. Lastly, open the `WMAppManifest.xml` file and set the `IconPath` node value to `wave_62.png` and the `BackgroundImageURI` node value to `wave_173.png`.

The XML should look like following code follows:

```
<IconPath IsRelative="true"
 IsResource="false">wave_62.png</IconPath>
...
<Tokens>
```

```
<PrimaryToken TokenID="SurfTileNotificationsToken"
  TaskName="_default">
  <TemplateType5>
    <BackgroundImageURI IsRelative="true"
      IsResource="false">wave_173.png</BackgroundImageURI>
```

How it works...

A Windows Phone application requires several icons at various sizes. Notice that we started with the largest icon and resized to each smaller size. This will ensure each has the highest quality resolution.

The application menu icon (62 px) and the start screen tile (173 px) are defined in the manifest file. These images must be located in the root project directory to be properly referenced.

The 200 px and 99 px icons will be needed during the app submission process. All of the icons must also be in the PNG format. JPG icon images will not cause a compilation or runtime error but they will cause errors during the marketplace submission process.

Submitting an app

You have arrived! You have built a Windows Phone application with all the bells and whistles, utilizing the SDK to its fullest extent and now it's time to share it with the world. Windows Phones can only install applications from the Windows Phone Marketplace. Getting an application into the marketplace can be frustrating if you aren't prepared. In this chapter, we will cover the submission process step-by-step and provide the tips/tricks you need to do it quickly and easily.

Getting ready

All of the official marketplace information is located at the following website:

`http://create.msdn.com`

First you will need to obtain an App Hub Membership. As of April, 2010 the cost of membership was $99 per year, although there are alternatives to purchasing a membership. For example, students can obtain membership for free through the DreamSpark program. Software startups in the BizSpark program have also been offered free App Hub membership from time-to-time. In addition, Microsoft has provided various promotional programs which offer membership reimbursement for developers who meet program criteria.

The good news here is that the membership is only required when you want to submit an app to the marketplace. This will allow you to defer the membership cost during the development of your app if necessary.

Part of the signup process includes an identification check to ensure the contact and tax information you entered is correct. An external organization (GeoTrust) performs this check. You will not be able to submit an application or unlock a phone until this step is completed. You should receive an e-mail or call from GeoTrust to complete the verification. This e-mail is commonly marked as spam, so keep an eye on your spam folder.

Check the certification requirements

The Windows Phone Marketplace has a certification process which all applications must pass before being made available to the public. As we have covered briefly, the certification requirements are clearly defined in the Windows Phone 7 Application Certification Requirements document. This is your guide to building an application that will hopefully pass application certification the first time.

Before submitting an application to the marketplace, you should review the certification requirements document to ensure you have handled all the requirements appropriately.

How to do it...

Perform the following steps to submit the surf updates app to the marketplace:

1. Open the SurfNotifications solution we worked on in the previous recipe. Change the currently selected build configuration in the **Standard** toolbar menu to **Release**, as shown in the following screenshot:

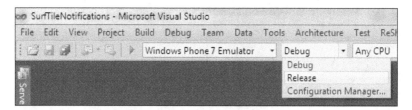

Or in the **Configuration Manager** (**Build | Configuration Manager**), as shown in the following screenshot:

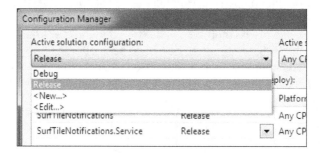

2. Build the solution and then open the **bin | Release** folder in the Phone Application project folder for the solution to find the `.xap` file:

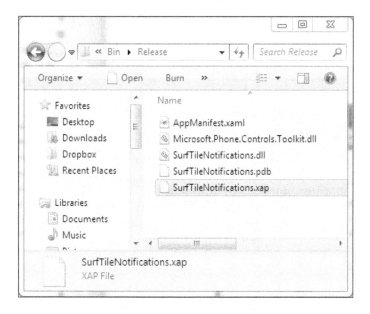

3. Log in to your App Hub account at `http://create.msdn.com` and open your Windows Phone dashboard, as seen here:

4. Click on the **submit new app** link at the bottom of the left pane:

5. Set the **Application name** field to **Oahu Surf Updates**. Leave the **Application platform**, **Default language**, and **Version** default values as they are

6. Click the plus sign in the box labeled **Application package**. A file dialog box will appear. Select the XAP file from Step 2.

7. Click the **Next** button at the bottom of the page.

8. On the description page, set the **Application title** to **Oahu Surf Updates** and the **Category** to **News & Weather**.

9. Set the **Detailed description** to the following:

   "Need to know what Oahu the surf is like at all times? This is the app for you. The information is made available by the National Weather Service. Have a favorite beach? You can specify a favorite to receive push notifications on the start tile for that beach."

10. Set the **Keywords** field to **surf surfing oahu updates**. Then click the **Next** button at the bottom of the page.

11. On the **upload app artwork** page, click the plus sign for each tile size and select the matching icon size you created in the *First Impressions* recipe.

12. Open the Oahu SurfUpdates solution in Visual Studio and start the application in the emulator, then stop debugging, go back to the emulator, and run the application again. Click the magnifying glass next to the emulator to set the zoom level to 100 percent. Take a screenshot using the *Print Screen* key, paste it into Windows Paint, and crop the image down to just the inner emulator window, which will be 480 pixels wide by 800 pixels tall.

    The zoom window is shown in the following screenshot:

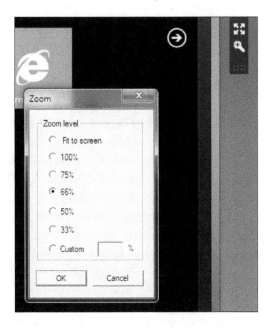

13. Click the **Next** button to continue to the **price your app** page.

14. Set the **Application price** field to **$0.99** and click the **Next** button.

15. On the **Ready to submit for certification** page, uncheck the **Automatically publish** checkbox.

How it works...

The following sections describe how the various stages of submission work:

▶ **Compiling the application for release**

The submission process will accept the application packaged as a XAP file. A XAP file is just a renamed ZIP file which contains all the necessary code files to run an application. Each time you build a Windows Phone application in Visual Studio, a XAP is created. The App Hub only accepts a release build, meaning that it was built with the **Release** build configuration.

▶ **Upload**

This first screen in the app submission wizard is where you identify the application for your dashboard and upload the application XAP file. The name field is only used for uniquely identifying the application on your dashboard. The name must be unique to proceed to the next step. You will receive the following error if it is not unique:

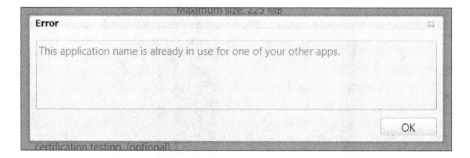

The Application Platform should be set to **Windows Phone 7**. You can also set the default language and the version number for your application if you like. The next field is for uploading your XAP file. Once the XAP is uploaded, it will be analyzed statically to read the application's capabilities for use in further screens and for various issues.

Next is a developer's notes field for storing private notes about the build/version.

The last two fields are testing related. Each application submitted to the marketplace is tested by a Microsoft testing team. The first is for specifying special notes for the testing team such as authentication credentials or usage details. The checkbox denotes the need for a technical exception which can add several days to the testing process. Checking this box should be a last resort.

Once all these fields are set, you can click **Next** or **Save & Quit** at the bottom of the page. The required capabilities of the application will not be displayed on the next screen until the static analysis is complete. Your best bet is to click **Save & Quit** to return to the dashboard and wait for the package verification to complete. The verification typically takes only a few minutes. Refresh the page periodically until the status shows **Package verified**.

Here is the unverified package view:

name	modified▾	status	action
Oahu Surf Updates	4/10/2011	✓ Submission in progress	Edit details

Here is the view once the package is verified:

name	modified▾	status	action
Oahu Surf Updates	4/10/2011	✓ Package verified	Edit details

Then click the **Edit** details link to go back to the **Upload** screen, where you will see the information you just completed, and then simply scroll to the bottom of the page and click **Next** to proceed to the next step.

▶ **Description**

This screen allows you to set some of the public information about your application including the application title, category, sub-category, detailed description, and keywords. These fields are required to proceed. There are other optional fields as well, such as ratings, legal URL, and support e-mail address.

The category, sub-category, and tags are especially important fields. They will be used in the marketplace search and browse areas, which will be the main way users can discover your app. Similar to HTML metadata tags for websites, you should think of all the tags that users could use to describe the application. In the same way, carefully consider the categories you select. Users will be browsing the marketplace using these categories looking for applications that interest them. It is in your best interest to choose the appropriate categories to entice the right users.

▶ **Artwork**

Obviously, this screen is where you set the marketplace artwork for the application. Three tiles and one screenshot are required. You can optionally add background art for use if your application is selected to be featured in the marketplace and up to seven more screenshots.

Details for preparing artwork were covered in a previous section.

▶ **Pricing**

Now it's time to price your application. There are many blog posts and articles on the web which compare free versus not-free revenue models. We will not cover that here, but we would suggest you do some research on the topic before making a decision.

The first option is whether your application supports Trial mode. Check this if you have added code to limit the functionality of your application based upon whether the user is in Trial mode. The next field, **Worldwide distribution**, specifies whether your application will be available to all markets or not. If checked, your application will be listed in all markets across the world. If not, you may manually select the countries in which you wish to make the app available by checking the boxes next to each country and their price at the bottom of the page.

Primary offer currency sets the currency for your application price. This currency is used to calculate the price in other currencies. The last field is the **Application prices**, which you can set in $1 increments between $0 and $50 and $10 increments between $50 and $499.

It is very important to note that the information on this screen applies to all instance of your application. For instance, if you are submitting an update for your previously published application, any changes you make to the pricing affect the app in the marketplace immediately, even if the update fails verification. This has caused problems for some developers. A common scenario has been updating an application to add trial support. The problem is as soon as the user submits the update, the trial option is enabled on the marketplace detail page for the application, even before the new XAP has been tested and deployed. This means that users can choose the trial option and get the app for free without the trial limitations. If the user never updated the app they could continue to use the app for free indefinitely.

To avoid this issue, you should submit any XAP updates first and after they are successfully verified, submit the pricing changes in a second submission.

▶ **Submit**

The last screen in the wizard is the final submission page. You have the option to review the application details you have set or the Windows Phone Application Provider Agreement. The last checkbox specifies whether you wish to automatically publish the application to the marketplace after passing certification. This may be useful if you want to release an application or an update to the public on a specific date.

▶ **Other general notes**

Microsoft has made submitting an application for the marketplace quite simple. They provide all the necessary tools to manage the process in a transparent way. The steps presented in this recipe assume no errors occur during the submission process. Occasionally errors do occur, but in the majority of cases the App Hub website clearly describes the problem and gives the information necessary to remedy it.

In the event that you have further issues that cannot be resolved on your own, the support team is available to help via the support page on the App Hub.

Finalizing a Windows Phone application and completing the marketplace submission process is a very rewarding process. It is not uncommon to fail the certification process. However, 62 percent of all apps pass certification on their first attempt. If you are in the unlucky 38 percent, don't worry; Microsoft provides detailed reasons and testing results to help you quickly identify the issue and resubmit the application.

When an application fails certification, you will receive an e-mail which informs you of the failure and directs you to your dashboard to retrieve the certification report. The report will detail reasons for the failure, citing the certification requirements and steps to reproduce the issue. Once you have resolved the issues, you can open the pending submission details, update the XAP, and resubmit.

There's more...

There is a comprehensive App Hub FAQ page with further details and answers to many common questions if you would like more information about the App Hub:

```
http://create.msdn.com/en-US/home/faq/windows_phone_7
```

Free app submissions

As an App Hub member, you are entitled to submit as many paid applications as you would like and up to 100 free app submissions. To clarify, these are submissions, not apps with unlimited update submissions. You can, for example, submit 100 free apps with no updates, update a single free app 100 times, or submit 50 apps with two updates. Additional free app submissions will cost $19.99 each. In general, Microsoft pays out 70 percent of the price of the application to the developer (other taxes or fees may apply in some countries). There is no pay out for free apps, so Microsoft limits the number of free apps a developer can submit. The 30 percent or so that Microsoft keeps pays for all the platform services they provide for the community.

Getting paid

Some of you are now asking, how do I get paid? There is a minimum threshold of $200 that you must exceed before you will be sent any money. There will also be a delay in payment due to collection times, which can vary between 15 and 120 days, depending on the user's payment method. As mentioned previously, you will receive 70 percent of the gross sales minus sales tax or VAT, if applicable.

Payment is made via an electronic deposit to the bank account specified on the **payee details** page of the **my account** section of the dashboard. Payments will only be made if this information has been completed and verified. You can see the status of payouts by clicking the **Access payout details** button on the reports page from the dashboard. Choose a time period and optionally a specific country or application to see the payout details. If your bank information hasn't been set or there is some other issue, a notification will be displayed at the top of the page.

Payment information incomplete. In order to be paid for application sales, you must provide your banking information. Enter your bank and tax information.

create a report

Download reports

You probably noticed the **daily download details** chart on the reports page, which shows the number of downloads for all your apps on each day for the last month. What you may not have noticed are the links to the right of the chart under the **top 5 downloads** section. If you click on any of these links, you will be able to create more specific reports for individual apps and different time periods. You can even see the raw download/purchase data by clicking the **data** option:

Localization

Windows Phone applications can be made to support multiple languages (currently English, French, Italian, German, and Spanish) using resource files in the solution. The MSDN site has a great article with all the implementation details at `http://msdn.microsoft.com/en-us/library/ff637520(VS.92).aspx`.

Once you follow these instructions and (re)submit the application to the marketplace, you will be required to enter description and artwork data for each language you added to the application. This will allow you to translate the application's description/metadata and use appropriate screenshots for the various languages you have supported.

Index

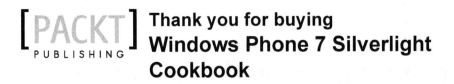

Thank you for buying
Windows Phone 7 Silverlight Cookbook

About Packt Publishing

Packt, pronounced 'packed', published its first book "*Mastering phpMyAdmin for Effective MySQL Management*" in April 2004 and subsequently continued to specialize in publishing highly focused books on specific technologies and solutions.

Our books and publications share the experiences of your fellow IT professionals in adapting and customizing today's systems, applications, and frameworks. Our solution based books give you the knowledge and power to customize the software and technologies you're using to get the job done. Packt books are more specific and less general than the IT books you have seen in the past. Our unique business model allows us to bring you more focused information, giving you more of what you need to know, and less of what you don't.

Packt is a modern, yet unique publishing company, which focuses on producing quality, cutting-edge books for communities of developers, administrators, and newbies alike. For more information, please visit our website: www.packtpub.com.

Writing for Packt

We welcome all inquiries from people who are interested in authoring. Book proposals should be sent to author@packtpub.com. If your book idea is still at an early stage and you would like to discuss it first before writing a formal book proposal, contact us; one of our commissioning editors will get in touch with you.

We're not just looking for published authors; if you have strong technical skills but no writing experience, our experienced editors can help you develop a writing career, or simply get some additional reward for your expertise.

Microsoft Silverlight 4 Data and Services Cookbook

Microsoft Silverlight 4 Data and Services Cookbook

ISBN: 978-1-847199-84-3   Paperback: 476 pages

Over 85 practical recipes for creating rich, data-driven business applications in Silverlight

1. Design and develop rich data-driven business applications in Silverlight

2. Rapidly interact with and handle multiple sources of data and services within Silverlight business applications

3. Understand sophisticated data access techniques in your Silverlight business applications by binding data to Silverlight controls, validating data in Silverlight, getting data from services into Silverlight applications and much more!

Silverlight 4 User Interface Cookbook

Silverlight 4 User Interface Cookbook

ISBN: 978-1-847198-86-0   Paperback: 280 pages

Build and implement rich, standard-friendly user interfaces with Silverlight and Expression Blend

1. The first and only book to focus exclusively on Silverlight UI development

2. Have your applications stand out from the crowd with leading, innovative, and friendly user interfaces

3. Real world projects which you can explore in detail and make modifications as you go

Please check **www.PacktPub.com** for information on our titles

Microsoft SharePoint 2010 Enterprise Applications on Windows Phone 7

ISBN: 978-1-84968-258-9   Paperback: 252 pages

Create enterprise-ready websites and applications that access Microsoft SharePoint on Windows Phone 7

1. Provides step-by-step instructions for integrating Windows Phone 7-capable web pages into SharePoint websites

2. Provides an overview of creating Windows Phone 7 applications that integrate with SharePoint services

3. Examines Windows Phone 7's enterprise capabilities

Microsoft Silverlight 4 Business Application Development: Beginner's Guide

ISBN: 978-1-847199-76-8   Paperback: 412 pages

Build Enterprise-Ready Business Applications with Silverlight

1. An introduction to building enterprise-ready business applications with Silverlight quickly

2. Get hold of the basic tools and skills needed to get started in Silverlight application development

3. Integrate different media types, taking the RIA experience further with Silverlight, and much more!

Please check **www.PacktPub.com** for information on our titles